To T

BLACK OR WHITE
NO GREY AREAS

BLACK OR WHITE
NO GREY AREAS

LEE CLARK

WITH

WILL SCOTT

Mojo Risin'
Publishing Ltd

Published in 2016 by Mojo Risin' Publishing

British Library Cataloguing in Publication Data:
A catalogue record for this book is available from
the British Library

ISBN-13:
9780993442445

Cover photograph
Andy Thompson, Singe Vert Photography

Including additional photographs
Adrian Clark

Cover and plate section design
Andrew Brewster, PrintNV

Printed & bound by CPI Group (UK) Ltd, Croydon, CR0 4YY

Proudly published up North

THIS BOOK IS DEDICATED TO

My three children, Jak, Claudia and Bobby
my wife, Lorraine
my parents, Robert and Joyce
my two sisters, Kerry and Beverly
and my brother, Michael

Thanks for your love and loyalty

CONTENTS

Foreword

1   Got the T-Shirt

2   Knitted Jumpers for Goalposts

3   Whatever Happened to the Heroes?

4   There's a Killer on the Loose

5   Kicked the Bucket

6   Tyne to Leave

7   Walk like an Egyptian

8   Prodigal Returns

9   Heard the one about the Dutchman, Knight and Geordie?

10   Greatest Newcastle United Side

11   Best of the Rest

12   Flying the Nest

13   The Boss

14   Terriers in the Doghouse

15   Feeling Blue

16   No, I don't like to be Beside the Seaside

17   Change of Climate, Foreign Food and the Language Barrier

18   Friends, Family and Struck by Cupid's Arrow

19   Thoughts of Chairman Clark

20   I Have a Dream

FOREWORD

I knew Lee Clark was a special talent from the moment I first saw him play. There were several others like him in the Newcastle youth squad and that is why I promoted them to the first team. There was little money for me to spend when I was manager at St James' Park so I had to invest in the kids. I also felt the senior players weren't giving me everything. I was left with little choice but turn to the talented crop of youngsters in our youth team set up. They may not have had any experience, maturity or wisdom, but they made up for it with enthusiasm, passion and a thirst to learn. The lads sometimes couldn't understand my accent, which we would laugh about, but there is no language barrier in football. I could get my message across because they were all intelligent youngsters.

We had some good times together and a lot of fun at Benwell, where we used to train. It saddens me that I couldn't develop and nurture the lads through to maturity. Nearly all of the boys I blooded went on to have good careers in football – although not all at United. The really gifted ones remained: Steve Watson, Steve Howey, Alan Thompson, Robbie Elliott and of course, Clarky, who was the jewel in the crown.

The young Geordie had the head of a veteran on his shoulders. He was so composed and confident on the ball you would forget he was still a teenager. The surroundings and intimidating atmosphere of St James' Park, and other venues on our away travels, held no fear for him. Nothing ever seemed to faze or bother my precociously talented midfielder, whether he was playing in the schoolyard, the back streets of Buenos Aires or the Maracanã Stadium in Brazil. He had the ability to block out any environment, enjoy and play his football.

My only surprise is Clarky never played for England. He was capped at every stage with the exception of senior level. It was tough for my young protégé because he was playing in the era of the so-called 'Golden Generation'. Yet several players in his position were capped for their country, during his time, who did not have the ability of my charge and neither did they deserve it. I've heard people say, "But he didn't have any pace." Why did he need pace? He could get away without having a burst of speed because of his all-round ability. Clarky had great vision, a wonderful first touch, could pass and score goals with either foot. In short, he was the complete midfield player.

I've watched my young playmaker's career very closely. It came as no surprise to see him follow me into management when his time as a footballer ended. It may have raised a few eyebrows with some people but not me. The same happened when I took my first tentative steps into the dugout. A lot of people didn't think I was management material. But Clarky has such a good football brain and knowledge of the game it was an effortless progression. He took to it naturally and had some early success in his managerial career. There've been a couple of setbacks, which happens to us all, even to those who went on to become greats in the game. But I'm sure Clarky will bounce back from those reversals of fortune and achieve much more in the game.

Buena Suerte,

Ossie Ardiles

PRAISE FOR LEE CLARK

"Clarky was a great lad and smashing footballer. He was hailed as the new Gazza when I left Newcastle. That is a lot of pressure to put on young shoulders but he handled it brilliantly. We had some great times at Benwell Training Ground when he was a kid in the youths and I was in the first team. I'm sure those tales will appear in his book. I hope you haven't put that story in about the industrial dryers? You have, haven't you? Bugger!" **Gazza**

"Lee was a good boy. With Gazza, he was the best player at Newcastle from my spell at the club. He was the sensible one and Gazza was the crazy one. Lee was still a schoolboy at the time. I told him to forget about school, stay and play with me. Unfortunately he had to go and finish his education. In my country it wouldn't matter. He played football the way it was supposed to be played – like a Brazilian. Lee had great technique, two good feet and very good vision. You could see from an early age he was going to be a star. I'm sure he has some great stories to tell about his career and I'm looking forward to reading it." **Mirandinha**

"There are certain things I look for in players. Crucial is their shape. They need to be athletes and I'm always looking for footballers with a good first touch. When someone rifles that ball at you, is it under control straight away or does it take two touches? A classic example at Newcastle was Lee Clark, who had the best touch of anyone there, probably as good as any I have seen. He wasn't blessed with tremendous pace. It is his control that is world class." **Kevin Keegan**

"It's fair to say, I knew it would be hard to persuade Clarky to come to Sunderland, with him being a Newcastle United fan. But I knew he couldn't drink, so after six bottles of Laurent Perrier Champagne, in Harper's Bar, Manchester, he shook my hand and agreed to sign for me. Clarky was a great link-up player. He could handle the ball, a very intelligent footballer and brilliant in the dressing room with the lads. It tells you everything about him that a diehard Geordie could win over the Mackems. But that is what he did with his performances on the park. He was magnificent for me: as a footballer and a guy, absolutely outstanding." **Peter Reid**

CHAPTER 1
GOT THE T-SHIRT

The infamous Sad Mackem Bastard t-shirt incident at Wembley will never go away. I get asked about it all of the time. And, still to this day, the feeling on Wearside is that I've committed high treason and should be punished in some way. In fact, there are Sunderland supporters today who would take great pleasure in seeing me hanged, drawn and quartered for the act.

There appears to be an overall impression that I was walking around the streets of London all day in the controversial t-shirt. That I'd woken up on the morning of the FA Cup final, gone to my wardrobe and thought, 'What disparaging t-shirt should I put on today? Should I wear my blue 'I ♥ Kevin Keegan,' my black 'I adore Newcastle t-shirt,' or the white one with, 'Sad Mackem Bastard'? I know, I'll wear the SMB t-shirt, that'll wind up supporters of the team I play for.'

The truth? I stepped out of a cab on Baker Street and someone whipped the offending article over my head as soon as my feet were on the pavement. And, to be fair, the t-shirt was Newcastle United supporters taking the piss out of me rather than me taking the piss out of Sunderland. I've said several times in the past that I regret the incident, and I do. But I had no control over what happened. It was good natured banter that got out of hand. If you study the picture and see my reaction, I'm looking down because I didn't know what was happening. I've got a floppy cricket hat on and I couldn't see what was on the t-shirt at first. I couldn't have had it on for more than 30 or 40 seconds. But in that time the cameras had the evidence. I was set up. Just imagine if Micky Gray, Gary Rowell or another die-hard Wearsider had played for Newcastle and they were at

Wembley to see their home-town team. I am sure Sunderland fans would've thought up or schemed something very similar for them.

I'd asked Peter Reid for permission to go to the FA Cup final to watch Newcastle against Man United as I had the previous year when my old team played Arsenal. He said the same thing, "As long as you don't wear any colours," as in black and white colours. I'm not that daft, although, people will say, 'Daft enough to get caught out.'

I was looking forward to the game and some downtime after a successful season with Sunderland. I went with my father-in-law, Paul Lamont, and a few friends. Ray Thompson, the Newcastle United kit man, sorted out all the lads with strips with names on the back. My old teammate Les Ferdinand arranged a night club on the Friday night for us and we had a heavy evening. On the Saturday we knew one of the Geordie lads who had a pub on Baker Street and agreed to meet some friends in there before the game. Later on, after the stitch up, I learned a couple of supporters were scheming and had the infamous t-shirt under wraps. We got to Baker Street and, no sooner had I stepped out of the taxi, than this t-shirt was being pulled over my head. If you look at the photo my arms are stretched out wide and then all of a sudden there were camera flashes going off in all directions. My father-in-law turned to me and said, "You're in trouble now, son, if that gets in the press."

I rang my agent to tell him what had happened and he told me, "Don't worry about it. We'll sit on it and see if anything happens." The story broke about three or four weeks later, on the day of the Northumberland Plate, commonly known as the Pitman's Derby, at Newcastle Racecourse. Why did it take so long to hit the newspapers? These were the days before an omniscient social media circus. There were no Twitter, Facebook or the likes of Snapchat. In fact, the Internet was still in its infancy. Furthermore, there were no mobile phones with cameras that could upload pictures to the Internet. The guy who took the photo, and sent it to the press, was probably using an instamatic camera. If I remember correctly, you could buy a film that had either 24 or 48 snaps. I'm guessing he had to use up the film before Truprint received it for development! (Other photographic developing emporiums were also available). That would explain the delay.

I was on my way to the race meeting and got a call saying the papers had got wind of it and would I like to say anything. I didn't want to say anything until I spoke to the club. Peter Reid was away in France so I had a meeting with Bob Murray, while Reidy sat in on a conference call with us. The fixtures for the new season were out and we were due to face Chelsea in the Premier League's curtain-raiser.

Reidy was in fine form, "You can fuck off, you little fucker. You're staying. You're not going anywhere. You're going to be in the team at Stamford Bridge."

After Reidy put the phone down, Murray turned to me, "Look Lee, I know the manager wants to keep you but it's going to be difficult after what's happened. In fact, it'll be impossible because the feelings among the fans will be high."

I had to start pre-season training with Sunderland and did the first ten days before my move to Fulham went through. There was a bit of banter from the lads taking the piss. But, all joking aside, this was a tough period for me because supporters were waiting at the training ground gates to shout abuse for t-shirt incident. The first day back at training, Reidy called a team meeting. At the time Allan Johnson and Michael Bridges were both in contract dispute. The gaffer was in fine verbal form. He'd give the *Viz* character Roger Mellie a run for his money when in this mode.

"I've got these two fuckers (Bridges and Johnson) who won't sign a contract. Well you've got two days to make your mind up or you can both fuck off. And this fucking lunatic is wearing t-shirts taking the piss out of the club! We've got half a squad but, fuck it, let's have a go at it (staying in the Premier League)!"

Supporters on both sides of the Tyne and Wear still ask:

Why did I sign for Sunderland when you're the quintessential Geordie prototype?

Why did you sign for our sworn enemy?

Cut him down the middle and he's like a stick of black and white Newcastle rock, they say.

I've been called all sorts of things by both sets of fans and some of them not very pleasant. But the truth is... Peter Reid got me pissed!

There were a few clubs interested in signing me when I made the gut-wrenching decision to leave my beloved Newcastle and make a career away from Tyneside. Man City, under Frank Clark, wanted to take me to Maine Road. Derby County, under Jim Smith, was another club who fancied me, while I later found out that Roy Evans at Liverpool had asked about my availability. That would've been a no brainer playing at Anfield. The Merseyside giants are a great club with a fantastic tradition. It was only when Paul Bracewell got sacked at Fulham and Evans came to Craven Cottage as interim manager that I was made aware of the Reds' interest. Evans told me he was put out that I wouldn't talk to him. But I didn't know. The club, or my agent, didn't tell me of Liverpool's interest at the time. Obviously, I was gutted I didn't get the chance to go and play for them.

I spoke to both Clark and Smith and was impressed by what they said. I had a lot of respect for Clark. He is a Newcastle United legend. He won the Fairs Cup before going on to greater things with Brian Clough at Nottingham Forest: winning the old Division One title and European Cup in the twilight of his career. And Man City was a big club. Obviously I knew Smith really well from his time at Newcastle. He gave me my debut after all.

Sunderland was the last club I spoke to. I didn't tell anyone I was going to talk to them and neither did I take any advice from friends and family. Maybe if I had, they would've talked me out of it. I don't know. Paul Bracewell played an important part in getting me to Wearside. He was Reid's assistant at the time. Brace was a bit of a mentor to me when he was at St James' Park in the formative years of the Entertainers under Kevin Keegan. Sunderland arranged a private jet to fly me to Manchester to meet Reidy. A private jet! He took me and my agent out for oysters and fizzy bubbles at some big city champagne bar in their big city centre. I couldn't believe what was happening; an ordinary working class lad from Pottery Bank eating oysters and drinking champagne. Talk about an Annie Hall transformation. The oysters were horrendous. I gave it a try, though. Truth be known, I'd sooner have a jar of mussels in vinegar, a bowl of whelks or a pickled egg than eat oysters. I was happy enough drinking the champagne though. We met about lunch-time and I was with him until about tea-time. He got me absolutely shitfaced, so much so, I decided to sign for the fiercest rivals of my home-town team.

What I liked about Reid was that he was deadly serious about his football, what he wanted and where I would fit into his plans. He was telling me he could get me into the full England squad, which was reassuring to hear. But he put me at ease straight away. It was as if I was out with a mate and we had a good laugh. And that's exactly how anyone expects to be treated. The Scouser is very good company – not just 'the Scouser' as in the Scouse folk in general – this one in particular is a sound bloke (despite his unfortunate head, as the Geordies are always keen to point out). Almost instantly I liked the guy and thought he would do well for me. One deciding factor of the move to Sunderland was that I didn't have to up sticks and uproot the family. I lived in Darras Hall at the time, my little lad, Jak, was only two and not having to move home appealed massively to me. And it was well documented that I was a bit of homer at that time and wanted to stay in the North-East.

When Sunderland put a private jet on for me to return to Newcastle, I was that pissed the flight staff weren't going to let me on. My agent, Paul Stretford, had to convince them it would be OK. It had to be, I was the only passenger. My father-in-law, Paul, was out in town with a few of his mates when I landed at Newcastle Airport so I decided to make a day of it and meet up with him. After all, I was in very good spirits. They were gobsmacked when I told them what had just happened. They thought I was taking the piss and wouldn't believe me at first. They looked betrayed – didn't quite go along with it. Then, after the initial shock and horror had worn off, I was fair game for sport and they started ripping the piss out of me.

Obviously, the financial package from Sunderland was great if not *crazy*. And with me being worse for wear when I met up with the lads on the Quayside, I was giving it the big one. Docked on the Tyne was a yacht, or so I thought. I turned to Paul, "With what I'm going to be earning I'm going to buy one of them," I said, nodding in the direction of the vessel with my proud face on.

Quick as flash he said, "Really? You must be on a good salary because that's HMS Newcastle! It's worth millions and belongs to Her Majesty the Queen's Royal Navy!"

We all just fell about laughing. I was on a good contract but not enough to buy one of the Queen's battle ships.

The day after I agreed to sign for Sunderland, I was out playing golf at Wynyard Hall with Paul. We got to the 16th and Lorraine, my wife, rang to say she thinks someone is messing about because she'd just received a call from the FA. The caller said the England team were away in Bulgaria or Moldova but there was going to be a squad announcement for La Tournoi. It was a mini tournament in France between the hosts, Italy, Brazil and England... and I was in! I thought it was a wind-up as well. I'd never been anywhere near the squad before and, the season that had just finished, I had been in and out of the Newcastle team. I summoned up the courage to ring the number, still not sure if it was for real, but it was the FA and it was all legit. I was thinking, 'Fucking hell, Reidy said he'd get me in the England squad but I never thought it would be that quick. That's 24 hours later!' He must have some clout, eh?

I sent a message through to Glenn Hoddle and his number two, John Gorman, saying I was delighted and honoured to be named in the squad. Although I'd agreed in principle to put pen to a contract on Wearside, I hadn't actually signed it. I told Hoddle my unveiling as a Sunderland player had been arranged for the day the squad were flying out to France. I asked whether it would be OK to join up later. He said, "No problem," and I could fly out on the Monday night.

My mind was swimming at this stage and I wondered whether my agent had inserted a clause in the contract stating a bonus for an England call up. I rang Paul Stretford and he said, "Leave it with me." So, while my agent, the Black Cats' chairman and manager were thrashing out the fine details of my contract, they were happy to insert the England squad call up clause because it was to the club's benefit. Having an England international on Sunderland's books would only reflect positively on the club. It was a statement of intent by the Wearsiders. Having a full England international in the squad would attract players who had similar ambitions to play for the national team. It has been said that an England call up is harder for those footballers playing in the North-East. My inclusion contradicted that statement. Get in!

I'd bought a pin-striped suit while I was on holiday in Marbella a few weeks before I signed for the Wearsiders. It was grey with a black stripe running through it. But for all intents and purposes it looked like it was black and white. I was also wearing a black and white tie. Brilliant. Sunderland was in the process of moving to the Stadium of Light and Reid's office was still at Roker Park. When I turned up Reidy was in *Dad's Army* 'Don't Panic!' mode.

"Fucking hell! You're wearing black and white, man! You can't be wearing black and white."

I was like, "What you on about? It's grey, man."

He absolutely slaughtered me for it in private, but in public, he was magnificent, saying a lot of complimentary things about me and making me feel at ease. One of the funniest moments of the press conference was, straight after, when we went back to his office for a celebratory drink. *Sky Sports News* was on his TV and the ticker bar was flashing... *Breaking News: England squad announced for Le Tournoi. New Sunderland signing Lee Clark is in the squad.*

Reidy's face was a picture.

He turns to me and says, "You little fucker!"

I tried to play it all innocent and replied, "What you on about?"

"You knew about that, you little fucker! That's why you got that clause inserted into your contract, you little bastard." He was priceless.

My old man came with me when I signed for Sunderland and he stopped with Reidy while I shot off to France. My new boss said, "It's OK, I'll look after him, son. I'll take him for a few beers."

After that, I never heard from my dad for a couple of days, which is quite unusual, so I gave him a call.

He said, "I felt terrible the next day. He can n'arf drink, can't he?"

My dad has always been able to handle his bevy but not on that Herculean scale. Consequently, he missed two days of work, ill, because of it. It was pretty standard after a night out with Reidy.

I got battered by the Newcastle lads when I turned up in France for the tournament. There's a picture where Alan Shearer has me around the neck. He's saying, "What the heck are you doing signing for Sunderland?" Maybe the words were a little stronger than that, to be fair. It looks like I'm laughing but I'm not sure it was fun because the swine was strangling me. It was like a home from home. Old teammates such as: Rob Lee, David Batty, Shearer, Andy Cole and Gazza were all there. But the other lads helped as well like Tim Flowers and Ian Wright. The same can be said about the up and coming boys at the time: David Beckham, Paul Scholes and the Neville brothers, Gary and Phil. I was an unused substitute in the three games and I was gutted, to be honest. It's all the more galling now when I look back and see players come on for 30 seconds in an England game and they're classed as internationals. When I look at the England players I was competing against, to the competition for places today, it was definitely tougher to get in the national side in my era.

Was I apprehensive about joining Sunderland? Of course I was. Who wouldn't be in my position? Somehow though, I managed to put a mental block on it. Newcastle fans didn't turn on me because I went back to St James' Park loads of times to watch my home team play. There was plenty of friendly banter. There was nothing aggressive and I never felt under threat. I got, "Coming to watch a big team?" and all of that banter. What I hadn't accounted for was how Sunderland fans were going to react to having a bona fide Geordie in their ranks; one of their enemies, if you like.

Admittedly, I was a bit nervous, tentative and apprehensive on the first day of training at Sunderland. Not only was I worried about the Black Cats' fans, but the reaction from the other lads was playing heavy on my mind as well. I'm a former Newcastle favourite and fan; Geordie through and through; club's record signing and not sure how people were going to take to me. I walked into the dressing room and see my old teammate, David Kelly, from Newcastle's 1992-93 promotion winning season. You ask any supporter old enough to remember Ned in his pomp and they will tell you he is revered as much as a Shearer, Milburn, Beardsley and all of those illustrious names from the Magpies' glorious past. His goals stopped us from sliding into the third tier of English football for the first time in the club's history. The following season his goals took us into the top flight and the hallowed Premier League. There were a few nods and the odd 'hello' as I walked into the changing room. Then Ned saw me and let rip, "Fucking hell, you must be getting some money to come here!" It was a proper ice-breaking moment and everyone in the dressing room fell about laughing.

Fortunately, I hit the ground running. I had an excellent pre-season, contributed to a good team performance in the club's first game at the Stadium of Light, a 0-0 draw against an excellent Ajax side. I then scored on my home debut in the ground's first competitive fixture when beating Man City 3-1. If I hadn't hit the ground running it could've been a lot different. I don't know how the fans would've reacted.

The results were awful at the beginning of the season. We won only one and lost three of our opening four fixtures. That inconsistency continued for a month or so, as we tried to find some fluency in our game. Then there was a bit of a watershed moment at Reading where we got battered 4-0. Incredibly, Reading finished bottom of the league that season.

Reidy went ballistic in the dressing room, kicked me up the arse and said, "I've wasted a right few quid on you!" He's what you might call a hairdryer manager. Think of the Tasmanian Devil sharing several pints of Nitro-glycerine with Yosemite Sam in a local pub. Yes, he's animated and loud but you knew where you stood with him. From that game on we hardly lost a match for the rest of the season. Sadly, we just got pipped to second place by Bryan Robson's Middlesbrough. Only a point separated the teams. The games against Boro were probably the difference because they beat us home and away to do the double over us. The Teessiders also beat us in the League Cup. This put us in the lottery of the play-offs.

We beat Sheffield United 3-2 on aggregate in the semi-final to win the right to play Charlton Athletic in the final. We got beat 2-1 at Bramall Lane before recording a 2-0 triumph at the Stadium of Light. The 1998 play-off final is very much fêted by the neutrals in the same way the Premier League classic between Newcastle and Liverpool is celebrated in 1996. It had everything: drama, excitement, a hero, a villain and, astonishingly, both of them were Mackems.

Clive Mendonca was a Sunderland fan playing for the Addicks. It couldn't have been scripted any better for him, as these things generally turn out to be. I've seen it so many times in my career where a former player or supporter returns to haunt his old club or boyhood team. The latter was the case at Wembley. Mendonca netted a hat-trick to inflict a devastating blow on his home-town club and also netted a penalty in the shoot-out.

The match ebbed and flowed in favour of both sides and finished all square, 3-3, at the end of 90 minutes. We then went 4-3 up against the Addicks in injury-time of extra-time. Our goal machine Kevin Phillips was already off the field. Reidy took me off as well because I thought I had cramp. Turns out I'd pulled a calf muscle. We thought we'd done it by that stage. But then Richard Rufus equalised to take it to penalties. Phillips was our number one penalty taker and I was number two. All ten penalties were scored and then we were into a nail-biting sudden death situation. No Sunderland supporters need reminding of what happened next as Micky Gray missed his penalty and we were condemned to another season in the Football League's second tier.

It was as if someone had died when we got back to the dressing room. Heads were down, there were a few tears and it was an emotional place to find yourself. Reidy declared, "We've got nothing to be ashamed of. We had a right good go at it and we'll have another go next season." He then told us the chairman had organised a party for the players and wives in Peterborough. The boss added we could still have a good night and that we deserved it for our efforts.

A big room was set aside for us to go and see our families after the match. The club was great with our nearest and dearest. They put them up in a hotel the night before the clash and really looked after them. The devastation was so bad after we lost the contest that Bobby Saxton got back on the team bus in his tracksuit and boots. He hadn't changed into his club suit. He was on a different planet and his emotions were running high. Saxton's wife had got Reidy's permission for the players' wives and girlfriends to join their husbands and boyfriends to go to the party on the Sunderland coach. When she got on the bus, Bobby exploded.

"Where do you think you're going? This is for the players and staff. Get off the bus!"

"But Peter said we could come back with you."

"Your mother never went down the pit with your father, did she?"

Saxton's wife was distraught. But we all were. The players' wives got off the bus and went on another one. Reidy's number two then turned on defenders Darren Williams and Jody Craddock and gave it to them big style, "You two fuckers have just cost us a place in the Premier League! I told you all week about looking after Mendonca!"

Williams and Craddock didn't need telling anything. They were just as devastated as the rest of us. The bus journey was horrendous for the first hour. The tension was excruciating. Saxton was sitting in the middle of the bus taking pot shots at certain players as they went past. It was horrific. Reidy eventually persuaded him to go and sit at the front of the bus in the end so we wouldn't be on the end of his cutting remarks. He eventually apologised to the boss and the lads for his outbursts. But the gaffer and everyone understood.

We went to the party, which was flat, and just went through the motions. It was an anti-climax. There was nothing to celebrate, so we had a few drinks to try and get it out of our system. We all took it badly but none more so than Micky Gray. It took all summer to get it out of his system.

Lionel Perez didn't have the best of games for us that day and I'm being polite. In fact, I took a call off Terry Mac a week or so after the game.

"What about Perez?" he said.

"I know, he was shit, wasn't he?"

He went, "No, we're going to sign him. What do you think?"

I was speechless! Couldn't believe they were replacing a fans' favourite like Pavel Srnicek – with him.

Kevin Phillips arrived at Sunderland around the same time as I did and what a great signing he turned out to be for £325,000.

Phillips got completely under every club's radar. Like all good strikers he had that selfish streak but you could tell straight away he had quality. He had a bit of a slow start but ended the campaign with 35 goals, linking up perfectly with Niall Quinn.

Phillips was a good lad but he was a typical striker who seemed to believe if he scored in a 2-1 loss, he'd done his job and he was free from blame. The team lost because it was everyone else's fault bar his. Sunderland was a big club but I got the feeling Phillips, after a couple of years of success at the Stadium of Light, thought he was better or deserved something bigger and better. Yet despite having a good career, and no disrespect to any of those clubs he played for, none of them were bigger than Sunderland. He went to smaller clubs with the exception of Aston Villa.

Sunderland made some great signings that season: Nicky Summerbee and Chris Makin came in. I think Allan Johnson might have been there already. Bridges couldn't get in the team. He was our substitute or super sub. He liked to have a laugh as did Gray. Our Mackem-born left-back was the butt of a few jokes because he loved himself. If he was chocolate he'd lick himself. He was Mr Flash, but in a good way. I heard Wayne Rooney knocked him out over a remark he made about his wife, Colleen. I wouldn't be surprised if it did happen because he was a cheeky bugger. When Mick McCarthy came in as manager at Sunderland, he had a team meeting telling players not to be extravagant or spend lots of money because dozens of people at the club were losing their jobs. The day after this chat with the players, Gray turned up to training in a brand new Ferrari.

I scored something like 13 or 14 goals in my first campaign on Wearside and the last four to five months were spent with me struggling with a double hernia problem. I could've got 20 goals had I been firing on all cylinders. But Reidy had asked me to continue playing. I had a lot of freedom to express myself.

Kevin Ball and Alex Rae played alongside me and they protected or looked after the ugly or defensive side of the game. And make no mistake about it, I was playing well. Ball was as much as a red and white as I was a black and white. And Bally and Gray became two of my best friends at the club. But there was never going to be a problem because they saw that I give my all when I was at the club.

Ball was great in the middle of midfield anchor role. He was a fantastic professional and trained hard Monday to Friday, kicking people in training in the process. He wouldn't try to do things he wasn't capable of. He would win the ball and give it to the ball players. He was a good man to have around for set pieces; very aggressive in the penalty area. You would never take the piss out of Bally, cut his clothes up or play tricks. He'd probably give you a good hiding. When I went to Sunderland I always thought Bally would be the one I had to win over because he was an adopted red and white. We became very good friends when we were at Fulham and ended up having a flat together for a few months. The lunatic had me doing sit ups before I was going to bed! If I give him the choice of going out for a meal and a glass of red wine or do 100 sit ups, he'd choose the sit ups every time. You could wash your clothes on my abs around that time, they were that hard and ripped. At least if I had a career-ending injury at the time I could have still made a decent living hiring my torso out to skiffle bands. Bally then moved on to Burnley and I was glad to see the back of him. Only joking mate!

I had an operation at the end of my first season to fix the double hernia problem and missed quite a bit of pre-season for the new campaign. Then the first game of the new term I broke my leg 30 minutes into the home contest with QPR. I cut across someone, he clipped my heels and my legs got caught up. I'll never forget it. The assistant physio took me to Sunderland

General Hospital in my strip. The nurse said, "If you're out tonight don't go dancing." But the club doctor transferred me across to the Nuffield in Jesmond and I was out injured until October.

Bizarrely, I had my father-in-law and a few friends at the match in one of the boxes and wondered why I hadn't heard anything from them. I was supposed to be going out with them after the QPR game. Turns out, because they're black and white, they'd closed the curtains because they didn't want to watch the match. They'd enjoyed the hospitality alright. They all got plastered, ironically, a different type to the plastering I was getting. They decided to watch the racing on the TV instead. None of them knew I'd broken my leg! Typical Geordies! *We'll come to your ground, drink your beer, but we're not watching your team play.* Lorraine, my wife, was away on holiday with the kids and saw it on the Sky Sports ticker bar.

Sunderland's chief executive, John Fickling, rang me up afterwards and asked if I wanted anything. I told him I couldn't drive now so he arranged for the club's car sponsors, Mill Garages, to send a car with a driver. It was only a seven series BMW. He picked me up and took me everywhere. Took me to training, the pub and restaurants and just sat in the car and waited for me. I didn't milk it, not much anyway. Well... it's not every day you get a chauffeur, is it? Reidy got wind of it and pulled me into the office to give me a bollocking.

"You fucking turn up in a seven series BMW! What do you think you're playing at?"

"It's not my fault. John asked if I needed anything. I didn't think he was going to send me a driver and a BM."

"All the fucking players will want one if they see that, you little fucker!"

I enjoyed my two years on Wearside. The club looked after me well and I got on with the players there. I had some fun winding up the lads – all good-natured banter. I was always reminded of my black and white heritage by the red and white contingent, so sometimes I would play up to it. It was never to the detriment or disrespect of the club. One part of my contract insisted that I got the best sponsored club car, which was a Jaguar. When I went to pick it up it was red with a white interior. I wasn't having that so I changed it to a black car with a white leather interior. The lads all slaughtered me for it, but I loved it; all good craic. I couldn't drive red and white, man!

At the same time, I played up to being a Sunderland player with my Newcastle supporting mates as well. There was this one time when I went around to my father-in-law's house. He's more black and white than Bertie Bassett's belly; a proper Toon fanatic. I knocked on his door and he wouldn't let me or my son, Jak, in his house until we took off our Sunderland tracksuits. He spoke to us through the letter box. He was apoplectic and gave me a right telling off.

"What if the neighbours see you?"

Paul reckoned he would've been shunned in the street or put in stocks and pelted with rotten eggs, cabbages and tomatoes. We gave in and changed out of our Sunderland kits and into some civvy clothes on the street before he let us in. You can't get more black and white than that. He probably bricked the chimney up so Santa couldn't get in.

Reidy was always up for some good craic. He was a proper man's man and a great man manager. He'd regularly come over and sit with me in the dining room after training on a Monday and say,

"Haway then, what are your mates all singing about me at St James' Park?"

I'd say, "They're just singing about your monkey's heed."

There was always going to be the unavoidable issue of him having a monkey's head. He loved all that though. He often went across to watch games in Newcastle and pop into the Black Bull opposite St James' Park for a pint. With the exception of The Strawberry it is the closest pub to St James' Park, staunch black and white and proper tough to boot. I mean, there aren't many people with the balls to go in there anyway, never mind if you're the manager of Sunderland! It just doesn't happen.

He came back and told me, "I had a great time. They were battering me, but I bought them all a pint and they ended up me best mates."

It never got aggressive with Reidy because of his nature. It was all just banter. He was always respectful to Newcastle fans and I reckon it was the same back.

Reidy was always good value whether he was losing it, having a laugh or being the manager. I got my mate Micky Holland a job at Sunderland. He's now a masseur at Newcastle. He ended up being Reidy's driver when he was on the piss. Micky told me he was with Reidy when they both saw Milton Nunez for the first time.

Apparently Reidy turned to Micky:

"Who's the black lad?"

"Which one?"

"The little fucker, there."

"That's your new signing, Milton Nunez."

"That's not the Milton Nunez I saw on the DVD. He was white and 6ft 4! He's black and 5ft 2!"

"Well you've just paid £1.5m for him, gaffer."

Apparently there was hell on that they signed the wrong player!

I loved my two years with Reidy. He was a great manager to play for. He was different to Keegan and Daglish but brilliant in his own way. He could rip your head off verbally within a second but you knew he was on your side. All that side of things was just business and you need to adapt your personality to deal with things. But outside of those dressing room situations, he was a top lad.

I was always a bit of a hot head in my younger days. When I came back from my broken leg, I made a couple of substitute appearances to ease myself back into it. I had about 20 minutes here and there and a game for the reserves in total. We were then due to go to Bradford, who were our rivals for the title. The manager named the team prior to the game and I was on the bench again. I'm thinking, 'I should be playing; they're our main rivals for the championship.'

In the first half we were terrible and I heard Saxton telling Reidy, "We've got to get him on." Reidy is telling him to 'leave it' until eventually I'm told to get stripped with 20 minutes to go. It was an eventful game because our goalkeeper Thomas Sorensen got sent off and Quinny went in goal.

I eventually got on the pitch and we won 2-0. We got back into the changing room after the game and Saxton says, "Right lads, everyone's off tomorrow; only the reserves are in."

"What time is training?" I piped up.

"No, you're off, son."

"I thought you said the reserves were in?"

"Please don't start, Lee, son."

"I'm coming in, so what time is training?"

I went into training the next day for devilment more than anything else. There was always an unwritten rule among the players and staff, if Reidy ever lost a game of head tennis in training, don't go and see him and have a go about something. He loved his head tennis and was as competitive as ever with the lads. Anyway, he'd lost at head tennis this day and I was waiting for him as he came to his office.

"Can I have a word, gaffer?"

19

"Yeah, what is it?"

"You bottled it last night, didn't you?"

"Bottled it?"

"Aye, you bottled it. You went with Kevin Ball and Darren Williams in centre of midfield. You played two centre halves in there against one of the best teams in the league! It says a lot about me that. I must be hopeless if I can't get in the team before them. Pick the phone up and see if anyone wants me. I'll leave now."

"Bottled it?!" Reidy shouted!

"Aye, you bottled it! I thought you liked to entertain. I'm not coming to Sunderland to be sub."

"You've been out for four months with a broken leg! You've just come back!"

"Doesn't matter; I'm your best player. I should've been playing."

"Look, you'll be starting against Bolton on Saturday."

"Too late now."

I then left his office leaving Reidy fuming. I saw Pop Robson, later, after a shower and he told me that he'd just had a meeting with Saxton and Reidy in his office. Pop said the gaffer was screaming, "What about that fucker? He's telling me I've bottled it! His craic is brilliant." Pop was another one I got on really well with. Pop was in fits. He said, "I can't believe you told him he bottled it. Never mind, Reidy loves you son."

Kevin Kyle was just a gangly 6ft 4 youngster when I was on Wearside. One day he went to see the gaffer and Reidy was thinking, 'What does he want? I don't even know the kid.' Maybe he was put up to this by the others, I don't know, but he wasn't the sharpest of tools in the box.

"I know you've got Quinny in the team and he's a big lad, and I'm a big lad," said Kyle. "I can miss sitters like Quinny if you want. I can miss-control the ball, trip up and fall over as well. I'm just saying cos I reckon I could save you some money. I'm only on £100 a week while Quinny must be on £20,000 a week."

"Are you taking the piss?"

"No gaffer, I'm not trying to be disrespectful. I'm just saying if you want to save some money, I can be as shit as him."

"Fucking get out of this office!"

Alex Rae was a good character. He always used to batter Quinny about his clothes. Quinny was a great fella; a nice man and a laugh a minute. There are a few players on the red and white side and black and white side who are respected and liked by both sides of the Tyne and Wear. You can name them on one hand: Sir Bobby Robson, Gazza and Pavel Srnicek spring to mind but Niall Quinn is definitely one of those.

Quinny was out with me and Micky Holland for a drink one day. I think it was a Sunday afternoon. We went over to this bar in Scotswood, the Sporting Arms. When I walked in everyone's shouting, "Clarky, how you doing, son?" and all that. They did the same with Micky. Then Quinny walks in behind us and the bar comes to a standstill. All eyes were on Quinny. But they were on us as well through our association. Sensing he had to do something fast to undo a potential tricky situation, the Irishman tells the barman to buy the bar a round of drinks on him. After that everyone in the room was his best mate. But that wasn't the half of it. We noticed the barman was serving drinks wearing a golf glove and sporting a cap on his head. Everyone in the bar seemed to be kitted out in Pringle or Argyle golf jumpers and t-shirts. There were several of the clientele walking around in golf shoes and playing pool dressed like Seve Ballesteros, even using a golf club as a snooker cue. It was madness, hilarious! Quinny's looking around the bar thinking he's just walked into Bedlam or some other mad house. I'm thinking, 'Just a regular Sunday afternoon in a local boozer.' We later learned there'd been a ram-raid at Ramside Hall and one or two of the customers had robbed the golf shop.

The initial disappointment of breaking my leg in the first game of the season to QPR was a distant memory and I was back in the side playing well and helping the side to maintain its lead at the top of the table. We'd only lost twice in the league by the time Leicester knocked us out of the League Cup semi-finals on aggregate. Promotion and the Premier League was not only a certainty, but it was well within our reach, and I was delighted to be playing a part in Sunderland's success. Nonetheless, it slowly began to dawn on me that Newcastle would be waiting for me in the top flight and this was a big dilemma.

After the second leg of the League Cup semi-final, I went to see the gaffer in his office. He was there with Andy Gray, although the Sky Sports reporter was there in a social rather than a professional capacity. They went back a long way and played together at Everton in the mid-80s. The boss asked what I wanted. At first I was reluctant to say it front of Andy. But Reidy just told me to spit it out, so I told him I wanted to move on. Said I'd had two great years at the club, but I can't play for Sunderland in the Premier League against Newcastle.

Reidy just turned around and screamed, "Fucking get out of my office! You're fucking going nowhere!"

Reidy thought it was the disappointment of getting knocked out of the League Cup after going so close. After all, I was a player who wore his heart on his sleeve. I couldn't hide emotions and disappointment. We had a proper sit down and talk about it later on. We'd just about sealed our return to the top flight around that time despite having only about two months of the season left. I gave my reasons to him again and he still wasn't having it. He wouldn't accept my explanation.

"We're going to the Premier League next season and I'm not letting my best player leave. You're coming with me."

We never spoke about it again after that and I played and helped secure the title, scoring at Barnsley in a 3-1 victory.

Even though my time at the Stadium of Light ended on a sour note, I'd like to think Sunderland supporters appreciated I was an influential player in a very good team during my time on Wearside. Sunderland fans knew where my heart lay but were happy as long as I did the business for them on the pitch. And they knew I always did that.

In hindsight, because of my background, it was probably a mistake signing for Sunderland. That's not to say I didn't enjoy my two seasons on Wearside. As you've just read, I had two of the best years of my life. But everyone knows I'm Newcastle through and through and I couldn't give 100 per cent for Sunderland against the club I love. And if I couldn't do that I'd have been cheating on Reid, his number two Saxton, the fans and all my team-mates. It was best that I went and Reidy knew how I felt before what happened at Wembley with t-shirtgate.

In the past, when I said I couldn't play for the Black Cats against the Magpies I was accused of being unprofessional. I don't think it was. I was just being honest. It was how I felt at the time and I still feel the same now. Ask any diehard Newcastle fan or Sunderland supporter and they'll understand. I know for a fact they will empathise with me. Playing for Fulham against Newcastle? That was never a problem. That was a very different situation. To understand, you have to know about the feeling between the two North-East clubs. People talk about the Old Firm game; the Merseyside and Manchester derbies; the north London contests and other local clashes. I'm sure they are passionate, feisty affairs with no quarter drawn. But the Tyne and Wear derby is something else. There is pure hatred, poison and venom. It makes (seemingly) rational people punch horses for God's sake. I wish that wasn't the case but it just is and always will be.

CHAPTER 2
KNITTED JUMPERS FOR GOALPOSTS!

There's always someone to piss on your parade, isn't there? Or just to dampen it so it won't even ignite.

I walked out of an exam at Benfield School. Not to be defiant, I just was being pulled in another direction. As I walked out, a teacher shouted I'd have no future. Those fearsome, menacing, and almost foreboding words roared from her mouth. There was no nicety, no encouragement to come back and try. Fortunately, that prediction didn't come back to haunt me. Although, to be honest, she could have been right. What was going through my head? I'm not sure. I just knew I had to get away from the place.

I was pretty focused at school and performed well until the last two years of my education. Did I take my eye off the ball (pun intended), as such? I probably did. But I was playing a lot of football for the school, Newcastle Boys, Wallsend Boys Club, Northumberland, England Schoolboys and, of course, United's reserves and youth team. Football was my life. I didn't have enough time to dedicate towards academic studies, so my schooling suffered in the end.

I'm not going to say I was an immaculately behaved, model student because that wasn't the case. In the end I just wanted to leave school as quickly as I could, join Newcastle and start an apprenticeship. To do this meant missing my exams. I had a dilemma because there were a few subjects I was interested in. In the end I didn't, or rather couldn't, go through with the exams. I got as far as sitting down and writing my name at the top of the paper. Then I thought, 'No, I don't want to do this. I'm not wasting my time in here for two hours to do something that will have no relevance to me in the future. Football is for me.' Of course, this was a ridiculous thing to do. I know that now. You always need a Plan B; something to fall back on. Without meaning to sound ancient, there were days when your parents used to say things like, "You need to get yourself a trade," because it was a given that you'd always be able to find work. It's a bit of a risk for us lot because many of us had the same 'I don't need qualifications' attitude. I was lucky to have had a relatively injury-free career – anything dangerous enough to draw the curtain on my profession and I'd be auditioning for *X-Factor* or tiling your bathroom. I'm hardly setting a good example to future generations because all young footballers should be encouraged to stick in with their studies.

I stood up in the exam hall and my geography teacher, Miss Larrow, shouted:

"Clark, where are you going?"

"I can't do this, I'm leaving." I replied.

And that is when she delivered the cutting lines: "I'll see you on the dole queue. There's no future in football, son."

A few years down the line I was invited to open a new gym at my old school. 'The irony,' I hear you say! I know! Robbie Elliott's dad, George, was a teacher at Benfield: a great man, tough but a good bloke all the same. The school was going to be an elite venue for gymnasts and athletes to train and make use of the amenities. The school had great facilities when I was there. There was an indoor swimming pool; tennis courts; several football and rugby pitches and an indoor area for basketball. I played for the rugby and cricket teams at Benfield. I enjoyed the rugby but found cricket too boring. I couldn't focus when playing. I was honoured to open the event. The school had bent over backwards accommodating me when I was a pupil so I was more than happy to return the favour.

I was an established Premier League footballer at the time and obviously the luxuries that come with it meant, among other

things, I had a nice car. And further karmatic ironicals ensued…
yep, you guessed it… the first person I bumped into on arrival
was Miss Larrow. She couldn't have been nicer, asking how I
was and that it was good to see me, etc. As I said earlier, I got on
with all of the teachers and especially Miss Larrow.

So I turned to her and pointed to the car.

"There's no future in football, eh?" I quipped.

There was no malice or spite or anything like that, just a bit
of good natured fun and we both had a giggle about it as we
reminisced over my schooldays. I could have been a twat about
it and so could she, but that would have been pointless and
childish. It was brilliant to be asked back – it's things like that
what make it worthwhile for us. People who say being asked to
do such things is a ball-ache have got to be lying.

My family lived in a terraced house in Pottery Bank, in the
tough working-class area of Walker. There were two pubs: The
Lord Raglin Inn and Ellison Arms, a general store, a chip shop
and, after a bit of a grassy area, you looked directly at the River
Tyne. In fact my back garden was about 500 yards away from
the banks of the Tyne. Me and my mates would often go under
the railway bridges down by the Tyne and make swings. My
mother was never happy when she found out we'd been down
there. She was always fearful of some tragedy lurking around
the corner.

Walker isn't the most affluent corner of the North-East. It's
not a bleak neighbourhood, in a Dickensian *Hard Times* or
Great Expectations sense, but it is a tough place to live. There
aren't many prospects for youngsters because the government
have continually failed to invest in the area. As a consequence,
it's easy to see how kids are seduced by an alternative lifestyle,
given there is little in terms of entertainment; other than crime,
villainy and drugs. Hundreds, maybe even thousands, of kids in

Walker become yet another failing statistic of society. Some have spent time as a resident in one of Her Majesty's prisons as a consequence of the choices they've made in life.

Good friends, very loyal to me, have taken a path which has led to crime and drugs. I had a tough choice to make when I was a kid and let them go. I couldn't afford to be mixed up with them or their life. It would've finished my career before it even started. It happened to David Roche later on. He was a good friend, fine footballer and eventually got a decent move to Peterborough, then Doncaster and finally Southend. But, unfortunately, he got mixed up an alternative lifestyle away from football.

My brother, Michael was another who fell foul of the authorities and later in his life spent time inside. Michael was involved in three armed robbery raids when he was younger. My old man said it would be better if he found another occupation because he wasn't very good at being a robber. He got caught every time (see, should have had a Plan B!). All joking aside, he did time in prison, came out but couldn't get a job. You're supposed to get rehabilitated when you go inside and it's supposed to prepare you for a life on the outside. You learn a skill or a trade like our Michael did. Unfortunately, it's a waste of time because as soon as an employer discovers you've got a police record they won't give you the job. This has happened several times to my brother. It's little wonder people go on to reoffend. The government want to have a hard look at this structure and fix it otherwise the social system will continue to break down. All the same, it was hard to take for the family.

My family were victims of crime, like many others in the Walker area. We got burgled and I had a few medals and trophies stolen. My old man was furious. He had a few of his awards stolen from his racing pigeons. He was very proud of the trophies he'd won. The crooks thought they could get a few bob to feed their drug habit. I knew who the thieves were. I had to go to their door and one of them got a good hiding for his troubles. I understood their reasons for doing it and it was sad. Once upon a time they were good friends of mine. They were desperate for the money and that was the only way they knew how. It wasn't even personal to them, but it was to us losing our valuables. I didn't know it at the time, but this was my chance to get out and escape from the pressures and temptations of crime. It eventually saw me play in the Premier League, get a record transfer and the money and riches from that set me up for life. If I didn't have football who is to say I wouldn't have been one of these lads. I'd like to think I wouldn't have taken that route, just because I was growing up in that environment, but who knows. As it happens I never had to that choice to make. Football, got in the way of everyday life. It *became* my life.

My first football memory is from about 1978, while I was a kid at St Anthony's School, in Walker, at the top of Pottery Bank. It isn't there now. This would have made me about six-years-old. My old school teacher, Jim Horrocks, approached as I was kicking a football around in the playground and asked whether I would be interested in playing for the school team, when classes finished, because they were a man short. I must have been decent because this was for the Under-11s. Mr Horrocks was a brilliant sports teacher and a good tutor in general. Everyone was in awe of him. He was very much a Dickensian type of character in stature: a huge, tall man, enormous beard and booming voice. But as you got older the fear factor between the kids disappeared because he was such a warm, lovable bloke who liked to laugh.

I couldn't wait to get home and collect my football boots, the hallowed £6.99 Woolworths' Specials, with the orange stripes down the side. Obviously this was all my parents could afford but I loved them because they were my first football boots. All the same, I thought I was the dog's bollocks in them. I remember the bus trip to Wallsend High Street to buy them with my mother. The excitement, trepidation and thrill of going into Woolies were almost tangible. You had to be a kid of a certain age to get the feeling. I couldn't wait to get home, try them on and then get out on the field so I could pretend to be one of my heroes playing for Newcastle. Thinking back, I seem to remember wearing them around the house.

Micky Edmondson, who runs The Back Page shop, in Newcastle, had been the main man at our school at the time. He was the star player because he turned out for Newcastle Boys, which was the area team. Micky was a prolific goalscorer and professional football clubs were looking at him. He was the one we all aspired to play like at the time (and I'm not just saying it so he stocks this book in his shops). I was substitute for the school team game but I got thrown on in the second half. I didn't think much about it, took it in my stride because I loved playing football. The lads were twice the size of me and double the weight, but it didn't matter because I treat the game as if I was playing in the school yard with my mates.

As the weeks went by I started to play on a Saturday morning. There was a pathway that used to run down the side of our school and a graveyard in Walker. That was our St James' Park or Wembley and where we used to play our school team games. Hundreds would come and watch us play. One week Brian Clark approached and asked whether I'd like to play for the famous Wallsend Boys Club. Brian recently retold the story in the press and apparently I gave him a load of cheek. As if that happened! I'm sure you're mistaken Brian, I was never a cheeky kid. Brian was, and is, a well-known figure among the local and junior football fraternity and became a Newcastle United scout. The likes of Alan Shearer, Peter Beardsley, Steve Bruce and, later, Michael Carrick and Fraser Forster played for Wallsend.

But there are literally hundreds who have made it as a professional footballer who once represented the famous North Tyneside club; many of them mates, like: Alan Thompson, Steve Watson and Robbie Elliott. Not a bad CV, Brian.

I went down to train with Wallsend. We'd do half an hour in the gym lifting weights, star jumps and burpees, then another half-hour training. Obviously I was getting impatient because I wasn't getting a game and didn't understand why. There was a rule, which is still in place now, stating you couldn't play competitively for a boy's club until you were nine-years-old. Obviously, I didn't know that at the time. I hassled to the point where the manager eventually relented and cough, cough, I played every week, under a different identity at the age of six and seven. The manager would tell me my new name every week and shout it from the sidelines. But once the game was under way I was in the zone and never paid any attention to whatever my 'name' was because it didn't register with me. He could have shouted Keegan, Supermac or Billy the Fish for all I cared, I still wouldn't have heard. I was too focused on the game to hear anything from the sidelines.

My early football skills were developed in a yard at the front of the house, which had a bin storage area. I always tried to kick the ball against the wall but on many occasions I cracked or smashed the kitchen window. The council joiner, or glazer, was forever around at our house fixing the result of my, not quite as yet, finely honed skills. If I was chased from the front yard by my parents I'd go to the square, nearby, which had concrete balls in situ at either side. My friends and I used them as the goals. I always played against the older lads, my brother and his mates, who were, sometimes, over ten years older than me. I always got one over them because, it was usually my ball and, if they upset me I'd pick it up and take it home! This was a regular occurrence because they were tough lads with a vicious sense of humour.

There was also a grassy area outside the flats at Pottery Bank where we used to play. We managed to knock up some goal posts out of scrap timber. I persuaded my mother to knit some nets for us. She was a prolific knitter and used to knock out some lovely jumpers; although there were a few horrendous ones in there as well. Yeah, we could have just used jumpers for goalposts, but why would you when you can have proper goals with nets? There isn't a better sight than seeing a ball hit the back of the net. Those games involved 15-a-side at times. On other occasions we would be playing three pots in or whatever took our fancy. After the game we would take them down carefully, and pack them at home until the next game, which was always the next day.

My dad was a Newcastle supporter, as was my brother Michael. My first game at St James' Park was in 1980 when my brother and his mates took me in the Gallowgate End. Bill McGarry was the manager and the team included Billy Rafferty and Bobby Shinton. I can't remember the game, unfortunately, although it was a bleak time for the club. I could've picked any concrete bollard to sit on in the Gallowgate at the time because it wasn't rammed the way it is now.

There was never a school uniform. In fact, I remember wearing an old England Admiral strip for school, from the 1982 World Cup in Spain. One day in Art we did some painting and before I knew it my beloved England top was covered in red paint. I was distraught. My mother did her best to get the paint off and I was lucky I didn't get told off. Ironically, Alan Thompson's mum was the school dinner lady and I had a few telling offs from her in my time. She was another who thought I was a cheeky kid! Slanderous, really!

My mum used to do the half-time oranges for the school team. She was always an enthusiastic participant and supporter, whereas my dad was the antithesis to that. He used to just stand and quietly watch. My mother got to see all of my school games because the old man worked 12-hour shifts as a dry liner on the buildings to provide for the family.

He played football in the army but not to any real level, nor did my brother Michael, who was more a cricket and rugby man. There was no genetic or generic family line of footballers to my knowledge. There was a cousin from my dad's side, Ian Mulholland, who went to Derby. He was an apprentice a few years before me but got diagnosed as a diabetic. There wasn't the science or knowledge on diabetes that we have today so he had to quit.

Arthur Appleton, a journalist and writer, once said the North-East was a "Hotbed of Soccer," and wrote a book about it. This was certainly the case in Walker. There were other teams in the Walker area like St Vincents, under Brian Simpson, god rest his soul, who had Paul Stephenson and Jeff Wrightson playing for him, while Ian Bogie turned out for West Walker. They all went on to play for Newcastle. These lads were all a lot older than me.

Things escalated at a ridiculous pace. I went from being a snotty nosed kid using his sleeve as a handkerchief in the playground, to the school team, boys club and beyond. There was always something happening. It may come as a surprise but I never thought I was a special or gifted footballer. I never dreamt in a million years, that when my brother took me to my first football match at St James' Park, I'd eventually join my heroes in later life. I didn't think it was possible. That was for other people, not for the likes of me. I didn't understand the process of how it worked and the thought never crossed my mind. I just carried on playing football for all of my teams.

I got to play for Newcastle City Boys, two years below my age group, at nine, in the Under-11s, while I was still playing for St Anthony's and Wallsend Boys Club. Things started to snowball from there with people taking much more interest. Peter Kirkley was the Youth Development Officer at Newcastle United and also involved at Wallsend.

One night after training Kirkley talked to me and my parents about joining Newcastle's Centre for Excellence, as it was called then, now, the Newcastle Academy. I went there from the age of ten. All of a sudden I had four football teams and found I was playing seven days a week and sometimes twice a day.

It was a surreal time when I was a teenager. There were regular knocks on the door on a Saturday morning, generally from representatives from different clubs the length and breadth of the country. They'd be interrupting my dad sitting in his string vest, like Rab C Nesbit, having his full English breakfast, asking whether I'd be interested in signing for them. On one occasion it was Alex Ferguson from Man United. I never had time to think. If I did, maybe my head would've exploded. But my upbringing helped because I was always grounded. I would never have been allowed to get above myself, if I had tried to give it the big one and pretend to be a huge star.

Joe Harvey was still around when I was a kid. He was Mr Newcastle: mentor to every manager, coach and scout who followed his exit as United boss in 1975. I was getting a lot of interest from clubs at the time and there was this match I was playing in for Wallsend Boys Club against a team from Norway. The game was put on at Benwell and Kirkley asked Harvey to come along and watch me. The club were about to offer me the contract of contracts if you like; never awarded to any youngster before. It was two years as a schoolboy, two years as an apprentice and two years as a professional footballer. In essence, they wanted Harvey's stamp of approval or blessing. It was dreamland. We won 9-1 and I scored seven. Apparently, Harvey said, "Do what you have to do to get his signature."

It's a shame because as a youngster I didn't know too much about United's former boss. I knew he'd been a player who had a bit of presence about him. But I had no idea what he'd done as a player and manager. In my humble opinion there should be a statue of him alongside Jackie Milburn and Sir Bobby Robson. Harvey was the last manager to win a major trophy and captained the club in the 1950s FA Cup final winning teams. Harvey's grandson, Gary, was at the Centre of Excellence, with me.

The club didn't just rest on their laurels trying to sign me. They didn't think, 'He's a Geordie lad and he'll sign automatically,' which, as it happens, I was and was going to anyway. As soon as I knew they were interested there was only one place I was going. They didn't know that. And there were about four or five clubs offering money to my family that would've made a hell of a difference to our lives. It would have set up the Clark family for life. My dad always let me make my own decisions in life; some of them have been right and some of them wrong. I often asked him for advice but ultimately the decisions have been mine.

Stan Nixon was the coach at the Centre of Excellence and, looking back, he was way ahead of his time. Even now when people talk about innovative training techniques, he was putting that into practise 30 years ago. Alan Thompson, Steve Watson, Robbie Elliott and Steve Howey were all part of this group. There were other talented kids there who, for whatever reason, didn't make it at Newcastle. Some went on to have a good career elsewhere and not just in football. There were several who didn't make it for attitude problems. I'm sure Nixon brought on and developed my ability to its maximum potential. A lot has been made of coaches not concentrating on the technical side and with the emphasis on running and fitness. You can't point that finger at Nixon. In all of our sessions he had the ball out and we practised on skills. The lads loved the training schedules they had under him.

I don't want to be disrespectful to where I was brought up because I am proud of where I come from. The east end of Newcastle is, and was, the making of me in many respects. I wouldn't want to change that. It gave me the grounding I needed and helped make who I am. When I became a successful footballer I always looked back on my time growing up in Walker with pride. I think that is what sets me out to be a little different to the players from my era because I've never tried to change; never thought I was better than anyone else or behaved like a Prima Donna. I've seen my brother and sister go without Christmas presents because I wanted a certain type of football boot. They were prepared to sacrifice that for me, which I always appreciated. I've never forgotten that. And I'm a fan at the end of the day. I'm like the supporters. I would've been on the terraces following the Magpies every week had I not been playing. Newcastle United recognised I had to leave Walker, however, and the environment, to be able to continue my development and progress. They wanted to take away any temptations that weren't law abiding. My family was part of a very loyal tight-knit community but had been victims of crime. Despite that, doors were just left open and friends were allowed to just walk in without knocking. And I would do the same at my friends' houses.

The club bought me a house in Mullen Gardens, Wallsend, when I was playing for England Schoolboys. My parents split up around this time and my father brought up me and my sisters, while my mother moved on. When I look back it's unbelievable how he managed to do it; working 12-hour shifts and then coming home to look after us. My older sister played a big part as well. I still get on with both of my parents and love them both. These things happen in life and you just have to get on with it. I wish it hadn't happened. I'd have loved for them to stay together. I always said to them, once I'd made it I'd buy them a house and a BMW. I hadn't realised it would be one house and BMW each!

It was crazy at this time. Like an explosion of activity in my football life. I was either at home or abroad playing in football tournaments and competitions for Newcastle against other clubs. This all culminated when I was selected to represent my country at Under-15 level. I was made captain and that was the cherry on the cake. I was getting national attention at this stage and ITV screened the game against Italy at Wembley where I scored a hat-trick. At that point, nothing could have been better... schoolboy captain of England, a hat-trick and on TV. It was a dream come true.

I remember playing in the Berlin Stadium against Germany. The stadium is famous for hosting the 1936 Olympics, where Jesse Owens claimed four gold medals in 100m, 200m, 4x100m relay and long jump. There were 50,000 people there when I played for my country and we got pumped 5-1. There were two sets of dressing rooms because the place was so big. One changing room, which was close to the pitch, was for half-time, and the one at the back of the stand, which was a bit of a hike, was used at the end of the game. There was a surprise for me coming off the pitch at half-time. Peter Kirkley popped his head out and said: "I've got someone to see you," and my dad comes into view. You might ask why this was a surprise, well, he'd never been abroad before and Newcastle had organised it all for me. Playing for your country is an exceptional moment in itself, but to share it with your father makes it extra special given the sacrifices he made for me. The result wasn't what I wanted but it was great to have my dad there to see me captain my country.

As a footnote, and you might laugh at this, but, family holidays were always spent at Whitley Bay Caravan Park. We used to travel in a taxi, because we never had a car. We thought it was great going in the taxi. It felt as if we were going on an Enid Blyton, *Five Go Mad*, adventure.

I played ten games for England schoolboys and captained them all. We played two games at Wembley. In the first I scored against Brazil in a 2-0 win in front of 50,000. Then there was the Italy clash where I netted a hat-trick in a 4-1 triumph. There were about 70,000 inside the stadium for that one. We also played Brazil at Roker Park, beating them 2-0 again. I netted in that one as well. The Brazilians didn't know what had hit them. Both squads travelled up together from Wembley to the North-East and stopped in a hotel in Washington. It started to snow when we arrived and the South American lads didn't know what it was. It was hilarious to watch. They were picking it up off the ground wondering what the hell the white stuff was. A cold wind blew from the north, and it made the trees rustle like living things. It wasn't that winter was coming, it was more like, "Bem vinda, lads. It's always winter. Get used to it."

We played in Switzerland, Wales and faced Northern Ireland at Carrow Road, Norwich. Brendan Rodgers was in the Irish squad. We bumped into each other in Spain a couple of years ago and had a chat about that. We also played against Scotland at Tannadice, Dundee United's ground. The only guys who went on to carve a good career from that time were me and Gary Flitcroft. Jamie Redknapp came in half way through the campaign and obviously went on to do great things. Rob Price was with Liverpool for a while and is now head physio at Hull City.

The Centre of Excellence at Lilleshall was going when I was playing for England Schoolboys and the staff tried all ways to get me there. But I was such a homer and wouldn't leave my beloved Newcastle. Bobby Robson was the England manager at the time and he came to see me. He tried to talk me around. He told me about all the benefits: that I'd be getting coached three sessions a day and schooling with the rest of the lads. Basically, I'd be living and breathing football. But I was doing that at home anyway so didn't feel the need to change geographical locations to do it.

I was the second Geordie in consecutive years to be named as England Schoolboys captain. I followed a lad called Shaun Murray, who skippered the national team the previous year. Murray was a fantastic player and I'd heard stories about the money his family were offered by several clubs if he'd join. I don't know if any of it was true. He decided to sign for Spurs in the end.

Murray played for Westerhope Boys Club and I'd go to see him if he was playing at Wallsend with his team. There used to be hundreds watching because he was such an incredible player. It's still a shock and surprise he didn't become a big star at Tottenham. I don't know what happened to him and why he didn't make it because he had everything as a footballer. He certainly didn't have the career his schoolboy days suggested he would have. He'd take the ball from outside his own box and just slalom through the opposition and smash it into the top corner with his left foot. It was brilliant to watch. Murray's story is perhaps a warning to wannabe footballers not to get ahead of themselves and think they've made it.

My recent ascent and success hadn't gone unnoticed among some of my peers. There were a few instances when I was targeted playing for Benfield School by people trying to carve a name out for themselves, for all the wrong reasons. There was this game at Monkseaton where I was getting roughed up by a couple of players. This never worried me. Coming from my background I regularly played with bigger, tougher and older lads. I've always been able to look after myself, so I was handling the situation. But I reacted to a challenge and the referee asked my school teacher to take me off before I got sent off. The game ended and I thought nothing of it until the next day. I used to go to the school library to read the newspapers and there was a back page lead in *The Journal* by Brian McNally, about my sending off. The piece also intimated I'd been misbehaving at school! I couldn't believe it. For one, I hadn't been sent off and two, I couldn't believe the interest over a 15-year-old schoolboy when there were stories of Newcastle and Sunderland to write about. It wasn't very complimentary to say the least. I realised then things would never be the same for me. My father was upset about the story because it wasn't a true reflection anyway; while I was upset, embarrassed and a little bit ashamed of the unwanted publicity given to my parents and the school.

My school teacher, Bob Hamill, like Jim Horrocks at my primary school, was brilliant in handling the situation. But my father was furious and we all wanted to know how the story got out. There was no social media or mobile phones back then. My father came into the school for a meeting and we later found out it was the deputy head teacher. His name escapes me. Why he did it, I don't know. I can guess the journalist in question was sniffing about and making calls after a tip-off. Maybe the teacher was being naive or trying to make a point. In general, I got on with most of the teachers. They were proud of what I was doing for the school and supported me. They'd had other pupils at Benfield, such as Steve Bruce before me, who went on to be successful. And they hoped I would do the same.

There was another incident when I played for Wallsend Boys Club, with an infamous referee from Walker. I can't remember his name but he wasn't very good. He actually sent me off in a game following an incident which wouldn't have even warranted a talking to by your average match official. He was later boasting, at a local working men's social club, of how he put me in my place. My dad was in the club at that time but didn't let on he was Lee Clark's father. That was his way. You wouldn't see him on the touchline watching me. You were more likely to see him standing in front of a hedge or by a fence observing the proceedings. This was another example of how things were fast changing.

Gordon McKeag, the Newcastle chairman at that time, pulled me and my parents into the office to tell us Liverpool had offered £250,000 for my signature. I was still a teenager, yet to play in the first team. McKeag told us the bid was substantially higher than what he could get for several of the first team at the time. The chairman felt we were entitled to know the club had received this considerable offer which, to be honest, would have set my parents and I up for life. My dad was great about it. He left the choice up to me. He always left these decisions up to me, regardless of being a young lad. This was despite having had many offers to go to clubs like Manchester United, Spurs and Ipswich before I was even 14. My mother was another who supported my decision. It was a great Liverpool team at the time, managed by Kenny Dalglish. Of course I wasn't going to go straight into the first team. I was going there to be nurtured in the same way Jamie Redknapp was developed. Obviously I was flattered. But I was never ever going to sign for anyone other than Newcastle United. I had no interest in going anywhere else. And to be honest, while we were in McKeag's office I'd become bored, lost concentration and zoned out of the conversation. The Newcastle chairman was a lovely bloke, but he could send a glass eye to sleep and we were in there for over an hour. Anyway, I wasn't going anywhere so what was the point of listening after that? My dream was to play for Newcastle and Newcastle only.

I used to play a lot of my youth team games as the supporting striker, now commonly known as the number 10 role, off Steve Howey, funny enough. Howey was originally a striker. We used to score a fair amount of goals in the Northern Intermediate League. I was a regular in the reserves as a 15-year-old. I'm not sure whether all of the accolades, compliments and interest had taken their toll around this time. For a good six months to a year after my 15th birthday I felt as if I'd stagnated. I didn't feel as if I was progressing as quickly as I thought I would. Or should. It was a tough transitional stage from playing against boys to facing men. It was a huge step physically and mentally. I did get help. I didn't go through it all alone. Brian Clark was there for me. He was a big mentor and still is to this day. Peter Kirkley was another, as was Colin Suggett and Jimmy Nelson. Despite all of this help, I knew I had to do it myself. I was determined to prove my worth and make it as a professional footballer. What happened next changed my life forever.

CHAPTER 3
WHATEVER HAPPENED TO THE HEROES?

Paul Gascoigne was Newcastle's star player when I signed schoolboy forms for the Magpies and he was still only a teenager. Gazza had everything. He could dribble, take on players, thread defence-splitting passes through the eye of a needle to the strikers and score incredible goals. Jackie Milburn, United legend, icon and star of three FA Cup winning teams in the 1950s, said he was, "The best player in the world," when interviewed on Saturday morning BBC show *Football Focus*. Wor Jackie got scoffed at by the programme's anchorman, Bob Wilson, at the time. Gazza then went on to show the world, and prove Milburn right, at Italia 90. I bet a few pundits were eating humble pie after witnessing United's former midfielder light up the tournament at the home of the Azzuri.

Everyone at the club knew Gazza was a special talent. He was the best player in the team as a teenager. He was also making waves around the country with his performances for the Magpies. People were fast becoming aware of him. If he hadn't injured his knee in the 1991 FA Cup final, while playing for Tottenham against Nottingham Forest, he would've become the best player in the world for a generation. He was unplayable in the 1990 World Cup and became England's talisman during the tournament.

I remember going into the office at St James' Park with my parents to sort out a first contract as schoolboy. Gazza was in the reception as I was going in. He shouted, "Take them for fucking everything, son. Take them for every penny!" He was brilliant. I was telling my son, Bobby, about him recently. Regularly, Gazza would finish training with the pros and then come over and join our sessions and Stan Nixon. He was never one of those professionals who was aloof or thought he was better than everyone. He took a genuine interest in all of us youngsters.

At Benwell Training Ground, when I was an apprentice, part of our changing area was the boot room. Gazza used to come in and have a laugh and a bit of joke with us. We were all in awe of him to be honest because we'd seen what he could do on the pitch. He was someone we aspired to. One of our jobs as an apprentice was washing and drying the training kit. We had these enormous commercial washing and drying machines. One time, Gazza climbed into one of those driers and told us to set it to mid-spin for ten minutes. He'd be saying, "Don't you dare put it on quick spin or I'll fucking brae the lot of you." We were crying with laughter, watching him get tossed around in there. And when he came out he'd go absolutely crackers. It was as if he'd taken some Class A drugs. I don't think it helped his mental state, but it was great fun at the time.

Gazza was always brilliant with me personally. There was this one time I was just about to play at Wembley for England Schoolboys. The full England team were inspecting the pitch because they were playing Czechoslovakia later that evening in a warm up match for the Italia 90 World Cup. Gazza saw me in the tunnel and shouted, "Clarky, how you doing, son?" I confessed I was having a bit of a nightmare because my dad couldn't stop for his game. The last train from Kings Cross was at 9.30pm.

Gazza said, "Fuck that son, tell him he can come home with me. Here's a ticket for the lounge."

He handed me a ticket for his game but I'm standing in the tunnel in my kit and ready to go on the pitch to play.

"Gazza, man, I'm going on to play now, how can I give him the ticket?"

"Don't worry son, I'll get him the ticket and I'll bring him home."

Amazingly, Gazza went into the players' lounge shouting, "Clarky's father, where are you?" Can you imagine anyone else of his stature doing that? Here was one of not only the best players in the country, but the world, because he proved it a month later in the 1990 World Cup. And here he was putting himself out for a schoolboy, a nobody really, someone with no promise of a future in the game.

My old man rang the following day and told me about his outrageous journey home from London to Newcastle in a Mercedes, travelling at average speeds of 120mph. They were cascading down the Coast Road, when all of a sudden some blue flashing lights appeared from the rear and the police pulled them over. Gazza wound down the window as the officer got to them. As soon as the policeman saw who it was, he says, "Alright, Gazza?" In his usual characteristic swagger, Gazza replied: "Hey, I'm sorry officer. It's not my fault. It's this fella here. It's Lee Clark's dad. It's his fault. He's been telling me to put my foot down because he needs to get to work." The officer just said, "No problem, Gazza, get yourself away." They got a police escort home with traditional blue flashing light. It was typical Gazza. He didn't have to do it, but he did. That was a massive part of his personality. Yes, he loved a laugh, joke and playing pranks but he was also a kind and caring man who always put others before himself. He had a massive heart of gold and he treat everyone the same. He didn't just do that for me, he did it for all of the other young players too.

I've been in a car with Gazza when he's somehow managed to procure a loud hailer. One time he drove us from Benwell to St James' Park shouting, "Vote labour!" He also used to take me to the Oven Door Cafe, on Nuns Moor Road, for their celebrated chocolate fudge cake. Former United manager Jack Charlton famously banned him from going. The fudge cake was to die for. It was a dream for us youngsters to have him around. We looked forward to seeing him every day because it was a joy to watch him train and play. But it was also special to be in his company because he was fun and, as Sir Bobby Robson once said, "Daft as a brush!"

I always get quite emotional every time I read, see or hear anything about Gazza. I saw the film, *Gascoigne*, recently and it pulled on my heartstrings. I wish I could turn the clock back for him, rather than myself. If only he got through the 1991 FA Cup final, things would've been so different for him. He was still a superstar and Lazio loved him... still do. He was still a great player. He was brilliant at Glasgow Rangers. I got into the England squad for La Tournoi, which we won in 1997, and he was the first one to meet me, make sure I was OK for everything. Of course the Newcastle lads were there: Rob Lee, David Batty and Alan Shearer, but Gazza just went out his way for me.

People have said, "If only Gazza had your temperament, Lee." But he was a genius! In any discipline of life there is always a chance a genius will go one way or the other; Gazza was like that. If he was playing now, in his pomp, there wouldn't be enough money to buy him. It was said about George Best as well. He would've won that Ballon d'Or every year, the one that seems to be won each year by either Cristiano Ronaldo or Lionel Messi.

Talking of South American footballers, I read an article someone had written with former Newcastle United favourite, Mirandinha prior to the 2014 World Cup in Brazil. Mira lives in Fortelaza, one of the cities where several games were played. I was flattered to read that the only two people he remembered from his time at Newcastle were Gazza and me. I was just a youngster, whereas Gazza was Mirandinha's self-appointed interpreter. I was lucky enough to catch up with Mira and his agent, Lee Payne, another ex-Toon player, earlier this year. Mira was in Newcastle to promote the opening of a Brazilian restaurant, Cabana, and he came to my house for dinner. It was great to see the little fella.

Alan Thompson turned up halfway through the meal. Tommo had been out for a few drinks with some friends but cut it short when he heard Mira was around at mine. Tommo was a little worse for wear to be honest and kept repeating a story of how Mira had given him a pair of sponsored New Balance football boots when he was a kid, and that he still had them in his father's garage. It didn't matter how many times Mirandinha told Tommo he was sponsored by Hi-Tech and not New Balance, he just kept repeating the story. It was as if the needle was stuck on a record. We were crying with laughter. Tommo just didn't get the joke! He thought it was us who were the daft ones and not him. It was a fantastic evening swapping stories from the old days.

I would often get invited to train with the first team when I was a schoolboy. And after I'd finished the first session I ever did with Mirandinha, our samba star said he'd see me at 10am for training the following day. I told our Brazilian international that I couldn't make it because I had to go to school. He replied, "School no good. You are going to be a big football star. Forget school and come here tomorrow and play with me." I was overwhelmed to hear that from our superstar striker. What a compliment. I was walking ten foot tall after that.

Mirandinha came to St James' Park with all the pomp, ceremony, hype and hullabaloo that surrounded the first Brazilian to play in the Football League's top flight. We'd seen him play for Brazil at Wembley against England and score. And then he went up to Hampden and was on fire against Scotland, setting up an outrageous goal with an audacious pass. We were thinking what's going on here? It was unusual because he would hardly pass at all during a game or in training. Mirandinha would shoot from anywhere. He had fantastic dribbling skills, close control and pace. Mira had all of the attributes that came with being a Brazilian footballer. And what a shot he had on him. For such a small guy he could smash the ball as hard as anyone I subsequently played with.

You can't talk about Mirandinha without talking about Gazza in the same breath. Gazza absolutely loved him despite the love-hate relationship they appeared to have on the pitch. They had loads of barneys on the pitch. But Gazza did love and care for him. Mirandinha couldn't speak a word of English when he first arrived on Tyneside. Whoever thought it was a good idea to have Gazza as his mentor wants their head examined.

After Mira's first game for the club at Norwich, Gazza set him up with the manager at the time, Willie McFaul, on the return coach trip back from the Canaries. He told him to rub his stomach and say, "Mr Willie, I am fucking starving. Can I have fish and chips?" Mira would be greeting people, shaking their hands and saying, "Hairy mot" thinking he was saying good morning. Wednesday was "Wankday" and there was a great one with Ronnie, who did the teas and soups at Benwell. Mirandinha had asked Gazza for the English word for coffee. The next thing we hear is our new Brazilian striker shouting, "Fuck off, Ronnie. Fuck off!" Ronnie was heard saying it was a bit disrespectful while everyone else is falling around laughing. But Mirandinha was a super guy. It goes without saying we'll never forget him.

Around 18 months after witnessing my first game as a supporter it was Kevin Keegan mania. The city went completely mental. It was incredible. No one could believe Newcastle United had just signed the current England captain, one of the most famous footballers in the world, and a global superstar, for only £100,000. Only three years earlier Hamburg had paid Liverpool a British record fee of £500,000. The Magpies were a mid-table Division Two side at the time. In today's terms it would be akin to Wayne Rooney signing for Ipswich, David Beckham penning a deal at Charlton Athletic or Lionel Messi going to Tenerife. It sounded like a fairy tale because it was such an unlikely story. Keegan, became my first real hero like he was for so many other kids my age.

I remember his first game at home against QPR. We were in the West Paddock behind the dugout for the match. And when Keegan scored, I got crushed, so some of the supporters picked me up and passed me to the back for safety. I generally sat on one of the concrete bollards in the Gallowgate End behind the goal. I had my pick of them. When Keegan signed for us we had to get to the ground for 1.30pm for an old-fashioned 3pm kick off. Before he arrived on Tyneside we could roll up ten minutes before the start and get in.

Arthur Cox was the manager who signed Keegan and his team from that period was brilliant. Newcastle, under Cox, was a team who would generally score more goals than the opposition to win, rather than grind out a 1-0 victory. If our opponents scored two then we would score three. I remember going to the games during the festive period back then and there was never any public transport. We used to walk from Walker to St James' Park, across Byker Bridge, past Manors and all of that. And back then we used to play the teams that were closest to us. I remember a game against Carlisle for some reason. I'm sure we beat them 5-0. But at that time we were scoring three, four and five goals in most games. But with Keegan, Chris Waddle and Peter Beardsley up front it was hardly surprising.

I got the chance to become ball boy on a couple of occasions during this period and wore that old sky blue Co-op tracksuit; bloody awful it was! It looked like a Coventry City tracksuit to be fair. There is some old footage of Alan Shearer wearing one in Keegan's last game at St James' Park before he's whisked away in a helicopter. Now that was in 1984 and they were still using the same tracksuits four years on. God knows how long they'd had them before that.

There was many a time when I had been playing on a Saturday morning and went to St James' Park caked in mud beneath my clothes because I didn't have time for a bath and wanted to see the game. It broke my heart when I saw Keegan leave in the helicopter after the exhibition match against Liverpool. Many thought it was a testimonial but he didn't qualify for a benefit match as he was only there two years. He used the match as a farewell fixture and all of the money raised was to go into a transfer kitty towards replacing him. I thought it was the end of the world when he left. I believed all of those special days were going to be consigned to the history basket and that was it.

Peter Beardsley replaced the retiring Keegan as my hero. He was the one player I loved to watch. Pedro did things you didn't think was possible. Then a few years down the line I got to play with him and I'm thinking, 'Wow, this is the stuff that dreams are made of.' Beardsley is a terrific example to all players who get a knock back early in their career. He had several rejections before Carlisle decided to take him on their books. From there he went to Vancouver Whitecaps, Manchester United, back to Whitecaps, then to Newcastle, Liverpool, Everton and back to us. He went on to be one of the best players this country has produced and one of the best in Europe. When Beardsley went to the World Cup in 1986 he made Gary Lineker. It was an ideal partnership and Pedro was the perfect foil for Lineker.

Beardsley was great with me when I was a youngster in his first spell at the club. He used to drive me from Benwell to St James' Park after training and gave me some sound advice when there were several clubs chasing my signature. He was sponsored by Puma and gave me a couple of pair of boots from the 1986 World Cup in Mexico. They were magnificent boots; you couldn't buy them in the shops.

We still had great players when Keegan retired but then manager Arthur Cox resigned in protest over transfer funds and Terry McDermott couldn't agree a contract. Supporters were wondering what was going to happen next. Yet it looked positive when local hero and World Cup winner Jack Charlton replaced Cox. Newcastle made a great start to life back in the top flight, winning their first three matches ensuring we had a decent start. Unfortunately, the way Big Jack had us set up playing meant he couldn't get the best out of Beardsley and Waddle. Waddle later left for Spurs as a consequence.

Ex-Newcastle shot-stopper, Willie McFaul took over the reins from Big Jack and was the manager I actually signed for. He was pushing to get me playing in the reserves while I was a schoolboy. He also tried to give me my first team debut before he got sacked, which would've made me the youngest player ever to play for Newcastle. Beardsley left St James' Park for Liverpool accusing the club of a lack of ambition. The £2m United received for selling Pedro was a UK record at the time. McFaul used the money on some high profile signings such as Andy Thorn, Dave Beasant, John Hendrie and John Robertson. For whatever reason they didn't gel and it didn't work out and our former Fairs Cup winning keeper was dismissed.

McFaul was the catalyst for my progression. He was the one who got me playing in the reserves at 15. The club used to pick me up from Benfield School to play for the second team. And I was playing against men. My first game was at Elland Road against Leeds United and Vinnie Jones broke my nose. He did it when we went up for a header. There were no words exchanged but my nose was all over my face and I was covered in claret. I'm thinking, '*What the hell was that* !?' It was probably Jones' way of welcoming me to professional football. The late Gary

Speed was playing for Leeds that day as well. Mick Martin was our reserve team manager. It was the best preparation for the first team. It's a shame it's gone now. There isn't a reserve league any more. You don't get that intensity and realism now. You were generally playing against players who were first team players, who were either coming back from injury or trying to prove they should be back in the team. It wasn't wrapping them up in cotton wool back then the way it is now. I also played at Liverpool, straight opposite Jan Molby, who was a bit of an Anfield legend.

Yet my career at Newcastle was nearly over before it even got started. I was mopping the dressing room out this one time, as apprentices and trainees had to do back then. There were still a few of the pros in there while I was on the mop. John Pickering, who was a first team coach under McFaul came in and ordered me to put the mop down before giving me the savaging of all savagings!

"We've had reports your school work is poor and that you've been misbehaving. You better start pulling your finger out and improving on that score, son, because, if you don't, you'll not be fucking coming here to play football!"

He made me feel like shit! It was embarrassing to be told off in front of some first teamers. It was deeply cutting and I felt ashamed. I was petrified and thought my world was crumbling around me. For a long time, after Pickering ripped into me, I thought I was going to be kicked out of the club. He was threatening to take away the very thing I always dreamt of doing. It didn't happen of course but it was a kick up the backside and I needed it; a cruel-to-be-kind message. I wouldn't say I was a cheeky kid. I gave as good as I got within my peer group but with the professionals and coaches I was quiet and respectful.

Apprentices don't do any of these chores now. It is outsourced to a cleaning company or whatever. It still causes a massive debate in football. There are some people in favour of going back to traditional football apprenticeships where the kids had to sweep up, clean boots and be a general dogsbody. But there are a lot of people against bringing it back. I'd be up for bringing it back. It didn't do us any harm. There was great camaraderie between us all. It gave us a good grounding and ambition to become a professional. It was a fantastic feeling when I turned pro and didn't have to do those jobs again. I reckon about 85 to 90 per cent of those apprentices with me at St James' Park went on to have a career as a professional footballer, although not necessarily at Newcastle.

My first wage, plus travelling expenses, was £38.50. I had to get the bus from Mullen Road, the 306 into town or the bus to Wallsend Metro, which would take me to town. I'd then get the 38 bus outside of the Odeon on Northumberland Street to Benwell. Then I'd start my chores: washing kit, sweeping up or whatever. We all had designated jobs and I was given three professionals to look after: Micky Quinn, Dave Robinson and later Frank Pingel. You'd get a physical and verbal battering off the pros whenever you went into the changing rooms with their kit. It was ritual humiliation and that was the norm. You'd try and get in and out as quickly as possible to avoid the abuse.

We'd have to clean the boots with a big wire brush and many-a-time you'd have cuts all over your hand from it slipping. We'd do double training sessions after we'd swept, mopped and brushed the changing rooms and communal baths. It was horrendous having to clean it with the carbolic soap. The bath was always full of pubic hair and crap. We, young lads, always hoped there would be some hot water left. But there would never be enough to fill it up again so we just had to top it up. We had enough on our plate trying to deal with acne and puberty without having to wash ourselves in this shitty bath.

One year we had to paint the changing rooms before the start of the season and it ended up in pure carnage. My job was to paint the toilets in the away team dressing room. I remember emulsioning the ceiling while standing on the toilet. I slipped and my foot went into the bucket. It was a proper *Laurel and Hardy* moment. Instead of just taking my trainer off, I'm walking around the facility leaving footprints all over the place. Youth team coach Colin Suggett went absolutely ballistic with me.

We had to be at Benwell Training Ground between 7.30am and 8am to get the professionals' kits ready. Training was 10.30am but the pros might come in at 9am and their kit, towel and boots had to be there, ready and immaculate or you'd get a hiding. Another job of mine was to make Jim Smith's coffee first thing in the morning. I'd never made a cup of coffee in my life before then and wasn't too sure how to do it. I got away with it, however, because every time I delivered the coffee to his office, it was filled full of cigar smoke and he couldn't see who it was. I'd slam the coffee down on his desk and just nash. Then a few minutes later you'd hear him scream, "Who made this coffee? It's fucking shite!"

Another job of mine was to polish the floors with one of those big industrial buffer things. I went to do the physio, Derek Wright's room, and forgot to put the soft buffer on the bottom of the machine. Off I go and, given Wrighty is a bit OCD, he's screaming, "Lee! What are you doing? It's chewing up the floor!" I'm going, "Sorry Derek, don't tell Suggy, he'll take it out of my wages." It was terrifying but we had great fun at the same time. Wrighty was great. When he didn't have anyone on the treatment table he'd join in the six-a-side games in the gym and smash us against the wall if he got the chance. He only did it to keep himself in work.

On a Thursday morning the apprentices all used to go to Wearside College for our day release BTEC course with all the Sunderland, Middlesbrough, Hartlepool and Darlington apprentices. It was great craic. We had a full day together and we'd be taking the piss out of each other, especially when we were about to play against one of the other teams. It was great fun and they were all good lads.

I remember on my 17th birthday Colin Suggett called a meeting and he's furious! He's screaming, "Everyone in the boot room!" We're thinking, 'Oh no, what's happened?' and, 'Someone's in for it!' So he's ranting and raving and I'm thinking, 'Hang on, he's already had a go at us for that, last week.' It just didn't make any sense. Then he turns to me and says, "Lee, happy birthday, son," and walks out the boot room, turning the light out as he leaves. All the lads jumped on me and there's boot polish rubbed in my face, Vaseline in my hair, deep heat up my arse and on my bollocks. The lights go on and I glance in the mirror and see something that resembles a black and white minstrel. My hair is standing to attention as if I've put my finger in an electrical socket and I can't stand still for the deep heat finding a fiery path on to my gonads and up my jacksie. Then I hear Bobby Saxton shouting, "Where's Lee Clark?" I jump out of the boot room and he goes, "Fucking hell son, what's happened there? Never mind, get your boots on, we're a man down, you've got to come and train with the first team." I'm thinking, 'Shit! My arse is on fire, my bollocks are burning and I can't stand still.' It must've been a Friday because Jim Smith kept stop-starting the practice match to go through a few things with the players for Saturday's game. I was in pain so I was running around to try and take my mind off it when he'd stopped to talk. The gaffer clocks me running and shouts, "Lee, for fuck's sake, stand still, will you!?" And then after the session Smith came up to me and said, "Well done son, you couldn't stop running out there." I couldn't tell him the reasons why and what happened.

The players were great and we all had a fantastic relationship. When Christmas was approaching we always made sure the kit and boots, of the pros we were looking after, were immaculate. We didn't want to miss out on a good bonus and, with Mick Quinn being my pro, I thought I was on to a good thing. He was the main man, banging in goals for fun and surely the best paid player at the club. You'd really push the boat out asking if they wanted a cup of tea, chocolate biscuit and all that spiel. We're talking between £50 and £100, which was a lot of money; two and three week's wages! Anyway, Quinny pulls me to one side and says, "Clarky, you've been brilliant for me this season. It's Christmas tomorrow and I'm going to make sure you get a good bonus." I'm thinking, 'Brilliant!' I must be getting a good few quid off him. Quinny was sponsored by Nike at the time. So the following day he turned up with this package for me, all wrapped up nice and that. I ripped into it and found a couple of Nike t-shirts, which had been sent to him from his sponsors. No word of a lie, I took them out and they would've gone around me three or four times. They were like double dust-sheets, a double bedspread and bigger than a two-man tent! I wanted to say, "You cheeky bastard," but couldn't, obviously, cause I'd get a hiding. Thanks Quinny! I really appreciated that Christmas present. There are some things you just don't forget.

Just before I turned pro there was a game where Newcastle played Coventry and Frank Pingel had scored an own goal with his head. I'm watching him and wondering what the hell is he doing with that own goal? So I'm in the boot room on the Monday after the game and picked up the Dane's boots. I turned to the lads and said, "What am I doing cleaning his boots? He's shite! I'm better than him." So I went up to him and said, "Sorry Frank, but I can't clean these anymore because I'm better than you." And because he was such a nice guy, he let me get away with it! Anyone else would've given me a right hook. I was out of order, regretted it and shouldn't have said it. But enough was enough; he was hopeless.

Scott Sloan came in from Berwick Rangers and what an arrogant fucker he was; always trying to give it the big one with us young ones. I was thinking, 'Hang on, you've come from Berwick Rangers, not Glasgow Rangers, and you're trying to tell us how to go on.' John Gallagher was the same. He came from Falkirk. The North-East wind used to blow him over. They were two super-arrogant lads. They treat us like shit and looked down their noses at us. Where did they go from Newcastle? Exactly, nowhere! Why they behaved like that when the big stars like Micky Quinn, Roy Aitken, Mark McGhee and Kevin Dillion, were brilliant.

I still keep in touch with Dillion. He is a great lad. He would regularly have stand up rows with the manager and go toe-to-toe with him. Us young 'uns would be shitting ourselves. McGhee was the same. It was generally in the practice match ahead of the weekend game. They'd be at loggerheads about tactics and how we should be approaching the game.

McGhee and Aitken were Scotland internationals. Aitken was the Scottish skipper at the time. Despite that the boss was telling him he was shite! McGhee's goal against Bradford in 1989 was nothing short of a world class moment. The youth team had been playing away and we got to St James' Park late. But we were back in time to see him pick the ball up and set off twisting and twisting and twisting. And before you know it, it's in the back of the net. He was a very intelligent footballer and it was no coincidence Quinny scored all of those goals. They were perfect foils for each other.

When I look back at the pros we had at the time: Quinny, McGhee, Aitken, Burridge and Dillion, they made us. By that, I mean the youngsters that came through and played in the first team. There were times when they were cruel, but it was a cruel to be kind scenario because they thought a lot of us. I know that because they spent a lot of time with us, kept us involved and never left us out. They wouldn't have done that if they didn't think well of us.

There were plenty of characters in the side and none bigger than John Burridge. Budgie was as mad as a box of frogs! At Maiden Castle, he'd regularly be walking around bollock naked with a hairdryer and diffuser in his hand trying to get his curls right. He'd be cracking the same jokes he'd been telling for about 40 years. No one would be laughing but himself. But on the other side, when he went on to the park to train or to play he was 100 per cent focused. Training was just as important to him as the games. He hated conceding goals whether it was six-a-side, match day or a kick about with kids in the park using jumpers for goalposts.

Budgie went toe-to-toe with our kit man, Chris Guthrie, once. Guthrie used to join in the games every now and again when we were short of numbers. He was an ex-pro and still had a bit of quality. But he was in his 40s at this time and, obviously, not as quick on his feet as he used to be. Budgie exploded with Guthrie because he felt he should've closed the marker down quicker. A few punches were exchanged before some of the lads intervened. But that was Budgie. He demanded proper application, dedication and focus from everyone. It was great for us because subconsciously we were picking up good habits from the older pros. It seems a lot of modern day players think they can just go through the motions during the week and flick a switch to turn it on, on a Saturday. You can't do that. You've got to have the same passion every time you train, never mind just during a match.

Steve Watson made his full debut on New Year's Day at Wolves and, being the youngest, he got the short straw and had to room with Budgie prior to the match. I did the same when it was my turn. Watto was into all of this WWE, which is broadcast from America at about 2am or 3am in the morning. But Budgie liked to go to bed early, despite suffering from insomnia. After dinner Budgie and Watto are watching TV in their room and our shot-stopper tells him to turn off the TV because he's going to sleep. But before he goes to sleep he hands Watto four oranges and says, "Just throw them at me at any time during the night so I can test my reflexes." He was actually wearing his gloves for bed; barking mad.

Budgie was way ahead of his time in terms of nutrition. His food intake before a game involved jars of Heinz baby food, with a tray full of nuts and raisins. His farts and shits were horrific! And he always went to the toilet with the bog door open so we could smell the aftermath. We all thought he was crackers but when football turned to sports science to try and improve the fitness and nutrition of footballers, he was proved right. Our typical pre-match meal was either: Dover Sole, vegetables or steak and the old prawn cocktail; sophisticated, eh? Now it's gone into a buffet mode with four of five options. Breakfast is toast, cereal, poached or scrambled eggs, beans or fruit; nothing too heavy that won't digest. After an away game it was back to the Wetherby Whaler. It didn't matter where we were in the country; could be London. It might be a three-hour drive but we'd still hang on despite it being an hour to get home from there. I first went there coming back from a reserves match. It was fantastic.

Talking of food, we used to hate it when Colin Suggett pulled us in to do something extra after training had finished because you knew you'd be left with the worst sandwiches. All of the prawn salad and chicken sarnies had been eaten by the time you got back in. We were always left with corned beef and beetroot sandwiches.

All the youth team lads got on really well. We were successful in the Northern Intermediate League and won it. It was a tough league and we had a couple of good runs in the FA Youth Cup. We lost in the semi-finals to Manchester City over two legs one year. Gerry Taggert and Neil Lennon were playing in the City side. We'd beaten Arsenal in the quarter-finals and Andy Cole was playing for the Gunners. The year after we got thumped off Liverpool at Anfield, who had Robbie Fowler and Steve McManaman in their line-up. You could tell those two were going to have great careers.

Jim Smith was another high-profile manager who had recorded success at his previous clubs. He was loud, had a deep gravelly voice and I was shit-scared of him! Smith gave me my debut. But I wish I could've played for him when I had a bit more experience. I would've been able to handle him a bit better. I said some of the experienced pros had stand up rows with Smith in training but it was worse on a match day at half-time. I used to shit myself! I wondered whether I was going to get it with two-barrels.

The senior players used to put towels over their suits in the dressing room after they got changed into their kit on a match day. I thought this is what you did when you were a first team player. I'm thinking, 'I'm having some of this'. It soon became apparent, however, the towels weren't some symbol of honour. They were there to protect the players' clothes when the manager was throwing full cups of tea at everyone.

Saxton was Smith's assistant and he was a big advocate of mine. He thought I was a good player and spent a lot of time with my development on a one-to-one basis. He understood the pressure that came with being a young precociously talented player.

I made my debut as a substitute at Bristol City, September, 1990, as a 17-year-old. I came on for Neil Simpson. It wasn't a surprise because I had been part of the first team's pre-season preparation in Scotland. I'd been an unused substitute a couple of times, so I was in and around the squad. I'd be there helping the kit man with the strips. The team had just come back from Hungary but they didn't want me to travel because I'd just played for England in a youth tournament.

Everything about first team football was totally different to what I'd been used to before: the speed of the game, physicality and the quality of play was a step above anything I'd ever experienced before. I came on after 35 minutes, so got quite a bit of game time. We lost 1-0 but I did alright and after the game received quite a bit of praise from the lads, the boss and the press.

My full debut was made on my 18th birthday at home against West Brom. Liam O'Brien scored in a 1-1 draw. I remember Brian Talbot was the Baggies' boss and Sam Allardyce was his number two. Talbot tried to sign me on loan before I got in the first team. Smith refused because there were several injuries and he couldn't afford to let me go. The boss told me to be patient because he would give me a chance.

I then scored a first goal for my home-town team with a rare header at Wolves in a 2-1 defeat, the match in which Steve Watson made his debut to become the youngest player to play for Newcastle. Smith would have a team talk after the pre-match meal and then he would name the team and subs for the day. I didn't have time to get nervous, although there were nerves; because it was so close to kick off. Smith was great with me. He'd had plenty of clashes with the senior players, but he never had a go at me if I made a mistake or didn't play very well. It was only ever words of encouragement. He handled my situation well.

The season before I made my debut, Newcastle lost to Sunderland in the semi-final of the play-offs. It was bad enough losing in the play-offs but being knocked out by your biggest rivals was devastating. It coincided with a political power struggle at the club. The Magpie Group were attempting to take over from the old regime so the club was going through a lot of turmoil at the time. I didn't know Sir John Hall when this was going on but I did get to know those in and around the controversial boardroom revolution, such as John Waugh, Malcolm Dix and Peter Radcliff. These guys were big United followers and took an interest in the youth and reserve teams, not just the first team. They were telling me that Sir John was a wealthy man, had vision and wanted to invest in all aspects of the club: the stadium, training facilities, first team and youth squad. With hindsight this was great for the club and me personally because I got a lot of support from the Halls and Freddy Shepherd. But at the same time it was a bit sad. McKeag was a nice man but didn't have the finances or vision to take the club forward. This isn't just a criticism of him because most of the board were old school and didn't know how to take the club forward and make progress.

All of this unrest behind the scenes manifested itself on the terraces because supporters wanted a change. They were fed up with perpetual mediocrity. This, of course, transferred itself on to the pitch and it affected some of the players. It hindered Smith's plans, which were ultimately, to get the club back in the top flight. We didn't hit the heights of the previous season when we finished third. But we had a lot of injuries that term. That was why a lot of us youngsters got a chance. There was always speculation the manager was either quitting or getting the sack after the play-off disappointment. I've subsequently met Smith in later life and wish I could've played for him when I was an experienced player. He was a good manager. He was successful and his teams always played good football. It was as tough managing Newcastle back then, as it is still now.

Ironically, Ossie Ardiles came in and decided youth was the future. The Argentine deserves a lot more credit than he gets for our future development. Ossie's first game as United boss was at home to Bristol Rovers. On the morning of the game he came to watch the youth team play at Benwell and win. In the afternoon he saw his first team lose 2-0 at St James' Park. The week after, against Notts County, there were eight players from that youth team game in the first team squad. Myself, Steve Watson, Steve Howey, Alan Thompson, Robbie Elliott, Alan Neilson, Lee Makel, David Roche, John Watson, Matty and Richie Appleby all played in some of the youngest sides ever to play for Newcastle. In fact the following season, away to Kenny Dalglish's Blackburn we had an average age of 21, which was the youngest ever side. We drew 0-0 at Ewood Park against a team that got promoted that term.

I'm sure the experienced players who were binned for us were miffed at being dropped. But they never took it out on us. On the contrary, their support and encouragement never wavered where we were concerned. There was never a team meeting where Ossie said, "Right, old players out, young players in." He just brought us into the first team fold and picked us to play. And during that time there was never any negativity from the terraces. Maybe that was because we were all local players, I don't know, but the support was fantastic and appreciative of the football being played. The games were always exciting. Unfortunately, our naivety let us down because we were so young.

One of our first Sky televised games was the Zenith Data Systems Cup game against Tranmere where we drew 6-6 and lost on penalties. There was another game when we were 3-1 up against Charlton Athletic and lost 4-3. The team couldn't see a game out when we were winning with 20 minutes to go. We would try and score more goals.

Ironically, further down the line that is what was thrown at us under Keegan's successful teams; and we had experienced players in KK's sides. Famously, against Athletic Bilboa, me and Philippe Albert were central midfield players in a UEFA Cup home leg where we were winning 3-0. That would've been more than enough to see us through the away leg. But no, we kept pushing for more goals and, consequently, got hit on the break and conceded two goals. It ultimately cost us because Bilboa won the away leg 1-0 and went through on away goals.

The supporters never ever turned on the gaffer either. Ossie was always a popular manager and gets a good reception every time he returns to Newcastle. I don't know how true a story this is but rumour has it that he funded David Kelly's £250,000 transfer from Leicester City. Apparently he gave the club the money as an interest-free loan and United paid him back after the Magpie Group takeover. What a masterstroke to bring him to the club in the first place. Ned not only scored the goals that kept us from slipping into the third tier of English football but his goals helped to get us into the newly formed Premier League a year later.

Kelly was a wonderful signing for the club: a big personality; a great fella and a brilliant guy. It's easy to see why he was such a success at Newcastle. He gave his all. His work ethic was phenomenal and he scored goals on top of that so it gave him more confidence. Ned was a huge crowd favourite at St James' Park. He scored something like 30 goals when we got promoted and then he got sold. That showed you the way the club was going at the time. It was ruthless on my old mate. He was a laugh a minute, right at the front of the queue with the jokes, got to know all our families and was great with us all. Ned, Brian Kilcline, Kevin Sheedy, Paul Bracewell and Barry Venison, were the new senior players at the club and they looked after us young lads in the same way the previous regime had.

When I was Birmingham manager and Ned wasn't working I'd get him tickets for the match because he is a big Blues fan. I'd do anything for him. He still keeps in touch to this day. Kelly could've stopped and fought for his place. He might have got about a dozen or so games that season but at the time he just wanted to play every week. Players from my era didn't want to just sit on the bench and pick up money for doing nothing, which unfortunately seems to be the way with many professionals these days. Playing was more important. There's hundreds who have hardly played any games in their careers yet have a healthy bank balance. Our mentality was different. We wanted something tangible to show from our 15, 16 and 17-year playing careers.

I know Pavel Srnicek mentioned in his *Pavel is a Geordie* book that he felt there was a lack of respect towards Ossie from the young players, but I don't think that was the case. We did have a giggle and carry on with the boss about his accent but he was very self-deprecating and laughed about it himself. He'd say, "Bibblybobbedyboo. You not understand, Clarky?" He didn't want to be called gaffer or boss, he just told us to call him Ossie. We all loved him.

Ardiles has to take credit from converting Steve Howey from a centre forward to a centre half. Most people attribute Keegan for that, but it was Ossie. People asked why he swapped Howey from front to back and the Argentine said, "He was shit as a centre-forward. He couldn't score goals. That is why I looked to play him as a centre half because he was a good footballer."

It was always eventful at St James' Park, none more so than when Justin Fashanu turned up at the club. He made his debut against Peterborough in the League Cup; in a game we eventually lost 1-0. The dressing rooms got robbed and Fashanu tried to claim for a watch worth over a thousand pounds. We never knew whether this was the case. The rest of us didn't have much to pinch as we didn't have anything of value. There was plenty of dressing room banter back then that would be seen as homophobic now. But it was all seen as innocent fun as to who was going to be sharing a room with him. None of us knew many black people never mind any gay people so this was all brand new to us youngsters. Fans were probably thinking, 'What's going on here?' But credit to Ossie for giving him a chance because nobody would touch Fashanu at the time. Looking back, though, Fash should be looked upon as a pioneer, the first openly gay man to come out in football.

Ossie also signed a guy called Gavin Maguire on loan from Portsmouth. He was a bit of a lunatic. He would just smash into everyone, even in training. He loved us young lads but would just kick us up a height! He was a tough, hard bastard.

All the young players were devastated when Ossie got sacked. We understand it now because it was touch and go as to whether we were going to stop up at the time. He was a manager who showed unbelievable belief in us youngsters. It was sad for me personally when he got sacked. I know it was for the best in the end because Keegan came in and we just took off after that. Ossie was a terrific fella but we had to accept his reign was over. It was time for a new chapter in the club's history. The king is dead; long live the king, as they say.

CHAPTER 4
THERE'S A KILLER ON THE LOOSE

You always felt like you were in the presence of someone great. He had magnetism, an aura and an awe-inspiring magnitude of charisma. He had this characteristic without even saying anything. And when he did speak, you listened. He was a fantastic footballer in his day, spoke a lot of sense. And when Kevin Keegan became our manager his personality, charm and appeal made us feel like giants in a Lilliputian village.

Keegan's instillation as Newcastle manager captured not only the imagination of the city, its fans but the club's players as well. We had no idea he was going to take over from Ossie. We, like the supporters, got our information through the media. Obviously, we were excited because of the impact he'd made at the club in his time as a footballer. We'd all watched his career closely and it was almost a fairy tale. The early rejection, working in a factory and playing in the old Fourth Division was later swapped for a glittering career with Liverpool, Hamburg, Southampton and Newcastle. He won titles in England and Germany, the FA Cup, UEFA Cup and the European Cup as well as being a double European Footballer of the Year winner. Not only that, he had the honour of captaining his country, England. Keegan was arguably the first modern day footballing superstar. There was glitz and glamour as well as the tears and tantrums. His life was played out in the full glare of the public spotlight but he handled it brilliantly, unlike a lot of footballers today, and became a role model for thousands of wannabes.

Keegan got accused of being out of the game for too long; that he'd be out of touch because he'd spent eight years on a golf course in Marbella. Mind you, all of that was being written by sports writers and journalists, not professional footballers, former colleagues or managers. Most sports writers are frustrated footballers. The majority of writers have never played the game at any level so a lot of them don't understand it. But, when you have the knowledge and experience, picked up as a player, at some of the biggest clubs in the world, it doesn't matter how long you've spent away from the game. It's not rocket science. The former Liverpool striker had an amazing eye for a footballer and how he wanted his teams to play. The club could have chosen another superstar manager and it might not have worked out because not all big name players become top managers. But with Keegan, Newcastle and the Geordie fans, it was perfect. All the pieces of the jigsaw fit perfectly. They had a special relationship with him as did all who played under him.

Despite what I've just said, my career appeared to be in the balance on his arrival. I clashed with our new boss almost immediately. I was a regular in the side under Ossie. But that changed under Keegan after a practise match on the Thursday before his first game in charge, at home to Bristol City. I had, what the lads will tell you, one of my many infamous outbursts on the training pitch. On this occasion it was against Alan Neilson, who is a good friend of mine. Not that this mattered, as my mates will also tell you. The new manager pulled me to one side and said words to the effect, that I 'was a talented footballer but no good to me if you're a hothead. We need people with calm personas.' Consequently, I was left on the bench for the visit of City and started only four of our remaining 15 matches that term.

Subconsciously, losing my rag, if you like, might have been a reaction to the fact that Ardiles had gone. I'd lost an ally in our Argentine manager and I was hurting for his sacking. He believed in me and we had a great relationship. It is hardly surprising I was pumped up in training. Yes, I was excited Keegan was at the club but at the same time confused about my mentor leaving. Looking back, my frustrations were probably all a part of my adolescence, growing up, dealing with becoming a young man and footballer. As a young man there are rarely any grey areas, you deal in black or white when arranging your lifestyle decisions, choices and opinions. Eventually the team got the results they needed to stay up so you could say the former Liverpool great was vindicated in his selection. He achieved what he had set out to do in staving off relegation.

You could feel the tension going into our last game of the season at Leicester. We had won six, lost seven and drawn two of KK's subsequent 15 games in charge. The initial feel-good factor had been replaced by a lot of trepidation and uncertainty. Newcastle was on the verge of going into the third tier of English football for the first time in their history. Nothing less than a victory would do. As it turned out we could have lost and still survived, but we weren't to know that on the pitch. Those were the days of the transistor radio. That's how fans found out what other teams were doing. It seems a bit prehistoric now but there were no mobile phones, Twitter or instant access to Facebook. Still, it was great to win our final two games and get six points to ensure we would stay up. I remember the bus journey back from the Midlands and the sheer relief of survival was substantial. There was no party or champagne but we certainly had a few beers on the trip back to Tyneside.

We weren't sure whether the gaffer was going to come back for the new season. His classic quote, "It's not like it said in the brochure," had us all worried. That was an absolute vintage Keegan line. Only he could've come out with that. But we loved him. Everyone at the club wanted him to come back after he kept us up. There was a danger it wasn't going to happen though. Later on, Terry Mac told me how they jumped in the car and headed home to their families with no purpose of coming back. At the start of the negotiations between KK and the United board, he wasn't getting the vibes the team were going to challenge for promotion to the Premier League. Keegan was never going to come back and be a manager for a team just treading water. Yet something changed during the course of the summer and he got the finances to start the process.

It seemed as if there was a great weight lifted off us when we returned for pre-season training ahead of the 1992-93 campaign. Doom and gloom had been replaced by optimism and belief. There was a bounce in everyone's step and we were all feeding off Keegan's ebullience and enthusiasm. John Beresford, Paul Bracewell and Barry Venison had joined us for pre-season training. They may well have been the only three signings Keegan made in the summer of 1992, but they were all experienced players who had a lot of ability and football to offer. This was proved when we embarked on an 11-game unbeaten run at the start of the season.

Bez could've signed for Liverpool. We'd seen how good he was in that successful Portsmouth team that got to the FA Cup semi-final in 1992. We might have struggled to stop up the term before but we knew we had some good players: Micky Quinn, David Kelly and Gavin Peacock all had quality, as well as the sprinkling of precocious youngsters in the group. It was a perfect blend.

I was handed a free role, almost, as the new campaign got under way, with Brace or Liam O'Brien sitting in for me, while I got forward to help out the attack. It was their unselfishness that allowed me to do that. The pressure was then on me to create goals for the team or score myself, because I'd left them alone in the middle of the park, under the vulnerability of a counter attack. This was how we felt when David Ginola joined us. He was a bit of a liability defensively. That part of the game didn't come naturally to him. But we didn't mind doing that little bit extra work because he was a match winner. He had the ability to turn a nothing pass into a goal or a chance for one of his team mates.

Keegan helped Ardiles' early development of Steve Howey. He didn't just become a centre back; he became a majestic centre half. He was big, strong and could compete in the air. Howey could play football as well. Sometimes when teams were dropping off he would carry the ball forward, pick a pass, score from open play or score from a set play. Becoming a top class defender was a natural progression for him.

Venners and Brace were a massive influence on me and the younger lads. They were senior players, trained well, spoke articulately and led by example with their performances. They were the catalyst for success in our promotion season. Pound for pound it would be very difficult to find a more consistent player at the club in Venners' time; whether it was at right back, centre half or the holding midfield player. The introduction of Venners, Brace and Bez was the beginning of KK raising the bar for the team, in terms of the quality he started to bring in. Rob Lee, Scott Sellars, Andy Cole and Mark Robinson followed soon after. Robinson was a perfect example of this because he never became a first team regular. He was a quality player who was a warning to those in front of him. They had to perform at a high standard because he was breathing down their necks. He may not have been in the first team but he contributed in a different way to the squad.

I wasn't a defender but we had some great ones at St James' Park in my time. I could reel them all off: Beresford, Venison, Kilcline, Howey, Watson, Albert and Peacock. What used to nark me and the other players were the accusations that we couldn't defend as a team. It was nothing more than lazy journalism because we were always in the top four in the defending stats for goals conceded. I feel critics took that game at Anfield as a model or stick to beat us with. It wasn't like that.

We didn't lose or win 4-3 every week under Keegan. I'd be surprised to find more than two or three of those scorelines in his five-year reign. It was harsh and I felt for our defenders and goalkeepers because of it. They got pigeonholed that they were letting the team down. This was far from the case. It was derogatory. It became an urban myth. And once it got drummed into the football supporting and reading psyche it was hard to believe anything else. You heard or read about it every time you picked up a newspaper or watched *Match of the Day* and Sky Sports: "Great going forward but can't defend!" Absolute bollocks!

We did have attack minded full backs but you can't tell me Venison didn't take pride in defending and keeping a clean sheet. The ex-Black Cats player was a winner in everything. He was the most professional, professional out of everyone. His will to win on a Monday morning at 10.30 was the same as it was on a Saturday at 3pm. It was phenomenal. And Pav touched upon this in his *Pavel is a Geordie* book. Keegan was in Venners' side in training and they had lost. The club captain hated losing and knew KK was the weakest link in his team that day. He told him it was time to pack up and be a manager. The incident with Venners came about because Keegan had lost the ball. He shouted, "You're too old now, you're past it, you're the manager, you shouldn't be training with us."

My thought process as I was driving to the ground before a game was: first and foremost, win it. Then it was hopefully play well enough to warrant an inclusion to play in the next game. It was never me before anything else. What was the point of playing well and losing? It was all about winning. The be all and end all were the three points.

Robert Lee came to us in the early autumn of our promotion season and was a different class. He might have been a bit of an unknown to Newcastle fans when he signed for us but we knew all about him from his Charlton days. He was always the Addicks' stand-out player. We were always concerned about him every time we faced him. He was a pass and move midfielder and when he moved from the right of midfield to the centre, it was never a problem to him. He did have a couple of tricks but he was more of a *get the ball into a striker's feet and get the return or second ball* or the old one-two player.

Lee for me was one of our blue chip players because he could play numerous positions at a very high standard. Like Venison, his consistency levels were phenomenal. He was a very humble man, likeable and bought in to the Geordie/Newcastle way of life; as did his family. He loved it up here. I got on really well with the Londoner and he was one of the best I've played with. He had the whole package. And I had no problem when our roles changed in the side and he became the attacking midfielder while I became the holding player. He was capped by England and was playing well. Sometimes you have to hold your hands up and admit you can't compete with that.

The standard of training increased tenfold when Keegan came in, quite simply, because of the high rank of senior player he was bringing in. It was ridiculous; unbelievably high and phenomenal, really. They were not only good players but great professionals. The bar was being raised all of the time and we had to step up to the mark or get left behind. And the likes of me, Elliott, Watson, Howey did. Both me and Watto got called up into the full England squad while Howey got several caps and was part of the Euro 96 squad. I'm sure he would've got more had it not been for injury.

Keegan would take the odd coaching session but it was mostly left to Derek Fazackerley. The boss was more a motivational coach. But KK would give them a heads-up to whether it was a defensive or attacking format, depending on the opposition we would be facing that weekend. Chris McMenemy did the same when he took over from Faz. The sessions ran like clockwork because the coaches had good players. Keegan was always on hand giving advice when we were playing because he was such a quality player in his day.

Terry McDermott, on the other hand, had a good rapport with all the players and was like a buffer between the lads and manager. He made them feel good about themselves. He was great at lifting the spirits of everyone, even those not involved in the team. It's tough when you're not in the starting 11 and you don't feel as if you're contributing. But Terry Mac was always excellent at making you feel you're still part of the bigger picture. I say he was a buffer but Keegan didn't really need one because he was always approachable. You could always go to him about anything, whether it was football matters or family related. But there were occasions when you didn't want to talk to the gaffer and you'd seek out his assistant. And of course there were things that the boss didn't need to know or, rather, you didn't want him to know. Terry Mac was perfect for that.

Arthur Cox was another good one to go to see. The former Magpies boss was as straight as a die. There was very good chemistry between all of Keegan's staff. But the boss was an especially inspirational man. Everyone was prepared to run through brick walls for him. He was honest, open and emotional. Terry Mac would try and keep us bubbling along with his humour when there were low periods or when we were having the odd blip. And we rarely did have the odd blip. We were always used to winning. There weren't many times we lost at home. But when we did it affected everything: your home life, social life and work. This was when the KK's number two came into his own.

Terry Mac's worst job was on a Saturday afternoon before kick-off. We'd be in the changing room and when he popped his head around the door we used to keep our heads down trying to avoid any eye contact. The lads knew he was there to tell a player the bad news, in that, he wasn't playing. The players turned this around and made a bit of a joke about it. We used to sit with towels wrapped around our necks because we called him the custard pie machine, and didn't want to get our clothes dirty from the custard pie he was chucking! He didn't enjoy that part of his job. But when we got the nod we knew Keegan wanted to see us to explain why he wasn't picking us for that game.

I was very much like the gaffer, in a lot of respects, because I couldn't hide my emotions very well. When he told me I was being left out, for whatever reason, I didn't agree with it. I always thought I should be in the team. We never had a shouting and screaming match. I respected the gaffer too much for that. He was honest enough to discuss his reasons for leaving me out of the side.

I won North East Footballer of the Year and swept the board with most of the player of the year awards in our 1992-93 promotion season. The North East Footballer of the Year Award was special because of the luminaries who had won it before, like Keegan and Peter Beardsley. And when you think about all of the quality players I was playing alongside, it made it all the more surreal. It was the first time I'd been to a black tie dinner. I am a Walker lad, remember, so yes, before you ask, it was a clip on tie, obviously.

In the October of the promotion season Keegan took the squad to Marbella for a training break. The trip was great: a bit of training, bonding and relaxing. Brian Kilcline and Derek Fazackerley nearly missed the flight from London to Marbella. They were sitting in the airport bar and didn't hear the call. Killer was wearing a brand new leather jacket and the pocket got caught on a stair rail and it ripped while he was rushing. Killer was always immaculately dressed: brogues, corduroy trousers and smart shirts, unlike the rest of us. And when we got off the coach in the Costa del Sol, our club captain tripped and the heel came off one of his shoes. He was walking lopsided while carrying his bags. The fact he'd had one drink too many wasn't helping the situation. It was like watching a car with a puncture or a bicycle with a buckled wheel. We were killing ourselves laughing.

After we won promotion, the whole team had an end of season trip to Cyprus. It was the famous or infamous holiday where Killer's ponytail was sheared off and his moustache got mutilated. Everyone thought it was me. In fact everyone was sure it was me. Even I was convinced it was me – but it wasn't! 100 per cent, it wasn't me who committed the treacherous act. Me, Watto, Tommo were having a few beers in Ayia Napa square. The rest of the lads had stayed, either, around the apartments where we were stopping or relaxing by the pool. We came back, saw Killer lying asleep and witnessed in astonishment that half of his tache had vanished and his mane of hair had disappeared. His ponytail was stuffed in a wine glass on a table by his side. Surreal wasn't the word. It was almost like a Biblical scene from *Samson* or the *Lion, the Witch and the Wardrobe*, where the evil White Witch had cut off Aslan's mane. Killer's hair was his pride and joy. It was clear he was sleeping off the intoxicating effects of an afternoon session because nobody would've dared to do it while he was sober. While the three of us stood there observing the horrific scene with an overpowering sense of foreboding; one of the lads told us we'd better watch ourselves because the finger of blame was being pointed in our direction.

The three of us looked at one another, turned on our heels and immediately legged it away from the apartments and scene of the crime. After about 500 yards of running breathlessly, I stopped and said, "Hang on lads, what are we running for? I know we've had a few beers but we didn't do it. We weren't even there." The three of us knew we weren't guilty but somehow the lads had convinced us we'd done it. I was a mischievous lad, who played pranks, but then so did the rest of the team. I was generally in amongst the high jinks and tomfoolery when it was going on but not this time. We returned and protested our innocence.

Venison, Bracewell, Sellars, Fazackerley, Youth Development Officer, John Murray and John Carver were all in the firing line. To say he was upset is an understatement. It all kicked off! Tommy Wright and O'Brien jumped in to try and calm him down because Killer went absolutely berserk! He was knocking people out left, right and centre. It was like a Popeye cartoon! It was pure carnage! The same happened to those who knocked on his bedroom door and tried to protest their innocence. A few were seen scuttling down the corridor on their arses! But the lads who did it took their medicine and realised they'd taken the joke too far. They must have, foolishly, drunk several pints of Dutch courage! Killer knew it wasn't us. He saw how upset and worried we were about it. Who were the guilty culprits? One or two of those named above. I'll let Killer name and shame them in his book.

Killergate aside, Keegan assembled a magnificent spirit in our squad. There were some great footballers in there and even better characters. I can't remember one bad egg KK brought to the club during his tenure. I never wanted to leave the place. Even on our day off, we couldn't wait to get back to work. I loved it. I think it showed in the way we played. And it demonstrated the togetherness we had as a group. We were all best pals and all got together with our partners. It was hard to replicate what we had as a group. The love and respect we had for each other was limitless. No one was left out of the group activities, from the youngest to the most senior player; we were all in this together. This transpired on to the pitch. When one of us wasn't playing well, you had a mate who looked after you and pulled a rabbit out of a hat to win the game.

There were other great guys behind the scenes as well, like Keith Beverage. I remember when we played Athletic Bilbao in the UEFA Cup away. Our physio was known to enjoy a cheeky drink or two. The night before the game he asked the barman for a brandy. The bar tender handed him one of those big gold fish bowl-type glasses and replied, "Yes sir, just tell me when to stop." Keith had turned away to talk to someone at this point and the barman just kept pouring until, before you know it, the glass is full to the rim. Yes, he did neck it all. Beverage by name… He was certainly eccentric and a joy to be around. We all loved and respected him. He had been at the club a long time and was a big Newcastle fan. He walked into a patio door when we were in Northern Ireland to play in George Best's testimonial. Thankfully there wasn't much damage, other than to the door. On another occasion when we were playing Metz in the UEFA Cup, Keith was trying to stitch a wound to David Batty's head while drinking a can of McEwan's at the same time. It was belly-achingly funny. Batts just shook his head and laughed. He had the perfect surname to suit his persona.

I've heard a lot of stories about certain football teams being a drinking club, but that was never the case at Newcastle. We all did go out together in the Keegan era, not so much before then. The young lads knocked about together but it wasn't such a massive thing when we were kids coming through. I wasn't a big socialiser anyway until I was about 20. I never saw any players breaking any drinking rules. You weren't supposed to drink 48 hours before a game and most players would have their last drink on a Tuesday if there was a match on a Saturday. The one time we broke this rule was the night we got promoted at Grimsby. We'd all had a good skin-full after the game and we had to play at home to Oxford two days later. We were awful. In fact we were that bad Keegan said he was embarrassed and disgusted by our performance and walked out of the changing room at half-time. We rallied after the break and managed to win 2-1 with me and Cole on the score sheet. The press wanted to know where the boss had gone. Terry Mac spun a line that Keegan's wife, Jean, was ill and left for that reason and not because we were rubbish. It was enough to put the press off the trail and kick us up the backside to play better in the second half.

We generally socialised on a Monday night if we didn't have a midweek game. You would really enjoy your Saturday night after a win, sometimes a Sunday, but we trained on a Monday still. It wasn't accepted by any of the pros if you trained poorly because you were suffering from a hangover. Fortunately that never happened with us. Our Christmas nights out became the stuff of legends though. We all went out in fancy dress one year. I was Barney Rubble and off the top of my head: Derek Wright was a pink fairy, Alan Shearer was dressed as Terry Mac, with the tash and curly perm and John Murray was Fabrizio Ravenelli. We started in the Black Bull by the ground and then walked into town and got as far as the Monument. All of a sudden a ball appeared from nowhere and we got in a circle and played one-touch. Within minutes there were hundreds of people surrounding us when they realised who we were. It was crazy. Big Les always laughs every time I see him because I staggered out of Legends bar with Barney Rubble's head under my arm and stumbled down Grey Street.

At Maiden Castle, where we used to train, we didn't have one big changing room, there were several in the corridor which could only hold between five and six players. We had loads of fun down there. Faustino Asprilla was always a victim of having his socks, shirts and clothing cut up. Mind, we would never do that to Killer. We wouldn't want the risk of getting a slap. You would often hear Tino screaming, "Fuck you! *Fuck you* !" He didn't speak much English but he could swear with the best of them. And then we'd see our Colombia international walking down the corridor in shredded clothes trying to find the culprits. The finger was always pointed at Shearer. But Tino bought into that camaraderie.

Tino was great fun to be around. He was a bit of a fruit loop and used to go and buy his clothes from the Walt Disney shop. He'd wear t-shirts with Mickey Mouse, Donald Duck or some other Disney cartoon icon. Me and Watto went around to his house in Darras Hall one Sunday to see if he wanted to come out for a drink. It was bizarre. His father was in the lounge, playing the bongo drums and Tino was nowhere to be seen. We found him in his bedroom lounging around. "Get a beer, boys," he'd say. I kid you not. He had an enormous fridge in his en-suite full of beer! He'd also take out a bottle of Tequila when we were on one of our social evenings. He'd hide it in his inside jacket pocket and take sneaky swigs when we weren't supposed to be looking. Me and a couple of the lads got wind of it and had a taste. It was like rocket fuel, about 90 per cent proof and he'd be necking it like pop! Crazy!

Tino used to have a chauffeur when he first came to Newcastle before he learned to drive. We all got sponsored vehicles and I remember the day he got his first car. He pulled out of St James' Park and you could hear the roar and screech of the motor as he tore up Barrack Road like a F1 driver. Moments later we heard an almighty crash and sure enough, our maverick Colombian striker shuffled back into the ground; walked up to the guy who was dealing with the cars, dropped a set of keys in his hand and said, "Tino need new car!" He'd only written it off! This was around the same time I was given an XR3i as a club car. It was a proper fanny magnet! But I made the mistake of tearing past KK and Terry Mac one day. After a short inquest, they found out it was me and I was downgraded to a Vauxhall

Vectra. After that, the lads were always calling me a taxi driver. It went from being a fanny magnet to a fanny repellent!

CHAPTER 5
KICKED THE BUCKET!

I honestly thought my career was finished at Newcastle after clashing with the boss at Southampton in our first season back in the top flight. Kevin Keegan was, and still is, an icon, legend and idol to tens of thousands of our supporters. If there was a poll for most influential managers or favourite players I'd be surprised if he didn't come out on top. It's fair to say that after my reaction to getting hooked at The Dell, I was hanging on for dear life. I didn't think there was a way back. But I was prepared to do anything to regain his confidence again, even if it meant I had to wash his car, polish his shoes, do his laundry or clean his toilet with my own toothbrush.

Ironically, I was one of the few players praised by the boss at half-time while a couple of the senior players were on the sharp end of his tongue. That was why I was surprised to see my number raised after the break. That's why I reacted the way I did. I nearly broke my toe in the process. It was a steel bucket that was kicked in anger. I was in agony, but didn't want to limp and double the shame and embarrassment of behaving like a spoilt child in front of the television cameras. I was off down the touchline towards the tunnel but Keegan got up and dragged me back into the dugout. It was a proper humiliation in front of the armchair viewing football world. It was like being smacked on the bum by my dad when I was a kid.

We eventually lost the Southampton match 2-1; a memorable game in its own right for those two brilliant Matt Le Tissier goals. Le Tissier seemed to do that every time we played the Saints, home and away. When we got into the dressing room after the match had finished, I got an absolute battering from Keegan. Then there was the seven hour plus drive in the coach back to Newcastle. I had plenty of time to reflect on my actions. Those long trips home aren't nice at the best of times but this was the worst of my Magpies' career. Around 15 minutes before we hit Durham, Terry Mac came down the bus and told me, "The manager wants you to go to Leicester tomorrow night and play for the reserves." My head was swimming with all sorts of scenarios, most of them bad. I slept on the events of the previous day and realised I'd made a massive error of judgement.

I went to Maiden Castle, where we trained, before I set off for the game against the Midlands outfit hoping to talk to the manager. I knocked on his door and waited nervously for KK to let me in. When I asked whether I could have a word, Keegan rebuffed my advances saying he wasn't prepared to talk to me. The boss told me to go and play for the reserves, do my best and that he needed time to think about what he was going to do. I knew it was serious. I was in trouble and had to do something about it. I thought I'd kicked my last ball for the club.

Knowing my career was hanging by a thread I hastily arranged a press conference in front of the TV cameras and apologised to my teammates, staff, supporters and more importantly, the manager. This got me back in the game, as you might say. Had I not done that I reckon I would've been kicked out of the club. I had disrespected the manager and the club in front of the television cameras; although at the time I did it out of frustration. I hadn't realised the gravity of the situation. As a player, to a certain extent, you're just thinking about yourself. You sometimes don't see the bigger picture. I certainly didn't at the time.

I was left out of the club's League Cup tie at Wimbledon a few days after Bucketgate, which is famous for Andy Cole going AWOL. Barry Venison and Paul Bracewell were rooming together ahead of the clash with the Wombles and they called me. Venners said, "I see your mate has backed you up like the good trade unionist he is." I hadn't clue what had happened or what they were talking about. Then, in plain English, "Coley's fucked off and no one can find him."

Although Brace and Venners were taking the piss, they were right; Coley had backed me up and apparently told Keegan my punishment was too severe. They had trained in the morning and our striker wasn't in the best of moods. He had a few words with the gaffer on the training pitch. Keegan told him, in kinder words than were actually swapped, if he wasn't in the right frame of mind he could re-evaluate himself. Coley did just that and buggered off. I know I was his pal but he would've done that for anyone if he thought it was wrong. That's the type of guy he is.

I'm not sure whether Coley's stand and subsequent actions had any influence on KK's thinking but we were both back in the side for the following fixture. Keegan pulled us both into his office and asked whether we were prepared to play. Obviously we were and, as these things work out, ironically, it was against Wimbledon at home, the team who had just knocked us out of the League Cup. The boss informed me I was playing but not in my usual position. I had to play on the right of a midfield four. There is no way I could play there as a winger because I didn't have any pace. But I was prepared to play anywhere. I was just happy to be back in the team.

Coley doesn't get the credit he deserves for his time on Tyneside. And I think it was simply because he went to our biggest rivals at the time Man United. The club could have turned it down but they didn't and let him go. He hit the ground running at St James' Park. I don't think it sunk in or he understood what the number nine shirt meant when I first told him. But he embraced it and scored an incredible 68 goals in 84 appearances. If they're not the stats of a goal scoring legend, then nothing is.

I remember the team was on its way to play Swindon this one time and Ken, the bus driver, called me on the phone saying the gaffer wanted a word with me. I'm thinking, 'Shit, what I have I done?' I thought I'd been caught misbehaving. I hadn't as it happens. KK told me that he'd signed my mate, Andy Cole, to look after me. This was a typical Keegan trait, building the squad when it was strong. Remember we had Gavin Peacock and David Kelly banging in goals for fun at that time. They were hardly a couple of slouches.

When I used to go away with England Under-21s I'd often come back raving about certain players, and Coley was one of them. We got on remarkably well considering our different backgrounds. I think it must have been one of my chats with Terry Mac. Our number two had obviously tipped off Keegan and they'd gone to see Cole and signed him. The game they saw the ex-Arsenal striker play in, impressed them both because he was injured and shouldn't have been playing. The Bristol City manager, Denis Smith, I think it was, tried to substitute him but Coley refused to come off. He wanted to stop on. This attitude and dedication, coupled with his ability, impressed the gaffer. He could see Cole was up for the fight when he could have easily ducked out.

I never tapped Cole or tried to pitch Newcastle to him or anyone. It was common knowledge the club was going places and we had tremendously passionate supporters. In fact, I knew of him as a 16-year-old when he played for Arsenal against us in the FA Youth Cup. We became pals when playing for the England youth team. We've been close ever since. Not long ago I played a little part in getting his son in at Bradford City. It goes without saying; he was a phenomenal number nine. You cannot argue with his ridiculous goalscoring record at St James' Park.

There has been a lot of mud slung in Cole's direction throughout his career: being arrogant and selfish are two of the biggest. I know him better than most but I wouldn't use either of those words. The one word I would use is shy. He never forces himself on anybody he doesn't know. He is polite and respectful to those people. Anyone who gets his back up, he tells them in no uncertain terms. He doesn't suffer fools gladly at all. He has his opinions but deep down he's a shy unassuming lad.

I remember Coley calling me this one day and asked, "You fancy helping me move into my new house?"

"Aye, of course mate. Where is it?"

"Crook."

"Where the fuck's Crook?"

"It's in County Durham. You're from this area, you should know it."

"You're right, I am but I've never fucking heard of Crook."

Anyway, I helped him move and around lunchtime we decide go to the local pub for a sandwich. It was a Saturday afternoon as it happens and we didn't have a game for one reason or another. When we walked in it was one of those classic moments where everything just stopped. Pints went down, music switched off and people stopped talking to stare at the pair of us. I'm sure I even heard a pin drop. I looked at the regulars, Coley looked at the regulars, I looked at Coley, Coley looked at me and we're both thinking, what's just happened? It's as if two aliens were standing in front of them. Obviously my old teammate is a black man and I'm not sure they'd seen any black men up there at that time. We couldn't get out of the pub quick enough. Not the warmest of welcomes to his new local!

At training on the Monday morning I pulled Terry Mac, "What the fuck are you doing putting him out there. Fucking *Crook*?" To be fair, you can't really blame the club for this one because Coley had asked for something outside of the city centre, away from the hustle, bustle and hassle of everyday life. And this was because he was a shy lad, maybe a bit introverted and uncomfortable being in the media spotlight. It was eventually resolved and the club got him an apartment opposite Jesmond Cricket Club.

Later on, me and Coley both bought an apartment in Greystoke Park, Gosforth, and lived either side of each other. This being the case we shared lifts into training each morning. It was his turn this day and generally we would go in quite early. So I waited and waited and he hadn't turned up. He wasn't answering his phone. I even knocked on his door and there was no answer. I thought, 'Fuck this, I'm not getting fined for being late,' so I jumped in my car and set off to training. Didn't really think that much about it because he regularly had family up from Nottingham or people from London and vice versa. Just as I pulled into Maiden Castle I got a call from him.

"Hi Lee, you OK mate?"

"Am *I* OK? I've nearly got a fine for being late, how do you think I am?"

"Sorry mate but I've had to keep this top secret but I'm signing for Man United."

I couldn't believe it. I was shocked to say the least. Several things were going around in my head but at the top of the list, 'We're losing our talisman.' You'd struggle to get a better pairing than Cole and Beardsley in the top flight at that time. Pedro's vision and first time passing and Coley's running. They were perfect for each other, moulded together. When our fleet-footed striker was on a run he didn't even have to think about scoring goals because it came so naturally to him.

We lost Cole to our nearest rivals but I thought Keegan handled it brilliantly. It was typically unique of him the way he confronted supporters on the steps of St James' Park to explain his actions. He understood the consequences but, knowing the gaffer, he always had something up his sleeve. Les Ferdinand was lined up, as it happens, but it took longer to get him over the line than he thought. He tried to get Big Les in while Coley was still with us. He wanted to play them together. KK and Terry Mac actually took him to Anfield to watch Ferdinand in action for QPR and asked whether he could play with him. Cole never left Newcastle because he was unhappy. He left because it was Man United. It's different for other players. For Geordies, it's a no-brainer, there's no other club you want to play for. Look at Alan Shearer; he could've signed for Man United.

There is definitely a bit of bitterness from people about Cole because he was a star on Tyneside. He achieved legendary status for his goalscoring. He wore the number nine; took on the pressure of wearing the shirt and was successful. It is a shame he isn't held in the same esteem as our other famous number nines. I'm aware he went seven games and two months without a goal. But this wasn't because he was going through the motions or unhappy. He wasn't that type of man. Even accusations that he'd been found out weren't true or couldn't be true because it wouldn't matter if defenders knew what he was going to do, they still couldn't stop him. Maybe he was carrying an injury. He had problems with shin splints, I seem to remember. It happened several times during his Newcastle career. The manager would never risk him if it was career-threatening. But Keegan knew even a half-fit Cole was worth having on the pitch because he could win a game out of nothing. He went on to win Premier League titles, FA Cups and a European Champions League winner's medals. He went on to become a better player.

Cole's sale was weird because we'd stopped becoming a selling club. We were a buying club then. Supporters were obviously concerned we were going to go back to selling our best players like we did in the 80s with Chris Waddle, Beardsley and Paul Gascoigne. This was never the case. Maybe KK thought Cole and Beardsley had ran its course and wanted to freshen it up with Ferdinand. Big Les's partnership with Beardsley was just as successful but different.

I went down to watch Coley's debut at Old Trafford against Blackburn Rovers, which they won 1-0 thanks to an Eric Cantona goal. There was a gentlemen's agreement Cole and Keith Gillespie, the makeweight in the £7.5m transfer, wouldn't play against their old clubs. But, as these things happen, we faced Man United the week of the transfer. I remember the game well; we drew 1-1. There's a great picture of Peter Schmeichel standing over me in the Black Bull opposite St James' Park, with my signed shirt for Pugger, who runs the Black Bull pub. I think I'm telling him to fuck off! It was a great game; atmosphere was unbelievable, as it usually was. And there were two great teams doing combat. Mark Hughes put them ahead and suffered an injury thanks to a Pav challenge before Paul Kitson levelled. It was tough for Kitson because he had to step into Coley's shoes. But it didn't matter who we got. It would've been tough for anyone to fill his boots. His goalscoring record was ridiculous.

I'm aware Cole was caught on camera singing an anti-Keegan song at the 1996 FA Cup final. I never saw it and was surprised when I heard the tale. Coley had nothing but respect for the boss and vice-versa. He loved his time at Newcastle. He would've instantly regretted it but probably got carried away with the moment. I would compare it to my t-shirt moment when I played for Sunderland.

Going into the 1994-95 season we were all full of optimism, of course. We finished third in our inaugural Premier League campaign and the team was both confident we'd improve on that the following term and maybe win a trophy. I missed the final two months of the 1993-94 season, and you could say I was in rehabilitation ahead of the new term. I had broken a metatarsal bone in my foot. Obviously a metatarsal wasn't as famous or sexy back then until some fella, who played in Manchester, lifted the profile of the bone before the 2002 World Cup. I think my first game back after that injury was in the second leg of the UEFA Cup against Antwerp. We had a lot of serious injuries that term. We were without Philippe Albert, Barry Venison and Scott Sellars for long periods and then we sold Cole. They were all big important players for us. No team would've coped with so many of its big hitters being absent. It is little wonder our season ended in a whimper. Although I'm guessing most Newcastle supporters would take a top six position now.

Albert's first day in Newcastle was a funny one. Traditionally, after our first day of pre-season training the squad would go to Jesmond for a bite to eat and then go in to town for an all-day session. The Belgium international had his medical on this day so didn't train with us. But he came to the Brandling Villa restaurant to meet us. This big beast with a tache; a Tom Selleck lookalike just turned up while we were eating. He was made welcome from the first minute and just bought into us straight away. It was like he'd been with us for five years. Albert was a fantastic guy and an unbelievable player. That goal against Man United in the 5-0 victory summed up what he was all about. He had the vision and ability of a number ten.

Our £2.7m defender took me out to this pub which sold all the foreign beers. Think it was called Beerex, around the back of the Civic Centre. He had me on this Lucifer beer from Belgium. I can't remember getting home. I think he carried me. Albert's signing summed Keegan up. Not only was he signing great players, but bringing fantastic characters to the club as well. It's obvious that homework on a player was done before he brought them in. You can't get that lucky every time. We were just as excited as the fans when Keegan signed a new player. Marc Hottiger was another great lad and a smashing footballer he brought in. And when you consider all of the different backgrounds we came from it was staggering how well we all got on.

There were never any personality clashes but there were confrontations just about every day with players because of the fierce competitive nature of the individuals. We all wanted to win. These were heat of the moment clashes that were forgotten about virtually immediately. That is one of the reasons I never joined in any football games in training when I became a manager. I know, if they have my temperament, I'll be kicked up in the sky by a player who is unhappy about being left out the side. I did that to Keegan, of course.

There was another time when I kicked off in training and Keegan wasn't happy with me so we were having this row as we were running together along the riverbanks at Maiden Castle. He was giving me a bollocking and I was trying to fight my corner. We never broke stride. But I was always kicking off in training. That was my nature at the time, unfortunately. Steve Watson, Steve Howey and Alan Thompson are my closest friends but we regularly fell out in training. It was never fisticuffs. It never came to blows and it was never a personal verbal attack. It was just business, I suppose. None of us ever backed down. Training was intense and we all wanted to perform to the highest level. Then after training was finished we'd go and have lunch together. We would sit and laugh and wind each other up about it. Players don't seem to police each other nowadays the way we did. It seems players now take everything personally.

Pavel Srnicek was a big brute of guy, an athlete. Every time I think about Pav's passing on, it saddens me because he was super fit. No one took the piss out of the big Czech because we'd seen him lose his temper a few times. You don't want to get into a row with a proper giant, do you? I was out of the team for some reason and Keegan was playing in the six-a-side game. He was on Pav's team. Pav rolled him the ball and I made no attempt to go for it and scythed him down. The boss went up in the air and spun before landing on his arse.

Keegan goes, "Fucking hell, Nash. That was a bit of a tough tackle."

I just shouted back at him, "Fuck off and get me back in the team!"

I think Pav thought, maybe, this fella needs knocking down a peg or two. I know I'm not the tallest player but because of his athleticism, he managed to kick my height. I thought he was going to kick me in the head. I nearly shit myself. It was as if he was saying, 'Keep behaving like that and I *will* kick you in the head the next time.'

There was a row between Shearer and Ginola at half-time in a game against Arsenal. Shearer was pissed off with the lack of service he was receiving.

"I fucking watched you last season put crosses in for fun, for Les to score. I turned to my Mrs and said, 'I'd get 50 goals a season playing with him.' But since I've been here you just keep cutting inside and having a shot, you selfish bastard!"

Ginola just jumped up and screamed, "Fuck you, Shearer. *Fuck you*!" They squared up to each other but no punches were thrown. Shearer just laughed it off.

I've heard people say Shearer and Ginola didn't get on, but that's bollocks. They were two great players striving to be the best in their profession and position. If they weren't like that you'd be asking why. They both had enormous respect for one another. It wasn't taken any further than the exchange of words. They didn't sulk or stop speaking to each other. Generally, you're chatting in the players' lounge after the game. Failing that the gripe would be all over by training on a Monday morning.

I gained a new nickname because of my explosive nature on the training pitch. On the way to our pre-season tour of Thailand

and Singapore, David Batty and a couple of the lads, had watched this movie, *Primal Fear*. The main character is a choir boy with a split personality, who turns into a serial killer. He was called Roy. Batts was quick to christen me with my new moniker when I kicked off in training shortly after. The lads reckoned I was a fun lad, popular and the life and soul of the party, off the pitch. But in training I flipped into this whirling dervish of fire and brimstone. There'd be many a time when Batts would say, "Oh no, Roy's coming out to play," and the lads would crack up, me too.

I'm not sure why I was ready to explode on a training pitch because in a game I rarely kicked off or got booked. I got sent off only once in my career for Fulham at Grimsby. I had controlled aggression and never wasted any time back chatting to referees. Being a manager now, I would have hated to manage me on the training pitch. I was a lunatic, a ticking time bomb and a mouthy little fucker. Sometimes you had to bite your lip but I couldn't resist it. There'd be carnage. Then I'd be the first to ask whether anyone fancied going for a beer. They'd be looking at me as if I was mental because only moments earlier I'd have kicked off about something. But it's like this, if I have to fall out with a mate between 3pm and 5pm on a match day to enjoy my weekend and the following week, I'm prepared to do it. It's all for the greater good.

CHAPTER 6
TYNE TO LEAVE

The debate, conspiracy theories and arguments over how we didn't clinch that elusive Premier League title in 1996 will go on forever. We all have our opinions or reasons why we didn't land the hallowed trophy of champions. I've heard them all and have my own, of course, but it goes without saying, it still hurts to this day that I don't have a Premier League winner's medal in my collection.

We ended the previous campaign in disappointing fashion. A top six finish wasn't even good enough to guarantee a UEFA Cup place. A lack of strength in depth in the club's armoury; injury to several key players and the controversial transfer of Andy Cole to Old Trafford were contributory factors. But our manager was determined, as we all were, to learn from those setbacks. If anything, he was even more bullish about our prospects for the future going into the new season.

There was a definite air of expectancy that enveloped the club as Kevin Keegan invested £14m supplementing our already gifted squad with the considerable talents of Les Ferdinand, David Ginola, Warren Barton and Shaka Hislop. We were also aware that our nearest rivals at Old Trafford had allowed Mark Hughes, Andrei Kanchelskis and Paul Ince to leave. That was a lot of experience, although it has to be said we never underestimated Man United. But while we respected the Red Devils it was all about us and what we could do. And on our day we blew everyone away.

Our style of play captured the imagination of the nation and installed us as the country's second favourite team. The gaffer wasn't one for the traditional pragmatic approach and we relished being part of that. It was a breathtaking paradigm of fluent, eloquent, one-touch football where attack became the best form of defence. This was no more personified than in Ginola, our new a £2.5m signing from Paris Saint Germain. The British footballing public had not witnessed his like before. Never mind that, *we* had never seen his like before. Most footballers seem to flourish when they have time and space. Our charismatic Frenchman, on the other hand, seemed to relish being heavily marked with his back to goal and with little room to manoeuvre.

With Ginola branding his unique style of wing wizardry on the left; Keith Gillespie providing a more traditional pacey role on the opposite flank; Peter Beardsley applying vision, awareness and ammunition in the hole and Robert Lee supporting a bludgeoning Ferdinand through the middle, we destroyed just about everyone who crossed our path in swashbuckling style. We led the Premier League table from the curtain-raiser and I read many a time that the championship trophy was already said to have been at the jewellers, with our name etched on it. It was no wonder that we got called The Entertainers. That's exactly what we were. And then it all went horribly wrong in late March. Why? More of that to come later.

At the end of the 1994-95 campaign, and before pre-season training had begun, me and a few of the other lads used to go into St James' Park even when we were supposed to be on holiday. We just loved being around the place. We were sitting in the reception area of the Milburn Stand this day having a bit of craic. The gaffer happened to be in at the time. We weren't sure whether he'd had his holiday and was back trying to sign players or not. There was always speculation we were after this player and that player. Ginola hadn't been mentioned at this point. His signing had been quick and out of the blue.

Keegan invited us into his office and offered us soft drinks and chocolate from his fridge. He pulled me to one side, away from the rest of the lads, for a one-on-one chat to talk about the forthcoming season. He discussed several tactical options: how, when he played with two strikers, Peter Beardsley would drop deep and make up an extra man in midfield with Lee and Gillespie. Keegan also confessed my exclusion from the side on several occasions was undeserved. KK explained he only did so to accommodate players with a bigger stature, such as Beardsley and Lee, who were both full internationals. So when he suggested whether I would be interested in this new defensive midfield role it came out of the blue.

In essence, when we returned for pre-season training, Keegan wanted me to take on the role in small games, whether it was six-a-side, eight-a-side, keep ball session, tactics' session and take it from there to see if I was suited to it. The suggestion was a shock but I just wanted to play for my beloved club. And if that was the only way it was going to happen I was going to do it. The way we played anyway, meant I was going to have a lot of the ball and that suited me down to the ground.

We started the pre-season build up and it was working well. I was on the ball more than I ever was in my former attacking role. I relished the new position and it became easy for me. I had the option of knocking the ball to the feet of Ginola on the left, hitting one over the top for Gillespie on the right, punch little ones down the side of the centre-halves or slide it in the spaces between the midfield and defence for Beardsley and Lee to get on the ball.

I have to say, Ginola was an incredible player and another great addition to the group. When he first came to Newcastle he was stopping in the Gosforth Park Hotel. Being two very important members on the social committee, me and Steve Watson decided to take him out to sample some Geordie culture. We didn't go as far as buying a Greggs pasty or a ham and pease pudding sarnie in a stottie, but we took him out for a few beers in some of the city's local hostelries. We started in the Three Mile Inn. But after a couple of hours, and one or two libations, our flamboyant Frenchman decided it was time to go back to the hotel for a sauna and massage. We weren't having that. The rule was that once we were out, we were out for the day! And by God didn't our France international suffer the following day in training. He was blowing through his arse while me and Watto kept up with the leaders. It is fair to say he was staggered by our appetite for a good time and the fact we didn't suffer in training the following day.

Big Les was another one happy to live the quiet life. Our new number nine confessed on his arrival that he never used to drink before he came to Newcastle. The Toon social committee can take credit for that one as well. Our £6m striker bought Andy Cole's old flat next to me when he moved to Tyneside. There was one night when the Paparazzi got a sniff that he had the famous model and television personality Dani Behr stopping over at his. Ferdinand asked if it she could stop with me for a short time while he got rid of the photographers. Obviously I was delighted to help out a friend and his damsel in distress. I said, "Not a problem Les, but I'm not too sure she'll be happy stopping with me knowing what I've got and knowing what you've got to offer." Dani turned up at one of our home games and it was pissing down. Newcastle supporters got wind of it as well and started singing a suggestive song about her and Les. We didn't take the piss too much because we didn't fancy a slap off him.

Ferdinand never wanted to leave Newcastle and although we've never spoken about it I'm sure he was hurt by the way it happened and how it was handled. The club agreed to sell him and then Shearer got injured but he'd already given his word to Spurs. Big Les wouldn't go back on his promise. He was a man of honour and integrity. He was given the nickname 'Sir Les' by the press and fans and it was fully justified. He's a total gentleman, one of the nicest fellas I've ever had the pleasure of knowing in football. He was a magnanimous man and an unselfish player. And what a footballer he was by the way.

Everything was going great until the last two pre-season games: one at Hearts and the other in Gary Mabbutt's testimonial against Tottenham at White Hart Lane. Keegan named the team for the match at Tynecastle and I'm not in it. I'm thinking to myself, 'Shit, second last game of the warm-ups and I'm not in the team. It doesn't look like he's going to start me for the first match at home to Coventry.' So I'm wandering around the pitch prior to the kick off with a face like a slapped arse. Keegan and Terry Mac are conversing on the pitch, witness I'm sulking and call me over. The boss asks whether I'm OK. I tell him I'm not, that I'm gutted and explained the reasons. But KK gave the reassurance that I was only being rested as I'd played in every game in the summer friendlies. The manager added he couldn't be happier with me and that it looked as if I'd played the role all of my life. Keegan also said I'd be starting at Spurs and in the first XI when the curtain was raised for the visit of Coventry to St James' Park on the opening day of the season. It was a typical Keegan moment. He had an incredible gift of lifting your spirits when they were down and making you feel like you're a giant among men.

I missed only two or three games through injury up until that fateful home clash with Man United at St James' Park, when we were 12 points clear. Man City away was my last game and I never started another that season. There were 11 games left and I was an unused sub in seven of them, coming on sub in the last three.

There are several theories as to why we blew our 12-point lead. The main catalyst for destruction, seen by many, was Keegan's decision to splash £7m on Colombian international

Faustino Asprilla from Parma. Another popular dynamic was the capture of David Batty. The boss believed we needed some defensive cover to protect the rich vein of attacking wealth and invested £4m in Blackburn's midfield enforcer as a consequence.

What do I think? I, obviously, believe Keegan shouldn't have changed anything up to that point. The stats back me up. They tell you I shouldn't have been dropped. There are various conspiracy theories and I certainly believe the boss should've just left Big Les and Beardsley up front and used Tino like he did at Middlesbrough that day as an impact player. He came on and changed the game when we were flat and needed a spark. Subsequently, we beat Boro 2-1. I'm guessing Keegan looked at the Man City game, where we drew 3-3, and thought we weren't solid enough defensively. And that's why he brought in Batts. If you look at the fixtures prior to the former Leeds spoiler coming in, from the beginning of January, we won five, drew one, lost one, scored 12 and conceded five. In the eleven games that followed without me: we won five, drew two, lost four, scored 14 and conceded 12. We'd only lost four in the previous 27 Premier League games so why try and change something that isn't broke?

Batty was a magnificent footballer. There was talk of Paul Ince coming prior to that but that was what Keegan was all about. He wasn't looking to replace me because he didn't rate me. He never wanted the team to stand still. He was always looking to improve, move it forward and take it to the next level. I never took it personally. We got on very well. I've read all of the comments about how, if you fell out with the boss, that was it, you were finished. If that was the case I wouldn't have played for Newcastle again after my petulant outburst away at Southampton and the infamous kicking of the trainer's bucket after my substitution. I never had a problem with Keegan signing anyone, Batty especially. He was top quality, England international, had experience, been there, done it and got the t-shirt. I never held a grudge and my respect for Keegan remains to this day; in fact it still goes through the roof.

I was never afraid of Keegan raising the bar every time because I believed I was a good player. I became an even better player because of all of these footballers he brought in. These players made my passes look great because they could read what I wanted to do. It's not rocket science. They were faster, more intelligent and skilful. That is why I found the holding role in midfield easy. I'm not being big headed. It would have been harder had I played in a lower division or been a non-league footballer because the standard is poorer.

Rumours were flying around in the media that we were going to sign Batty before he came in, as these things do. And Batts turned up on one of our Monday nights out, down Julie's night club. Beardsley stayed behind and brought him to the Quayside to meet us. It was the first time I'd met him. He was, and is, a good lad. We had a few beers together and all of the lads were taking the piss about him coming in to take my place. It was all good craic and banter. Batts and I became really close friends, or as close as you could get to him. He lived in Wetherby (handy for the Whaler) and was a real family man. He was a funny lad, real dry sense of humour. It never affected our relationship and I admired him as a footballer. I think he could have covered himself in even more glory had he changed his style. You talk about two-footed players and he was up there with the best of them. He could ping passes over any range with two feet. But he played the defensive midfielder role differently from me.

As the title was slipping away from us, or we were losing games, I never witnessed a lack of fizz or enthusiasm in the training camp. We'd never been in that position before or experienced it. There was only Beardsley who had won a title before Batts turned up. Venners and Brace had gone by this stage. We all felt the defeats and were hurting as a group. If we lost a game on a Saturday, Sunday or Monday; the following training session we would be low because we were unhappy about the defeat. There would be no laughing and joking then. But then we would pick it up again after a couple of days.

Did the boss's mood change in this time? What you see is what you get with Keegan. He can't hide his emotions. You know when he is unhappy or happy. I am the same. You can tell within seconds of seeing me what my mood is like. He was our leader and when he felt low so did we. There was never a time when teammates were having a pop at each other during the run in that season.

Towards the end of the 1995-96 campaign there were a few players who had a crisis of confidence because results weren't going our way. Players weren't playing to the same level and self-belief dropped, which is natural. When you're a player of a certain level, a lot of the time, it's what's going on between your ears. Your self-belief and confidence goes. You certainly see it with goalscorers. I've been lucky that I've played with some fantastic forwards in my career who were phenomenal strikers. When they're in a rich vein of form it's instinctive and they don't think about it. But if they have a lean period, it's weird, because they tend to over think things or try too hard, if that makes any sense. So when things aren't going for you the way they were and the goals and wins start drying up, you do have a few doubts and question your own ability.

After the Spurs game at the end of the season we didn't want to come out on the pitch and do a lap of honour. The only reason we came back out was to show some appreciation to the fans. It was never a lap of honour. There are only six teams who have won the Premier League since its inauguration in 1992. We were so close yet so far and we could've added to that. We were deflated.

We had a very vocal dressing room and, although we were all low, several players tried to rally us saying it was a great effort, we should be proud of our season and we'll come back and have another go next term. We thought, 'Yes, it makes perfect sense. We've had this experience and we're better equipped now.' It didn't mask how low we all were. But it was a fantastic achievement. We knew once we got back for pre-season training the boss and Terry Mac would be lifting our spirits to go again after our break.

I heard Keegan had offered to resign at the end of the season and it wouldn't have surprised me if he did. He was an emotional guy and a bit impulsive at times. We never got wind of it though. He was desperate to win the title. Maybe he thought he had failed. No one else connected with the club thought that: the players, staff or supporters. But I bet he thought that. Second to him wasn't good enough. That was his nature. But he came back after the summer refreshed, signed Alan Shearer and his enthusiasm was back tenfold.

We were on our way to Thailand and Singapore for a pre-season tour in the summer of 1996. Just as we boarded the plane and the doors were about to shut the manager jumped up, grabbed his carry bag and disembarked. We knew something had happened but didn't know what. Keegan then joined us in Thailand a day or so later. We'd heard and read the speculation we were in the running to sign Shearer. But rumours surrounding the club were rife and we didn't know how true it was.

The boss got the squad together on his arrival in the Far East and said, "If you don't realise that we're one of the biggest teams in Europe and the world, you will now. We've just broke the world record transfer fee to sign Alan Shearer." Shearer then joined us a couple of days later. It was a *wow* moment. But I think deep down we weren't really that surprised because Keegan continually did this with the standard of player he kept bringing in. Every season the players were bigger, better and more high-profile. We were excited all the same. The squad was confident it could win the title without Shearer coming in but his signature obviously made us stronger.

Sir John Hall, his son Douglas and Freddy Shepherd need to take a lot of credit as well. They were always looking to expand the brand. They travelled all around Europe and the world looking for innovative ways to take the club to another level, and sign the best players of course. Sir John bought some land at Woolsington for a state-of-the-art training facility with hotels and a health spa. Unfortunately, that one didn't get off the ground but they were always trying to improve.

There's been a big deal made of Shearer demanding Ferdinand's number nine shirt. It was written that the incumbent holder of the jersey was widely upset about having to hand it over. I can't comment on whether that was true or false, although if I had to guess I'd say it was incorrect. He was more upset about taking my number ten than giving up the number nine. Being the gentleman, and all round good guy, that he is, Big Les wouldn't take it at first. He said, "It's Nash's number." It didn't sit well with both Les and I at the time but the club insisted he wore the shirt. He took it badly and so did I. This was another example of when the club thought, 'He's the local lad, it doesn't matter what he thinks, he'll just accept the decision.' I'd had that feeling for a while. If the club were thinking that, they'd be right. Shearer and Ferdinand got on like a house on fire – on and off the pitch. But it is impossible not to like Big Les; everybody loved him.

I was at a bit of a crossroads in my career at the end of the 1996 season after being pushed out of the first team picture. I'd had chances to go to other clubs before but never contemplated it. Celtic with Tommy Burns, who was the manager, was interested in taking me as was Brian Little at Aston Villa. They went through the correct channels and I spoke with Keegan about it. There was never any official meeting. His door was always open and we'd often go in and have a chat, drink of pop and a chocolate bar. Thinking back, he was probably sounding out my feelings on such things. But I didn't want to give up the dream of playing for my home club without fighting for a place. As much as I was frustrated at the end of the campaign I wanted to prove my worth. I knew I was good enough. Keegan knew I was never going to let him down, whether coming off the bench or being recalled to the side in place of someone else.

It only hit home that I'd have to leave when Keegan left. I remember coming on as a sub when we beat Tottenham 7-1 and playing a big part in it. We blew them away like they were a lower league club when they were one of the best teams in the country. We did the same against Leeds United a few days later. That ended 3-0 against one of the best young sides in the Premier League. I wasn't aware he'd tried to resign after the Boxing Day game at Blackburn, where we lost 1-0. But when we went to a bitterly cold Charlton Athletic and drew 1-1 in the FA Cup I remember the manager getting on the bus and keeping his woolly hat on. We're thinking, 'What's going on there?'

The day after the draw at Charlton Terry Mac called a meeting at Maiden Castle. It was quite emotional. He told us Keegan had left and that he and Arthur Cox were taking charge in the short term. We were absolutely devastated. If Keegan hadn't brought us to the club, he had nurtured and developed the young lads that were already there when he joined. We all ran through the proverbial brick wall for him. We never felt like he'd let us down.

Stories broke soon after about having to balance the books and we began to understand. The club had become a PLC and he'd stopped enjoying being the manager because of what that entailed. Apparently he had to raise between £5m and £6m before he left. In essence, it was the sale of big Les. He was fine about moving lads on to bring in new players, but having to sell players to balance the books wasn't what he was about. He wanted the club to be different. He didn't want the club to go back to selling a Waddle, Beardsley or Gascoigne. When Sir John Hall initially came in they didn't do that. They started buying players to compliment the best players rather than flogging them.

I was back in the side at this point, doing well and enjoying my football. I was playing as a narrow right midfielder, because let's be fair, I didn't have any pace. I provided the assist for Lee to score against his old club at The Valley. We went to Villa, in the game after Keegan had left, and we went 2-0 up. I scored before it finished 2-2. I actually hit the post in the last couple of minutes which would've made it 3-2.

Kenny Dalglish came in and we'd gone from one former iconic player to another, who was also a fantastic manager. While we were all devastated Keegan had gone, the Scot coming in kind of softened the blow if you like. Shearer and Batts had both played under him and won the Premier League. He was very different to KK. You could read Keegan any day of the week whereas Dalglish would keep things tight and inside. He was very protective of the players even when the performances were poor. In private he was a funny man full of humour and liked a laugh. As players, we were all in awe of him for his achievements.

Dalglish's first game was the FA Cup Third Round replay against Charlton. Me and Shearer both scored in a 2-1 victory. I was on a roll. Not only was I starting games but scoring as well.

My confidence was sky-high. We then went to The Dell and I scored again, before Newcastle United nemesis Matt le Tissier scored yet another wonder goal to draw 2-2. He must have loved playing against us. It always seemed to be a world class finish every time he played. Then we faced Forest at home in the next round of the FA Cup and the new boss pulled me into the office. He said, "Look, wee man. I'm leaving you out today." I asked for a reason. He replied, "There isn't a reason. It's just because Peter Beardsley is fit and he's the club captain." That was the definitive moment. In my heart of hearts, I knew, it didn't matter what I did on the pitch I was always going to be down the pecking order with the likes of Beardsley, Rob Lee and Batts always coming before me, no matter how I was performing. This was hard for me. But for the remainder of that season I made it hard for the manager to leave me out, giving it my all.

I went to see Dalglish and he was brilliant. He said he wanted me to stay, that I would be a valuable member of the squad but he couldn't guarantee I would start every week. He wanted me to sign a new contract but also said he would understand if I wanted to leave. In hindsight, when I look back I wish I'd stayed. I probably would've played 25 to 30 games anyway. And the Scot only lasted a season after I left. We don't really live and learn, as we'd like to think we do. We just do whatever we think is best or right for us at the time and deal with it.

The players liked Dalglish but, let's be honest, he wasn't as open as Keegan. I really enjoyed playing under him and he had everybody's respect. He'd join in training and be the best player. He had a great sense of humour and we would've done anything for him. He was thorough and delivered a team talk in a different way to KK. He was a bit more tactical, discussing strategy on a board, while giving you information about the opposition; whereas Keegan was more open about the way he felt. Does that make you a more negative team? It shouldn't really. Does it make you a bit more aware of your opponents and make you nervy? It shouldn't, but maybe it did.

Dalglish moved training from Maiden Castle to Chester-le-Street because he didn't want people or supporters seeing the everyday happenings at the club. Maiden Castle was a council training facility so he couldn't stop people coming in. He had more control at Chester-le-Street over the comings and goings. It goes without saying Dalglish was more private than Keegan. He didn't want the club washing their dirty laundry in public, as such.

The new manager, however, made some bad signings when he settled in. He made some captures that looked good on paper but didn't work out. One of the biggest enigmas was Jon Dahl Tomasson. Just look at the career he had after he left Newcastle. Look at the teams he played for and the trophies he won. He won a Champions League medal with AC Milan. I think Dalglish wanted to pair up the Denmark striker with Shearer but our £15m striker got injured in the Umbro Tournament at Everton to scupper the plan. It was around the same time he allowed Ferdinand to go to Tottenham. Who knows what would have happened had Shearer not suffered that injury. Tomasson could've gone on to be a great. We'll never know. It just didn't happen for him. I remember Tino put him in on goal in the opening minute of his home debut and he missed. It seemed to affect his confidence and he struggled after that. You can't say he was a bad player. It just didn't work out for him at Newcastle.

There were several players Dalglish brought in and people were wondering if they were direct replacements for the players that left. For example, Des Hamilton was thought to have been brought in for me. Batty could be cutting at times. There was this one time after training when he turned to Des and said, "I know you've signed for United, but do you think it's the wrong

United? Do you not think Rotherham is where you're supposed to be and you took a wrong turn somewhere?"

I have no axe to grind with Dalglish over his part in the club's history. I know he wasn't very popular with supporters in his time at St James' Park. But, as much as it hurt to see the team struggle, I'd gone and had my time. The club hadn't forced me out. It was my decision. I didn't feel as if I got a fair crack of the whip at times and I can back that up. I was an easy option to leave out for the so-called big name signings. I was the local lad who wouldn't moan or sulk because I was just happy to be playing for my home-town club.

When I had to make the difficult decision to leave it was a wrench. I was giving up the dream of playing for Newcastle. You don't just walk away from that on a whim, not when you're a Geordie. But I was a footballer who wasn't playing football and that is what I wanted to do. I couldn't not play football, even if I was wearing black and white on the bench. There were three incredible footballers in: Beardsley, Lee and Batty, playing in my position. There was no shame in being unable to dislodge them from the side.

I knew my time was up at Newcastle. I'd scored three goals in three games from midfield and we hadn't lost a game and yet I was out of the side. The manager even said it had nothing to do with my performances. The writing was on the wall. Even the games that I didn't start I was still making a contribution. I remember the Leicester City game at home. We were 3-1 down when I came on and we won 4-3, Shearer bagged a hat-trick and I was involved in the winning goal. But the quality of player I was up against made it difficult. Well, impossible. I fully understood that. It goes without saying I left with a heavy heart.

CHAPTER 7
WALK LIKE AN EGYPTIAN

He'd always say it. "Prince Philip is a Nazi," and "The Prime Minister is corrupt," were just two of the more captivating and unconventional opinions made by my former employer, Mohamed Al-Fayed. I'm sure there were more but he certainly wasn't shy in sharing his views of the world. I can't talk about my time at Fulham without discussing the club's enchantingly eccentric, colourful and charismatic former owner. Al-Fayed was seen as a divisive and extremely dangerous character in the political world to paranoid members of parliament, but to us, a sincere, warm, caring and humorous man.

It's often underestimated how much the Egyptian-born businessman achieved at Fulham Football Club. This may sound a bit dramatic but I shudder to think what would've happened to the Cottagers without his chivalrous intervention. The West London outfit were on the brink of extinction prior to his involvement. Fulham were bottom of the Third Division, racked with massive debts and plunging head-long into oblivion before Al-Fayed's philanthropical gesture to invest in the club. He essentially rescued the famous ailing outfit from certain death. It's nothing short of a miracle what happened next.

The former owner of Harrods declared Fulham would be a Premier League club within five years. He delivered that promise in four. The Cottagers' meteoric rise through the leagues was nothing short of a fairy tale and *Schoolboy's Own* stuff. It could have been a story straight from the pages of *Roy of the Rovers* . Al-Fayed had bought the Freehold of Craven Cottage, and the club, for less than £7m in 1997. But by 2001 Fulham had risen out of the Football League's fourth tier like a phoenix from the flames and into the promised land of the

Premier League. And we secured our top flight League status in swashbuckling style after a record-breaking points tally as champions of Division One, now the Championship.

Al-Fayed was great to me, personally, and to all of the Fulham players. We were like his extended family. He was big into family life and on a match day he would spend an enormous amount of time fussing over our wives, girlfriends and kids, making sure they were happy and had everything they needed. There is no doubt he was absolutely eccentric. Some might even say he was barking mad. But one of the best I've ever had the pleasure of working with. We had some unbelievable times with him. When we won promotion to the Premier League he closed off the main restaurant to the public for our party. In each corner of the eatery there was an international theme: Italian, Indian, Chinese and another, which escapes me. When you went for a glass of champagne the waiting staff would pour a glass and then give you the bottle. It was everything you could think of and much, much, more. Money was no object.

Each member of the team got a Harrods discount card. And when I was made captain I got a Harrods Gold Card. The perk of having one meant I got free parking outside of the store. Me and Lorraine were in the Harrods store restaurant one day and Al-Fayed clocked us. He came over and asked why we were drinking champagne. I explained it was my birthday. He snapped his fingers and, as if by magic, another bottle of bubbly arrived for us. My boss then told us to enjoy our lunch and he would look after the kids for an hour, so we could spend some quality time together. The kids came back with several bags full of gifts and toys. The bags were as big as the children. Mohamed just gave them the run of the shop. When we used to go back to Harrods my son, Jak, would always ask whether Mr Al-Fayed was going to be around. This is just one small example of the man's generosity and kindness. One of Al-Fayed's signature themes was a gold bullion bar made out of Belgian chocolate. After every home game we'd come into the changing room and one bar was left for every player by his changing peg.

The club's supremo often had celebrities in the changing rooms before and after a game at Craven Cottage. Michael Jackson, Tony Curtis, Geri Halliwell and Rory Bremner were just a few well known visitors to SW6. When Wacko Jacko turned up he had some guy throwing rose petals down for him to walk on. It was surreal, exactly like *Coming to America* . I remember the chairman shouting, "Hide your cocks lads, Michael's coming!" We were all in hysterics but this was just the norm to us. When Ginger Spice came to see us he said, "You can't be playing football with a full bag, you need to get rid of it. That's what Geri is here for." We were going, "You can't say things like that!" but she just laughed and took it in the spirit and good fun it was intended. It was unreal, weird and fantastic all at the same time. We didn't know what to expect next. In fact, I was having a medical at Harrods one day, stripped down to my birthday suit and the famous Italian superstar actor Sophia Loren walked by as if it was the most natural thing in the world. Al Fayed said, "Here is an athlete," as they walked by. I made a double take in case I was seeing things. It was times like this when I thought to myself, 'I've certainly come a long way from Pottery Bank.'

We had excellent training facilities at Motspur Park, New Malden. It was a Grade II listed building that was developed into a state-of-the-art sporting facility for over 150 members of staff. Several international football teams have held training sessions there, including Brazil, Colombia, England, South Korea and Sweden. The arena stand was used in the 1981 film *Chariots of Fire*, which Al-Fayed's son, Dodi exec-produced by. But money was no object and this was just another part of the owner's grand scheme.

Al Fayed had big plans for Craven Cottage but more often than not his proposals hit the proverbial brick wall. The ground was in a residential area by the River Thames and getting planning applications pushed through proved impossible in the end. Players couldn't park around the ground. We had to go and park in a nearby school and wait for a minibus to take us to Craven Cottage. The Fulham chief wanted to build the stadium higher; have underground parking and apartments on the back of the Riverside Stand. But the Johnny Haynes Stand and the Cottage were both listed buildings and no matter what happens in the future they can't be touched. In the end Al-Fayed's hands were tied. We spent two years at QPR's ground, Loftus Road, while Craven Cottage was being developed. The owner did the best he could but was ultimately powerless to fulfil his vision and long-term grand plans.

Why didn't the club fulfil its potential and ambitions under Al-Fayed? The rejections for planning and development played big parts in it. The chairman was obviously ambitious but sometimes it felt like he was having a love-hate relationship with Fulham. There were times when he was in love with the club and other times it felt as if he wasn't in love with it. When he adored the club the finances were there and he would spend, spend, spend. Then, on the other hand, he'd change his mind and would be looking to cut costs. There was no real consistency.

It would be fair to say our owner was quite a volatile character at times as well. But then aren't we all when things aren't going for us? He'd often make speeches at one of our Christmas parties or an end of season get together and launch into one of his, "Prince Philip was a Nazi," tirades or openly discussed government corruption. It was hilarious stuff. The lads just put it down to his eccentricity and the frustrations of not being able to take Fulham to the next level. Mind you, he did take charge at Craven Cottage not long after he lost his son.

There was a strong possibility he was still grieving the death of Dodi in that high profile car crash in France with Princess Diana.

Al-Fayed's idiosyncrasies aside, he went out of his way to ensure me and my family were settled at the club. It was important to him and I appreciated it. While I was fine with the move it took Lorraine a little longer to settle in the country's capital city. Lorraine, Jak and Claudia came down initially for a year. The kids were in a Montessori Nursery in Barnes, near Harrods Village, where we lived. They were originally Harrods warehouses, which were converted into houses and apartments. But it was difficult for Lorraine. She was alone most of the time when I was at work and the kids were at nursery. She didn't get any time to spend with friends and she became a bit homesick. Lorraine decided to move back up north so I got myself a flat and I'd fly back on weekends to see the family.

The club were aware of my wife's decision to move back to Newcastle. But, when Fulham wanted to extend my contract, they made it clear that a new deal would be offered only under certain conditions. One of those stipulations was a commitment from Lorraine to return to London with the kids. With that in mind we decided to look outside of the city and found a place in Epsom, Surrey, before moving on to Kingswood and bought a beautiful house there. We found a nice neighbourhood and ended up having a happy, fulfilling time. The kids loved the school they were at and Lorraine met some good friends. It probably helped that five or six of the Fulham lads were living in that area as well.

Al-Fayed knew the importance of having a settled family because an unsettled domestic household can have an effect on your game. The Fulham chairman actually pulled a few strings to get our kids into the schools we wanted, which were full when we enquired. I think a couple of Harrods' hampers helped ease the process for the school on its fête and summer fair days. It was never any hassle or a problem for him. He was a one-off and a brilliant ally to have in times like that. You just knew you could always rely on him to help out when you were in need.

I'm aware my move to Fulham kind of contradicts claims of being a homer, but that was the case when I was younger. I didn't want to leave the home comforts of Newcastle. But after my spell at Sunderland turned sour I was keen to get away from home. And when new Cottagers' boss Paul Bracewell showed his cards, I jumped at the chance. Brace played a big part in my move to Wearside. He was a bit of a mentor to me when I was a kid on Tyneside. I also saw what Kevin Keegan was doing at the West London club, prior to becoming England manager and before Brace took over. I wanted to be part of the Craven Cottage revolution because it looked like a club on the up. KK had taken the newly ambitious outfit from the third tier of the Football League into the second tier. They were spending crazy amounts of money on players and cash seemed to be no object.

Fulham made it clear they really wanted me when I decided to leave the Stadium of Light. It was a no-brainer after that, once they made their intentions clear I wanted to go there. Bracewell broke the Fulham transfer record for me, paying £3m, and the Cottagers continued to break the transfer record for the first four to five years at the beginning of Al-Fayed's reign as owner. The club put me in a hotel on the outskirts of Richmond Park at first. It is a beautiful part of the world. I didn't start well and struggled for form during the first couple of months. It wasn't because I felt unsettled. I never ever felt the urge to get on a plane or train back home to Newcastle. Looking back, maybe it was because I didn't have the Lorraine and the kids around me. They came down to London later than I did, in the September.

Questions were being asked about whether I was worth the money the club paid for me. I didn't hit the ground running at all, but then all of a sudden it just clicked. The catalyst was scoring against Norwich in the League Cup in a 4-0 triumph. I felt that was the game where I proved to the fans, staff and everyone at the club what I was about. I already knew, but it was like I'd reassured myself as well. My confidence levels just escalated after that and I kicked on. I started scoring goals, winning player of the month awards and scooped the player of the season trophy in my first two years.

It was always on my mind as to whether I was doing justice to Brace. I wasn't firing on all cylinders. And when he lost his job it was tough. You think, 'Have I played a part in that?' But you're a professional at the end of the day and you have to move on. I don't want to sound callous here because I was upset Brace lost his job. But after he left it gave me a chance to play for another great manager, so every cloud has a silver lining, as the cliché goes. Karl Heinz Riedle, who stood in as caretaker manager, brought in Roy Evans to help out. Evans was his former boss at Liverpool and part of the famous Anfield boot room dynasty. He'd seen it all, got the t-shirt and DVD. It was a brilliant short period under him. Riedle may have been in the twilight of his career but he was still a quality player and professional.

When a manager leaves there's always the odd player happy to see him leave, usually those not being picked for the team. That applies to whether the boss was Keegan, Kenny Dalglish, Peter Reid or any manager. But the majority enjoyed playing under Brace. We weren't terrible by any stretch of the imagination but obviously not good enough to get into the automatic promotion or play off positions. The chairman was very ambitious and that was the least he expected. He wanted Premier League football ASAP!

Jean Tigana was named as Fulham's new boss after Evans and Riedle's brief tenure at the helm. The Frenchman immediately set about changing the philosophy of the club and we kicked on to even greater heights. Tigana was a member of France's legendary 1984 European Championship winning side, playing alongside Michel Platini, Alain Giresse and Luis Fernandez. He also won a Ligue 1 title in France, as manager at Monaco. Tigana was a bit of a pioneer in sports science and medicine. I think the French were one step ahead of everyone back them. The new manager took us to the Pyrenees for pre-season training. Generally, you don't go back to training after the season's end until July, but we were back in early June.

I knew about sports science but this was a different level to what I was used to. We had x-rays on our teeth, for example. The doctors reckoned that any infection or problem with our wisdom teeth could leak into our body and cause a breakdown somewhere. We had a hardcore of about six or seven British lads in the squad in their late 20s and early 30s and we all thought it was surreal. It's hard to change the attitudes of seasoned professionals at that age but we all bought in to it.

The squad also went to Clairefontaine in France, which is the national school of football over there. We had three weeks of training with three sessions a day: 6am, 10am and 3pm. It was the fittest and leanest I'd ever been. My fat percentage was six per cent. Our diet changed and the menu changed. We were taking supplement or vitamin tablets. I was low on iron so I took something to help combat that. The attention to detail was ridiculous. We did a lot with the ball but it was fitness as well. We did gym sessions as a group to become more powerful both individually and collectively.

When the international breaks came around, those who weren't away with their national side went to France and we'd have a friendly. One time we played in a six-a-side tournament with AC Milan, Marseille and FC Porto. Tigana also took us to a vineyard that he owned in the South of France. It was a bit of an eye-opener. I can't imagine a British manager taking you to his vineyard. The British equivalent would be to open a boozer or a newsagent. But it has to be said, Tigana's innovative methods took us to a new level.

Tigana loved the 'never give up' British mentality. He tried to build on that and get the best out of us. He was well aware the club had the best players in the second tier of football and, with our fitness levels, we dominated the majority of games. In fact a lot our games were won in the last ten minutes because our superior fitness kicked in when the opposition were tiring. I remember a game against Barnsley, who did well to hold us to 0-0 until the last ten minutes. We dominated possession and then they tired and we obliterated them. And the options of players we had were incredible. The manager rarely had to do a team talk on the day of a match because all of the prep work had been done during the week. I was thriving in the team, playing well, scoring goals and happy to sign a new contract.

Tigana was a relaxed guy with some fantastic ideas of how he wanted his team to play. He gave off a Cool Hand Luke persona to the outside world, and was like that to a certain extent. But he was also a humorous guy who could be ruthless when it was needed. He commanded respect because of what he'd achieved as a player. He was a fantastic footballer in his day. The ex-Les Bleus star never tried to change our personalities, just tried to change us as players and make us better. He gave us a shape and an idea of how he wanted us to play. But at the same time we got a lot of freedom to make our own decisions on the pitch.

The Frenchman added some good players to the side. John Collins, who he knew from his time as Monaco boss, was brought in from Everton. Louis Saha was a fantastic signing. Saha was brilliant in the lone striker role for us. He was a steal at £2.1m from Metz. The France international was electric; had a great leap and you'd be hard pressed to find anyone who was more successful than him at Fulham in performance terms. He could jump incredibly high and bring the ball down on his chest, where mere mortals would struggle to do the same. Saha had great pace, good touch, two quick feet and his heading ability was superb.

I remember when we went to Old Trafford and comfortably won 3-1 with goals from Saha, Steed Malbranque and myself. It wasn't a fluke; we could've won by more. We went to Highbury the week after and drew 0-0; a lot of which was down to Edwin van der Saar. Arsenal had a lot of class at the time with Thierry Henry, Robert Pires, Patrick Viera and the likes of Ashley Cole. But to take four points from those two games was the sign of a good side.

I've played with some great goalkeepers in my time: Pavel Srnicek, Steve Harper, Thomas Sorensen, Shay Given but van der Saar had something different about him; such a presence. He was definitely a *wow* signing. It was a measure of the club's ambition that we signed arguably the best goalkeeper in the world for a snip of £7m. The Holland shot-stopper was another brilliant fella; down to earth, sociable with the wives and girlfriends and helpful to the other lads. I'd often sit with van der Saar on the bus and talk about his Italian days at Juventus and, in general, pick his brains. I was surprised he stopped at Fulham for so long. Not being disrespectful to my old club but it was only a matter of time before Man United or another big club came for him.

Tigana had us set up to play a different way to other sides in the division. Luis Boa Morte and Malbranque played on the flanks, Saha through the middle and I played in behind the striker. I'd drop back to make a midfield three, when we weren't attacking, with Mark Pembridge and Sean Davis. Davis was a good young player coming through. He played in every division in Fulham's meteoric rise. That has got to be some sort of record. He got some good moves after he left SW6 but another one robbed of becoming an even better player because of injury. Then there was Sylvain Legwinski, Bjarne Goldbæk, who sometimes played on the right, Steve Finnan at right back, Rufus Brevett, left with Alain Goma and Zat Knight as centre-half. Goma was an accomplished defender. I'm not sure why it didn't work out for him at Newcastle. I do know there weren't many centre halves as fast as him. He seemed to pick up a lot of injuries, though, and couldn't get into any rhythm. He was a nice guy, quiet, unassuming and respectful.

Junichi Inamoto was playing for us around this time. He was unique because he was the first Japanese player in the Premier League and we had a huge Asian following because of him. He'd get two huge sacks of fan mail every day. That support kind of compensated for the supporters who decided to stay away when we played at Loftus Road. Not sure there'd ever be a *Inamoto is a Geordie* t-shirt, like.

There was an accusation the Japan international was only there to tap into the Asian market. That was unfair because he was a better player than he was given credit for. Maybe he wasn't good enough to get in that great Arsenal side but he was talented enough to be successful for us. He was a quiet, respectful, hardworking lad, who still socialised with us. I don't think he touched alcohol but it didn't stop him coming out with us. At Newcastle, Peter Beardsley didn't drink but he'd often come out with us. Pedro would often end up as the taxi driver to his own detriment. He'd often have to pull over in lay-bys for those who'd had one too many. I don't think he enjoyed that role. The biggest problem with Beardsley being sober was that the next day he would retell the night's activities much to the embarrassment of the guilty.

Fulham spent something like £49m in 40 days one term. It didn't really work out for Steve Marlet, an £11.5m capture from Lyon, but that happens sometimes. Not all signings are a success, it doesn't matter how much you pay for the player. Martin Djetou, came from Parma on loan, and could play centre half or in midfield. He was a smashing player. Brian McBride came in and was another brilliant signing, although a different type of player to Saha.

Boa Morte was a bit of a hot head at times but worked tirelessly up and down the flank offensively and defensively. He didn't mind the ugly, dirty work and always got stuck in. He could play in a two-man strike force or operate as lone striker as well. The Portugal international was very flexible. He was one of the most popular players in the dressing room; absolutely loved by everyone. He was a bubbly character who loved a laugh and a joke but deadly serious on the pitch. Like Faustino Asprilla, you could play tricks on him like cutting up his clothes and he would laugh about it. With Tino we'd cut the arms out of his shirts; toes out of his socks and put Deep Heat in his underpants. We wouldn't dare do that to Brian Kilcline, because we'd probably get a right hook! Killer was immaculate every day, unlike the stereotypical jeans, t-shirt or tracksuit footballer. He took pride in his appearance and we wouldn't dare touch his stuff. The same goes with Malbranque. He was a fantastic footballer but was a bit of a quiet and insular guy. You wouldn't play jokes on those characters. But being at Fulham was like my time at Newcastle because we all mixed and got on socially.

We finished 13th and then 14th in the Premier League in our first two seasons back in the big time but, by the end of the 2002/03 campaign, Al-Fayed decided he wasn't going to renew Tigana's contract because the club struggled in the bottom half of the table during his last term in charge. It was sad to see the Frenchman leave Craven Cottage. We'd achieved a lot under his stewardship. But the team found it difficult in his last season because of our involvement in the UEFA Cup. We qualified through the Intertoto Cup and played our first game on July 6. We'd played seven games before we kicked a Premier League ball in anger. Thirteen fixtures were contested in the Intertoto Cup before we saw off Dynamo Zagreb and Hajduk Split in the first two rounds of the UEFA Cup. Hertha Berlin eventually knocked us out in round three.

I don't think it helped Tigana or Fulham's cause playing at Loftus Road. We spent two seasons there and it was tough for everyone involved; mostly for the fans. It's like Newcastle being asked to play at the Stadium of Light. We'd play alternative weekends and alternative mid-weeks and they'd change the signage from QPR to Fulham inside and around the ground. Things like memorabilia and pictures etc. It must've taken a lot of effort to do. Obviously the supporters weren't too keen on the move so the club had to appease them somewhere along the line. We had some unbelievable times, games and wins there. There were a few stay away fans but I think the majority came around.

It got a bit messy in the end and the club took Tigana to court, claiming he had wrongly overpaid for certain players but the charges were eventually dropped. The former France international then took Fulham to court for wrongful dismissal and won. When the results weren't going our way the relationship broke down between the pair. I know Tigana was involved in an agency business before he became a manager. But we were never party to what was going on. Al-Fayed's decision to let Tigana go opened a new chapter in the club's history and our controversial owner decided to appoint Fulham's former captain.

Keegan signed Chris Coleman for Fulham when they were in the third tier, now League One. He was far too good for that standard. He was a class act. The Welshman was a big and powerful football playing, left-footed, centre half. Like myself, Coleman could see the ambition of Fulham and that's why he took an initial step backwards to go forwards from former Premier League champions Blackburn. When I arrived in the Championship, he was still head and shoulders above the best centre half in the division. He was a great captain, leader and a big personality in the dressing room. He was fantastic with the new players and their families helping them to settle in and I became very good friends with him.

Unfortunately, Coleman had a horrific car crash that nearly killed him. Ironically we had arranged to go and watch Newcastle play Spurs at White Hart Lane the day it happened. But he cancelled because he had to pick up his kids. Then later on he swerved to miss a deer on a road near where he lived. His car spun out of control and flipped over. His legs were jammed and he couldn't move to get his phone. The Welshman lay there for ages and thought he was going to die. He later told me petrol was leaking inside the car and saw sparks coming from the engine. Fortunately, a passer-by found him and called the emergency services. God knows what would've happened had this guy not found him. Coleman broke both legs, had pins put in his ankles and a muscle was removed from his arm and placed in one of his legs because the damage was so severe.

I went to see my good friend and playing colleague in hospital. He saw the look of horror on my face. Quick as a flash he quipped, "Fancy a bit of steak tonight, son?" He was a funny guy and always a one with a quick one-liner. I didn't know what to say but I was distraught for him. Coleman tried to make a comeback and pushed himself to the limits. I went to see him play in the reserves but you could see in his eyes that he knew he would never get back to the level he once played at. It must have been devastating for him to call time on his playing career.

I never thought Coleman would become a manager. I thought he'd move into the media side of football and become a pundit because he was very articulate. But full credit to Tigana, he saw what a great leader Coleman was and asked him to join the coaching staff. He took to it really quickly and became a very good manager. The ex-Wales international ended up being the youngest ever Premier League manager.

Coleman wanted me to play a different role to that of Tigana, ironically, against Newcastle at our temporary home, Loftus Road. We were drifting close to the relegation zone, while United were in with a shout of winning the title. It seems a lifetime ago that my home-town team were actually challenging for the Premier League. I scored the winner past Given, ten minutes from the end in a 2-1 victory. We had five games left of the season and we won three of those, drew one and lost one. Coleman got the job permanently after that.

The Welshman received tremendous respect from everyone as a man, player and leader. We'd seen him conquer adversity in one respect. Most people wouldn't have even tried to get back to playing again. It was great to see him flourish as a manager and he created a great atmosphere at the club. He was bubbly in a Keegan way and had us in the top five in his first full season in charge ahead of the January transfer window. There was speculation Man United were after Saha. But the gaffer was told by the board Saha wouldn't be sold. And because of that Coleman didn't line anyone up to take his place. The inevitable happened and he was sold for £17m.

Saha, unfortunately, didn't have the best of times at Old Trafford because of injury. He did have success there but Man United fans wouldn't have seen the best of him, which is a shame. He was a humble, quiet and unassuming lad who always wanted to get better. I'm sure his time at Newcastle was valuable to his learning curve. He was a young lad back then under Ruud Gullit and very raw but he would've got a lot out of watching Alan Shearer go about his business. I'm sure that held him in good stead for the future.

Talking of injuries, I had between 12 to 18 months out with Achilles' problems, which overlapped Tigana's tenure and the beginning of Coleman's stewardship. Initially I was out for four months with an Achilles on my right side. I'd taken the ball around Mark Crossley in training and it felt as if I'd been shot in the back of the leg. And then my left side went soon after at St Mary's Stadium against Southampton. While I was waiting for the operation I was still able to take part in the training sessions. I couldn't do any more damage anyway.

Tigana had picked a team to play in a forthcoming match against Liverpool around this time. A couple of days before the game he set up the first team against reserves in a practise match. I moved freely and played well and the boss put me in the squad after I came through the following session. He said I would be used in the last ten to 15 minutes if the team needed a change or maybe had an injury. But six minutes into the game Davis picked up a knock. I turned to Collins and said, "You'll need to warm up." To my surprise Tigana tells me to get stripped. It shocked me because I hadn't played for weeks and all of a sudden I'm going on to compete against Gerrard and Xabi Alonso – two of the world's best midfielders. Nothing to worry about there, eh? Then, as I ran onto the pitch, I felt my Achilles pop. It would have been embarrassing for me to tell the boss I couldn't go on. I played about 75 minutes of the 80 that was left, trying to hide it before being substituted. How did I play? The best I can say is that I ran around. Just. I wasn't moving freely at all. I told Tigana when I came off and he was apologetic but it wasn't his fault. I was a senior player after all. It didn't do any more damage because it had already been done.

I had surgery on both my Achilles. The club thought it might have been my wisdom teeth infecting my body, so they had them taken out. They sent me to Paris for that. I was also sent to the French capital to see a top of the range specialist chiropractor, Philippe Boixel. Gerrard and Michael Owen, from Liverpool were there at the same time. The Reds boss was Gerard Houllier, so it must have been a French thing. The Brazilian Ronaldo, who was at Milan, was also there. None of this would have been cheap. And I was going once a week. I'd fly out on a Wednesday morning, have an hour's treatment and then fly back. That's what the club was prepared to do for its players. It felt nice to be valued.

My career nearly finished early because of the Achilles problems. After the operation and rehabilitation, I was struggling. I'd do all of the work in my training shoes yet when I put my boots on it felt as if someone was using a Stanley knife down the back of my Achilles. I went to several specialists in France and England before spending 17 days in a sports rehabilitation clinic in Salerno, Italy. It was a beautiful place on the coast. The diagnosis revealed scar tissue was causing the problem. I worked with a doctor, Victorino Testa, who was recommended by a Doctor Mafuli, an expert I had seen in Stoke. Mafuli operated under a local anaesthetic, so I was wide awake, while he was trying to scrape away all this scar tissue. He couldn't get rid of it all. Testa was an expert in fibrolytus which was a procedure that broke down the scar tissue using deep massage. You can't do this with your hands or fingers, it was done with metal hooks. You could actually hear it breaking up or snapping. I'd be swimming and doing cycle rides around Pompeii while this was going on to keep up my fitness. Suppose there are worse places than this to spend your rehabilitation.

I was in the last chance saloon with this. If it didn't work my playing days were over. I know it's a perfect opportunity for an

Achilles heel pun, but it's just too soon. With this injury, you're supposed to have the procedure once every five days but, because mine was so severe, I had it every day for an hour. It eventually worked but I had to go into training at 8.30 every morning before the lads to prepare for the 10am session. I was in my early 30s around this time and still felt I had a lot to offer. That's why I put myself through the pain barrier threshold. I have huge scars down the backs of my legs as a reminder. The injury was just wear and tear and not exclusively for explosive or quick players. I don't think I ever had a hamstring injury. I wasn't quick enough.

I remember my last game for Fulham at Craven Cottage against Norwich. We beat them 6-0 and sent them down to the Championship. The number of Canaries fans that turned up for the clash was phenomenal. They took the whole of the Putney End. The match was sold out and we walked into a sea of canary yellow. The result for us didn't matter. Win or lose our position was fixed in the league. Norwich needed to better a rival's result and we expected a tough fixture where they would murder us; but it didn't happen. It was probably one of the easiest Premier League games I've played in.

My contract was running out that season and there was never talk of being offered a new one. I did broach the subject with Coleman and he said they were waiting until the end of the season. I knew in my heart of hearts there would be no offer. I was the team captain, a big earner and the club were trying to change its philosophy from what it was previously. That was the summer my old mate Andy Cole and van der Saar also moved on. Looking back, it was a big decision for the manager to make from a friendship point of view as well. After the Norwich game I asked what was happening. "Things were still progressing," and they were, "Trying to find a solution," to keep me. I would have accepted a new contract on a reduced salary but the club never offered or discussed it with me. It was just words really, but none of them were positive ones.

I got a call on the morning of the FA Cup final from the chief executive, Lee Hoos, to ask whether I could come in on the Monday after the Norwich game to talk about it. I couldn't because of a family holiday commitment. Instead they asked me to go in that afternoon, which I did. There was no manager or coaching staff, just Hoos, who told me the club wouldn't be offering a new contract. I felt a little bit let down because the manager didn't speak to me personally. I felt as club captain I deserved that from the boss and a friend. There's no doubt I would have made it difficult for him, questioning his reasons behind the decision. Hoos said things like, "We didn't want to make a derogatory offer." They didn't know what I would've accepted though. I was gutted. I was happy at Fulham and money wasn't my motivation. I wanted to play for a club I loved playing for. It should have been my decision to say whether the offer was a derogatory one or not. We were happy living where we were. It always feels wrong to be told something like that in such a manner; as though the club's been a bit cowardly or that you don't matter. I didn't put my house up for sale straight away because there were clubs interested in taking me on.

Coleman rang me a couple of weeks later. By that time my anger had subsided and I think he accepted he could've done it differently. I can empathise with him because I've been in that position as a manager. He was still relatively young and inexperienced in a lot of ways. You make a decision you think is right but then in hindsight it's not. I wasn't happy with the way it was handled but I'd built up a strong relationship as a captain to manager and also a friend to friend bond. It's all water under the bridge now and it's never affected my friendship with my old colleague and boss.

I had a great relationship with the fans and I'm humbled every time I go back to Craven Cottage. The supporters are very passionate about their team. I know Fulham aren't a club the size of Newcastle United but it didn't make them any less loyal. And they had a hardcore support following them home and away, who'd been there when they finished 91st out of 92 clubs in the Football League. Within five years of that finish the club was in the Premier League. That was an astonishing achievement. Being at Fulham was one of the best times of my career, if not *the* best. I loved it.

The club had a rich heritage and in Johnny Haynes they had one of the all-time greats of the game. He's one of the most unassuming guys you'll ever meet. He's had a stand named after him, and rightly so. Fulham is a good club to its former players. The red carpet is always rolled out for me when I go back as a pundit or a manager. I went back as Blackpool manager and we drew 2-2 after going 2-0 up. I got a great reception. I have great memories of the place and I'll never forget my time at Fulham.

CHAPTER 8
THE PRODIGAL RETURNS

Newcastle supporters might be surprised to read I was reluctant to rejoin my beloved home-town club when an offer to return was put to me. It should've been a no-brainer really, certainly with no new contract forthcoming at Fulham. But I was tentative because I didn't want fans to think I was returning to the Magpies out of charity or nepotism. Of course, that couldn't have been any further from the truth. Once I'd made it clear to everyone the contract offer had to be on merit and not benevolence, I was happy to sign. I also had to convince myself it wasn't some altruistic gesture by the club. If it was, I wouldn't have come home.

For the first time in my career I was in limbo and without a club. It was a new experience for me. I had always been in demand, under contract or had an ambitious club wanting to take me on. Now there was no demand and I was out of contract. But at only 32-years-of-age, I still believed there was life in the not-so-old dog. Despite that there was never a time, during this period, when I thought, 'That is it, my career's over.' I've always believed in my ability and was confident in finding another club.

My agent spoke to Harry Redknapp, who was Southampton boss. He showed some interest in taking me. Playing for such a charismatic manager appealed but it didn't go much further because he swapped Southampton for Portsmouth. Leeds United, under Kevin Blackwell, was having a sniff at me at the same time but, again, it never got any further than a few conversations with my agent. Leeds and Southampton could've happened had I pushed it but I was just waiting, maybe hedging my bets to see what else was out there.

I started pre-season without a club and began to train on my own. Trying to keep fit this way is tough, quite simply because there is no interaction with other players. Out of the blue, Terry McDermott called and invited me to come and train at my home town football club. McDermott was still at St James' Park under Graeme Souness. They'd had a conversation and made it clear I was more than welcome to come back and make use of the facilities, while looking for a new club. I was in two minds, given my history with United. It didn't feel right somehow. Maybe my pride was getting in the way. From the outside it would look as if I was going back cap-in-hand, like Oliver Twist, but that wasn't the case. Terry Mac called a few times and I was grateful for the invitation but turned it down. He was like a persistent Jack Russell tugging on your trouser leg, so I thought, 'Bugger it, why not?' There's only so much fitness you can do on your own.

My base training was good when I arrived at St James' Park. I'd always taken pride in my fitness. After a couple of weeks, I was still without a club but making good progress with my condition levels. Souness called a meeting around this time and let me know the staff were impressed with what they'd seen and would like to offer a contract. I let him know the doubts and anxieties I had about returning home. He understood my fears and told me not to worry about it. The manager made it clear I wouldn't be playing every week but intimated I could be an important member of the squad. Souness was keen for me to mentor the younger players and added the club would help with my aspirations to become a coach if I took this on board, which I was more than happy to accept.

Yet despite the elation I was feeling of being back on Tyneside I was saddened to discover how much United's stock had fallen. The Newcastle United I left in 1997 was in the Champions League and challenging for the Premier League title.

The squad was bursting with incredibly gifted footballers, players with good character and attitude. I returned to St James' Park to find, overall, the antithesis of that. The standard of player was poor, the attitude of many, atrocious, and the relationship between players and supporters appeared to be fractured and broken.

Newcastle was aware of my coaching ambitions and great in helping me because the courses were expensive. I've been a scholar of the game from an early age and had studied several managers and coaches while I was still playing. I got my first coaching badge at 19-years-old and the first team I looked after was Walker Central, a boy's club where Shola Ameobi started. I was forever taking notes after sessions I'd taken part in for future reference. Then there was the added bonus of being mentored by former Magpies favourite Tommy Craig. He was a top coach.

Craig would take me and Alan Shearer out for sessions on an afternoon when everyone had gone. He'd keep some youngsters back and mentor us through drills we'd have to do in the process of getting our badges. He'd point out what we'd done right and wrong and offered suggestions and pointers to improve and make training better. He played an early and important role in my coaching career.

As for the playing side of things, I thought the odd League Cup game or substitute appearance might come my way but didn't envisage playing in as many games. It came as a surprise to get into the 20-man squad at Arsenal in the 2005 campaign's opening fixture. I then came off the bench at home to West Ham for my second debut, 14 years after my first appearance, which was a special moment for me. My first start was at Blackburn where we recorded our first victory of the new term. Shearer and Michael Owen netted in the 3-0 triumph. I always had a good personal record at Ewood Park.

I felt comfortable when I got in the team. I didn't feel as if I was the weakest link or struggling at all. It was a great way to finish my career. I scored a first and, what turned out to be, final, goal in my second spell in the New Year's Day clash at St James' Park with Middlesbrough. It must have been in the last minute because I remember Shay Given being up for the corner. We drew 2-2. Being able to top and tail a career at my home town club was exceptional. I never thought that would happen to me. Even though I never had the success of my first spell it was still an achievement in one sense because we qualified for Europe.

There were some exciting young players in the Magpies' dressing room. Jermaine Jenas, Kieron Dyer, James Milner, Titus Bramble, Charles N'Zogbia and Steven Taylor had played a lot of games for being so young. Then there were the more experienced lads like Shearer, Given, Stephen Carr and Robbie Elliott were back at St James' Park. Owen had also signed for the club that summer. Despite that, I felt the quality of the group was nowhere near the previous squads I'd been a part of under Kevin Keegan.

A 32-year-old Lee Clark wouldn't have got a sniff in a Keegan squad. The chairman, Freddy Shepherd, was still providing funds for his managers but the players coming in were nowhere near the standard I'd played with before. Gary Speed, Craig Bellamy and Jonathan Woodgate had left. Some of the replacements, the likes of Albert Luque and Celestine Babayaro, came in commanding massive transfer fees and on enormous wages, yet lacked any commitment. Babayaro was a strange one because he was successful at Chelsea. He did have talent. Souness has gone on the record to say he didn't sign Luque but I'm not privy to that information. Regardless of whether the team won, lost or drew, it didn't affect how they felt. For someone like me, it was particularly galling to have that type of personality in the dressing room. What's the point of playing for a club if you're not that bothered about the result? I just didn't understand it. You can't play for the Toon and not know the pride and honour you're playing for.

There were other players who tried their best but just weren't good enough for where Newcastle should have been going. I don't know who was scouting these players. Jean Alain Boumsong and Amdy Faye were two good lads who fit that description. Boumsong wasn't a player at a level I was used to playing alongside. I remember a training session before the curtain-raiser at Arsenal in 2005. Dean Saunders was trying to go through a drill to contend with Denis Bergkamp, and Boumsong just didn't or couldn't get it. Bergkamp was the classic number ten who dropped off in the hole, turned and orchestrated moves and caused chaos if you allowed him to. It was hard to stop him slipping balls to Thierry Henry. They were two world class players and many teams, better than ours, had tried and failed to combat them. Boumsong said he was happy for the Dutchman to turn, face up and get in a race with him. We couldn't believe what he was saying about a man of Bergkamp's quality. The Frenchman also wanted the fullbacks to cover him, his centre half teammate to pick up the striker and the midfielder in front to drop in, protect and cover him, which more times than not was me. Basically, he wanted everyone to do his job so he could be free to wander about. He should never have been at Newcastle. He wasn't good enough.

Faye was a canny lad and good professional, but again, I don't think he was good enough to be playing for the Magpies. He wasn't hard to manage, like: Babayaro, Boumsong and Luque, for different reasons. With Babayaro, did he put the work in or did he just go through the motions on some days? The Nigeria international become a drain on the manager. Being a manager myself, I know how the Babayaro's of this world can be time-consuming when you're trying to get a session going with your group of players.

Souness was seen as a divisive character by fans and it got to the stage where, no matter what happened, the supporters weren't really going to accept him. But I got on very well with him. As a senior player I learned through him how to manage different situations. When the supporters turned on him he never once brought it on to the training ground or into the dressing room before a match. The Scot always tried to give players confidence and encourage them. He was really good with the youngsters as well. His coach, Dean Saunders, was the same. Supporters from the outside won't believe me when I say this but the former Liverpool and Rangers boss was a good man. He was a proper players' manager. But it didn't work out for him. We did have a lot of injuries around that time, and when results aren't going your way you ultimately pay the price with your job.

There were several mitigating circumstances as to why supporters didn't take to him. I know they weren't happy Sir Bobby Robson was fired. He sold Bellamy who was a popular player on the terraces. But ultimately, a lot of his signings didn't work out. The gaffer also fell out with Alan Oliver, a journalist, who worked for the local *Evening Chronicle* newspaper. The chairman told Souness he had to try and get along with Ollie. The Scot replied, "I'll snap him in half if I get the chance."

If Souness was ever under any pressure you would never think it, because he didn't show any signs of emotion. One of his favourite phrases or catchphrases was, *a proper man* and that's what he was. I spent hours with him talking about his career. It was a pleasure to listen to tales from his playing career, simply because he was a great in his day. He was voted by Liverpool supporters as one of the greatest three players ever to pull on a red shirt, alongside Kenny Dalglish and Steven Gerrard. That's not bad company to be in, is it?

Souness had success as a manager. He'd won a lot of trophies home and abroad. I have a lot of respect for him and enjoyed working for him. I've been lucky with the managers I've had. I've treated them with respect and received the same back. He was possibly the right man at the wrong time. It was always going to be tough replacing Sir Bobby. Just look at the problems Man United have had with managers at Old Trafford since Sir Alex Ferguson retired. You can say the same about filling Shearer's boots at St James' Park. It's impossible. The club tried to get Owen to fill that void as a long-term successor. The ex-Liverpool striker was a top drawer player but it didn't work out.

Owen was a humble man for what he'd achieved in his career. He was a magnificent goalscorer. But you got the feeling it wasn't a long-term commitment for him at St James' Park. He probably wanted to go back to Liverpool. But the Reds wouldn't or couldn't raise the funds when he was leaving Real Madrid. I can understand that. Being a Geordie, the only team I ever wanted to play for was Newcastle, but circumstances dictated otherwise. I don't think many people begrudged him that. We certainly didn't see the best of Owen and that was down to some serious injuries as well.

Shearer had to change the way he played after several career-threatening injuries and so did Owen. The former Liverpool man lost the blistering pace he once had as a youngster, and in his early 20s. Shearer reinvented himself, certainly under Sir Bobby, and had an incredible twilight to his career. There was a clamour to get him back in the England team after he retired after posting some impressive performances in the Champions League. Yet when Keegan came back he recognised Owen's shortcomings, if you like, and played him in the hole as a number ten behind Mark Viduka and Obafemi Martins to great effect.

There is a preconception Souness was a volatile man or had an explosive personality. He did lose his temper every now and again but I never witnessed any personal attacks or fall outs with players. He said it how it was and delivered criticism in a good manner. I know he had a problem with Bellamy but that was an isolated incident and most of it was of the Welshman's making.

I saw Bellamy in the latter stages of his career and it looked as if he'd matured a lot. And when you see him speak on television you get the same feeling. He was a fantastic player. I remember him breaking through as a youngster at Norwich City. He always had an arrogance about him, which was what made him such a good player. Watching as a Newcastle fan he was certainly impressive in the domestic and European programme. I remember seeing United in the Champions League. They lost the first three games of their group yet qualified after winning the final three matches; culminating in a ridiculous result in Holland against Feyenoord. Then they progressed to the second stage and got some great results against Inter Milan and Bayer Leverkusen. Mind you Shearer was brilliant in the tournament too. But Bellamy always seemed to push a self-destruct button. He always got involved with players, officials and team mates. I often wondered whether any of this was necessary. He could've been an even better player had he not had this tumult in his life. I would've loved to play alongside him. He had a bit more than just pace to his game, he had great technical ability as well. Obviously he wasn't as good a finisher as Owen but he still got his fair share of goals as well as being a creator of goals. He was perfect foil for Shearer but always clouded in controversy. I've heard stories about his Jekyll and Hyde nature. It's all second hand information passed down, but apparently he'd speak disrespectfully to the coaching staff before behaving like a perfect gentleman.

It didn't feel the same when I went back, despite there being some great lads at the club. Shearer, Given, Harper and Elliott were lads I'd played with previously and got on well with. And the night we got done 3-0 at Man City, Andy Cole had a field day. Coley terrorised us. The manager called a meeting the following day and told us he'd been sacked. We thought he was getting us together to talk about the loss at Eastlands because it wasn't a good performance. Souness had dealt with this type of thing before and was philosophical about his dismissal. But the boss was upset because he'd lost his job. Saunders was very emotional. The Welshman got up and spoke to the group. He spoke highly of the club and how big it was and it got to a few players. But ultimately the Scot left because of results and recruitment. They both weren't good enough. He knew that.

Glenn Roeder took over as caretaker manager when Souness was sacked. He was a steady pair of hands. I'm sure the chairman was looking to bring in another manager but Roeder won the job with the results he got on the pitch. He was an incredibly popular captain in his playing days, an excellent football playing centre half and he deserved a shot at the title, if you like, after steering Newcastle into Europe with a seventh place finish in the Premier League.

All of Souness's staff left apart from Terry Mac, and Shearer came in to assist Roeder. Shearer's title was more ceremonial than anything because he's always been a figurehead at the club. I'm not sure what happened or why, really, because almost immediately we started winning games. Roeder's first game was a 2-0 victory where Shearer broke Jackie Milburn's goalscoring record. We then went to Villa and won 2-1 and remained unbeaten for six games before three reversals in a row. But after that we continued our good form until the end of the season, which ultimately ensured Roeder landed the post. What did he do differently? He made a couple of changes in personnel but that was about it. Maybe some of the players had a look at themselves, felt responsible and thought they needed to do a bit more. Gave themselves a shake? Probably. It was long overdue.

We finished the 2005-06 season with a flourish and the chairman rewarded our caretaker manager with a two-year contract. Roeder set about changing the mentality of players in pre-season and was determined not to sign those who were more interested in fleecing the club and increasing their bank balance. I remember sitting in the office with the club's former skipper and some of the coaching staff on August transfer deadline day. The manager wanted a different type of striker to what he had at the club. Antoine Sibierski was thrown at us and seemed a perfect fit.

Sibierski played more like a number ten than an out and out striker. Keegan had signed him at Man City so that was a good sign. But the first thing that struck us about Antione was that he was a brilliant lad. He didn't get the pulses of the fans racing. The Frenchman wasn't what you'd call a marquee player and, in fact, there was a lot of negativity around his signing. It wasn't his fault, of course. Newcastle generally captured big name players at the time. It gave me great pleasure to see him win over the supporters and become a crowd favourite. The ex-Man City man scored some important goals for us and put in some great performances. You always want the good guys to have success and do well. He is a top, top guy and someone I still keep in touch with.

On transfer deadline day, or the run up to it, the manager, coaches and recruitment staff get together and discuss potential signings. There is a database of players that have been identified as possible targets. These had been built up over the years, through tip-offs, scouts and suggestions. Roeder sent me out to watch players all of the time and do match reports on the opposition. For example, if we needed a left-back I'd suggest one. Nigel Pearson would add his suggestion. The recruitment staff would have a player or two in mind, while the manager always had his own ideas. We'd come together and talk about the players, get reports on their characters or if it was a foreign player we might need to see some footage of him in action. The manager might want to go and see the player himself if you've flagged up someone. The boss might decide he trusts your judgement if he can't go and watch them in action. This is what happened with Martins. Ironically, I was sent to scout Fabricio Coloccini in Spain. He became a fans' favourite after I left but I didn't rate him. Yes, he had a good touch, pace and was an excellent footballer, but he played as an individual and not for the team. At the time he didn't have good positional sense for a centre-half.

Roeder signed Damien Duff for a snip at £5m. He arrived at St James' Park with a fine pedigree; winning countless trophies at Chelsea to boot. He also had a stack of international caps, which would fill the mantelpieces of several players. He was the Republic of Ireland's outstanding player in the 2002 World Cup. But what struck me with Duffer was that he had a lot of self-doubt. He always looked at things he hadn't done well in a game rather than what he had done well. The glass seemed to always be half empty, but he was always looking to improve, which is a great attitude to have. From what he'd already achieved, he was humble and down to earth but low on confidence and self-belief; staggering for such a fantastic footballer. He was another who desperately wanted to do well for United but it didn't happen for whatever reason.

Scott Parker was an excellent player for Newcastle in the short time he was at the club. His problem, initially, was that he tried to pigeonhole himself as a defensive midfield player. The former Chelsea and Charlton man was a box-to-box midfielder. He was a brilliant lad and one of the best I've had the pleasure of playing alongside and coaching. Parker always wanted to do extra work after training was finished. The Londoner constantly wanted to learn and talk about the game and did himself a disservice as a defensive midfielder because he had more ability than that. He could score goals, pass, tackle and get across the pitch quickly. Parker was a pivotal player for Roeder, despite being a Souness signing.

I had Tim Krul and Fraser Forster playing under me in the reserves. Krul came from abroad and it was clear he had ability at a young age whereas Forster hadn't played a lot of football until he was 14. He was more of a rugby lad. Terry Gennoe was the goalkeeper coach around this time and was asked to have a look at Forster. He got him down to the academy and saw something in him. He could hardly kick the ball and, was so inept at times that, he threw the ball into the goal on the odd occasion. But Gennoe saw something in the raw teenager. I remember one of my first games in charge of the reserves against Blue Star at the Wheatsheaf in the Northumberland Senior Cup. The Hexham-born keeper took up a yard turf when trying to take a goal kick. The ball was slapping no more than 20 yards. But with Gennoe's faith in him and Forster's great attitude and work rate, the ugly duckling turned into a swan, just like in the Hans Christian Andersen tale. There was a reserve game against Middlesbrough, where we lost 2-0 or 3-0 and after the game I was having a cup of tea with Sam Allardyce and he said he'd never seen a goalkeeping performance like it in his career. It could've been 10-0 or 12-0 if it wasn't for Fraser.

Alan Thompson came in after me and had a big hand in helping to develop Forster's career. He got him a loan move to Celtic, who eventually signed him. He also had another couple of spells at other clubs. He had a successful period at Norwich, helping them to promotion from League One to the Championship under Paul Lambert. The big keeper also had brief spells at Stockport County and Bristol Rovers as well. Forster has gone on to prove to be a fantastic goalkeeper at Southampton and a regular in the England squad. Why did Newcastle let him go? They had two extraordinary shot-stoppers at the club the same age. They obviously felt they couldn't keep both him and Krul happy so decided to let Forster go.

I was reserve team boss around this time under Roeder. Tommy Craig had moved on as part of the new managerial reshuffle. I read there was a bit of controversy surrounding Craig's exit but I don't think it was anything more than Roeder wanting his own men in. We had some good youngsters in the second string at this time. Andy Carroll was one such player. He was unplayable at times. We went to Everton one evening and he mullered former Magpie Alessandro Pistone and another senior Toffees defender, whose name escapes me. His headers, touch and finishing were spot on that night. After the game, Walter Smith and Archie Knox, who were involved with the Scotland team, asked whether he had any Scottish roots. He did but Carroll never followed up their interest. We sent the young Geordie to Preston under another former Newcastle coach, Alan Irvine, where he didn't do too bad but he didn't do great either. In training he was a hard worker. He would stay behind and do some extra work. Carroll was a bit erratic at this time. He was like a baby giraffe. There'd be times when he'd put a 30-yarder in the top corner and then in another drill he'd completely miss the ball. But he worked hard and made a success of his ability. He's quite unique in this day and age because there aren't many target men strikers of his ilk around. I was proud to be part of the staff when both Carroll and Krul made their United debuts in Palermo in the UEFA Cup, which we won 1-0 thanks to a Luque goal.

There are foreign players who don't pick up the tempo or ferocity of the Premier League and this was Luque's problem.

He wanted to play at his own pace rather than the pace of the game which isn't possible in England. He didn't hit the ground running and then the manager who signed him was gone eight months later. He didn't help himself because he wasn't prepared to fight for a place. I didn't perform to anywhere near the level I used to play at but I fought to get there rather than throwing in the towel. The Spaniard just didn't have that mentality.

Emre Belozoglu was a great fella and smashing footballer. I once had him, Joey Barton and Abdoulaye Faye play for me in the reserves at Man City. The day before the game in training, Barton and Emre had a bit of a barney. Barton had gone in late on the youngster, James Troisi, in Emre's team and he didn't like it. The Turkey international was a tough guy, like a little wrestler, despite him being a brilliant technician with the ball. I was in the middle of it trying to separate them. It then carried on into the dressing room. Barton actually apologised to Troisi but our Aussie youngster, obviously still feeling a little aggrieved at the tackle, didn't accept the apology with the good grace that was intended. Barton, not happy with the youngster's response, said, "Someone's going to get a slap today, just make sure it's not you!" Troisi didn't respond to Barton's bait.

I was worried the bad feeling between Emre and Barton might carry on into the game the following day because nothing had been resolved. I've seen Emre kick off a few times and was an antagonistic sod with the best of them. I've witnessed some colourful language with opposition players about their ethnicity. It's wrong but for some reason it's generally accepted in Turkish culture. There was an incident down at Everton with Joseph Yobo, I remember, when we lost 3-0. Earlier on in the season, when Big Sam was Bolton boss, he came in and told Roeder he wasn't happy with Emre and was going to report him for foul and abusive racial language towards El Hadji Diouf. In the end nothing came of it.

I had a couple of 16-year-old kids in the reserve team that evening and didn't want them to be affected by some bad feeling between two of the first teamers. I called Barton and told him to make his own way down to Manchester and we would meet him at the stadium before the game. He was a former City player so had contacts down there. There are generally only two reasons for first team members to play for the reserves: coming back from injury or they need to top up on their fitness if they weren't selected for a first team game. And I have to say, Barton, Emre and Faye were first class on the night. There was no problem. They were professional from the first minute to the last and we won. They made my job easier because they directed operations on the pitch and set a fantastic example to the kids. The youngsters, if they didn't know it already, learned how first teamers conducted themselves when dropping down into the reserves. They didn't sulk and moan, they got on with it. And I have to say I never had any senior professionals sulk or moan when they stepped down to play for me at Newcastle.

Barton has been a controversial figure throughout his career and it was no different when he came to Newcastle. The Scouser was left out of the 16 for the match at Wigan on Boxing Day and was furious about it. Barton wanted to know why he was taken to the North-West and yet wasn't involved. But Allardyce refused to talk about it. He told the former Man City man he would see him the following day to discuss it because he wanted to concentrate on the game. I don't know whether this was still playing on his mind that night when he was out in his home town of Liverpool. Consequently, he got into a fight, the result of which saw him jailed for nearly three months. But Barton was a big player for Newcastle and I don't know why Big Sam left him out.

Martins, like Barton, was another erratic player, at the best of times, but for different reasons. He had ridiculous ability but you didn't know what you were going to get from him. Could he be unplayable? Yes! Could he sulk? Yes! He was a player you always had to push, cajole and coax to get the best out of him. He had fantastic talent but was equally unpredictable. We went to White Hart Lane and won 4-1 in a game where Martins scored a worldy and was unplayable. I remember the first couple of games of Big Sam's reign and he was outstanding. He netted a brace in the season's curtain-raiser at Allardyce's old club, Bolton. It brought a comment from the manager who said, "He's a scorer of great goals rather than a great goalscorer." I think that summed up Martins perfectly.

It has been said and written that maybe Jermain Defoe would've been a better bet than Oba for the same money. But Martins came with a good pedigree from Inter Milan. I prefer players with Premier League experience or British players but this was Roeder's choice at the time. I know my old boss had worked with Defoe at West Ham and had first-hand knowledge of him. But I'm not aware as to whether he was either available or whether the manager even wanted him.

I thought Taylor was going to play for England. He was a young centre-half and you rarely see an 18-year-old playing regularly in the top flight at that age. He had all the attributes: aggression, never-say-die attitude and he enjoyed defending. I remember at the end of one session he came to me with a bag of balls asking to do more work. He asked if I could hit the ball as hard as I could at the goal line so he could try and head it away. A strange request because I thought he was going to ask something else, but there you go. He didn't stop many going in but he was keen to try.

Taylor had all the characteristics to become an England international. Injury held him back in one sense and on another maybe past national team bosses were a bit worried about calling him up because he was prone to the odd gaff in a game.

At international level you're playing against the very best strikers in the world and you can't afford that luxury because you'll get punished for it.

Bramble was another on his day that was up there with the best young centre backs in the country. But as everyone pointed out, his concentration levels let him down. He had two great feet, could hit an excellent pass, quick, strong, but then he would just switch off as if he was day dreaming. When he was focused and switched on he looked a top class centre-back. But you knew that a gaff was just around the corner, no matter how hard we tried to get him to concentrate. We used to sit him down and show positive clips of a game and then show the mistakes that undid all of his good work. You wouldn't expect a non-league player to do some of the things he was doing never mind a Premier League star. It was incredibly frustrating for the managers and coaching staff.

Dyer was another incredibly gifted player but he can count himself unlucky because he picked up so many injuries. He could run quickly with the ball; see a pass and make and score goals. He had fantastic fitness levels. He once missed a few games because in training he got hit in the eye by a pole we used to run around. One time he slid into the advertising hoardings behind the goal at the Gallowgate. He got a gash in his ankle that kept him out for a few games.

I believe there are footballers whose bodies can't take the physical aspects of Premier League football. It's incredibly intense and rigorous and will put a great deal of stress and demand on their physicality; so much so that the body can't take the day in and day out of training and games. Maybe Dyer was one of those. He was a nice guy but at times he could be a bit moody and disrespectful to some of the senior people at the club. He wasn't particularly respectful to Sir Bobby Robson at times; which made the press.

One of my biggest regrets in football was not playing for Sir Bobby. I would've loved playing in the team he built at St James' Park. Everyone has a great Robson story and my favourite is when he was at a book signing. There was a queue out the door a mile long and the ex-England boss turned to one of the staff and asked how many people were left because he was getting tired. The member of staff replied there's hundreds Bobby. Robson signed his next book as Bobby Hundreds instead of Bobby Robson. There was another time when Shearer was having a celebrity golf day down in Surrey when I played for Fulham. I was on Robson's table with Charlie Woods and Freddy Shepherd. There was a magician there doing a card trick and he asked the former Magpies chief for the time. Robson looked at his wrist but didn't have his watch on because the magician had taken it without him knowing. The magician pulls it out of his pocket and Sir Bobby says, "That's unbelievable son, fantastic. Any chance you could get rid of Marcelino for me?"

I remember all of the commotion after the Sheffield United home game where we lost 1-0. Supporters gathered outside the Milburn Reception shouting for our chairman's head. We'd just played in the UEFA Cup at Palermo on the Thursday night and the club decided to take the TV money so we had to play at tea-time on the following Saturday rather than play the game on the Sunday. We knew it was a huge risk with physical implications to the players in regards of recovery time. We stayed in Palermo after the game, recovered the players on the Friday morning, flew them back in the afternoon and straight into a hotel trying to get the recovery levels back. It was too short a time really and we weren't surprised when we lost the game.

Roeder suffered a little in his second season because we struggled with inconsistency. We had a great run in the UEFA Cup but our Premier League form suffered and the chairman decided to let Roeder go. It has been suggested he was too much of a nice guy and couldn't control the big characters in the dressing room but I disagree. He had a tough streak in him. I'm not so sure he lost the dressing room but there was a diverse set of characters in there that maybe weren't all pulling in the same direction. They all should've been speaking English in the dressing room and they weren't at times. That wasn't the manager's fault, it was down to the players. It's too easy to point the finger at a manager.

I got on really well with Allardyce when he took over from Roeder. I spent three to four months with him on the coaching staff. His attention to detail was second to none. People might say you can blind people with science, given his obsession with stats, but I reckon there's room for both. He never interfered with what I was doing when I used to be the manager of the reserves back then. The reserves have now been scrapped and in its place, we now have the Under-23s, where you can play four over age players in the team. He would tell me if he wanted some senior players to play and sometimes ask if I could get them to play a different role to what they're used to playing. Then he would let me get on with it. Big Sam would get me involved with the first team and I really enjoyed the short time I spent with him.

I would have loved to stop at Newcastle in a coaching capacity but I was both impatient and ambitious. I had to leave to progress as a coach or manager because my line of progression was blighted by Steve Round and Nigel Pearson. They were joint assistant managers under Big Sam. They were both very good coaches. Pearson was a great tutor and I got on really well with him. I watched his sessions, how he delivered, spoke to people and used to sit and pick his brains. He was and is a leader. He was like that in his playing days for Sheffield Wednesday and under Bryan Robson at Middlesbrough. He is a top guy and went on to show what a top manager he is. He did a great job at Leicester turning them around from what looked like guaranteed relegation fodder before setting the foundations of the Foxes' Premier League triumph in 2016.

The press had a problem with Pearson's manner, but I liked it. He doesn't suffer fools gladly. If he's not happy he'll tell you. There are managers who can tell people what they want to hear and hide the truth but there are others, like Pearson and myself, who can't hide the truth and want to say it as it is. As a consequence, it generally gets you into trouble or causes controversy. Then there's times when you know the truth but don't want to say it for fear of bringing about more problems.

Allardyce has an image of pragmatism, set pieces, long ball game and that his teams play back to front. I was never in a team meeting where he said smash the ball up field. He did practise a lot on set plays and he was pragmatic but it was never route-one stuff. He never brought in a big target man. Mark Viduka came in but he was a technical player, who liked to play football. Unfortunately, he has this reputation and it has been difficult to shake it off.

Admittedly, Allardyce was another one not really accepted by supporters but he lost his job because Ashley took over the club and wanted his own man in. Big Sam was very good at delegating work. He got his coaches to deliver the sessions he wanted and then became hands on a couple of days before a game. There was a lot of emphasis on sports science, which I know frustrated a lot of players because they were being monitored continually. Some players felt they weren't doing enough training to keep up with the levels of fitness needed. There were some strong characters in the Newcastle dressing room and I felt they didn't really buy in to his way of thinking. That didn't help his cause I suppose.

Big Sam has another stigma attached to him that he's a fire-fighter. That he's been brought in to put out the blazes and save struggling teams or turn around their fortunes in such a short space of time. Allarydyce's appointment was his chance at a big club to kick on. He probably feels, like me, had Shepherd stayed, things would've been different.

If Shepherd was still at the club, no, I wouldn't have left St James' Park. I got the feeling there would've been opportunities for me at Newcastle if Ashley hadn't taken over. But I'd been offered a big challenge in East Anglia and had the chance to go from being a reserve team manager to become an assistant manager at a fantastic club in Norwich City. I didn't realise how good a club it was until I got there, mind. I'd known Roeder for a long time and we had a good relationship. Going to Norwich was never going to be a problem because I knew who I'd be working with. It was still a tough decision to make because I was enjoying what I was doing. Big Sam didn't want me to go but understood my reasons and ambitions.

Shepherd played a big part in my coming back to Newcastle and I had a great relationship with him. He also played a big part in my career and my family's life. We have a connection as we're both Walker lads. The company he owns now, Triple S Sports and Entertainment Management, are my agents. My agent, Paul Stretford, the boss of the company has looked after me since I was a 16-year-old. It obviously had a huge impact on me when Shepherd left Newcastle, or rather he was bought out by Ashley, when he was lying on his sick bed. Who knows what would've happened had that not happened and he remained at the club. I probably wouldn't have joined Roeder on the coaching staff at Norwich.

CHAPTER 9
HEARD THE ONE ABOUT THE DUTCHMAN, KNIGHT AND THE GEORDIE?

There were a couple of opportunities to go back to Newcastle between leaving in 1997 and my eventual return in 2005. The first time is quite an amusing tale. Not long after Ruud Gullit replaced Kenny Daglish as manager, the Dutchman came to the Stadium of Light to watch Sunderland play with coach John Carver. About 20 or 30 minutes into the game Gullit turned to JC and said, "I like the number four. I think we should sign him," or words to that effect. And who was wearing the number four shirt that day? That's right, you guessed it, yours truly. For whatever reason the ex-Holland legend didn't make the connection between me and Newcastle. Carver was astounded at first. He thought his new boss was on a wind-up. He said, "Are you taking the piss? The number four is Lee Clark. We can't sign him. We just flogged him to Sunderland last year. There was hell on about it at the time."

Would I have gone back if there was an opportunity? I would have bitten their hands off. Would Sunderland have let me go? I very much doubt it. I imagine there would've been more hell to pay on Wearside if the former Chelsea boss had got his way. Apparently Gullit took it to boardroom level that he wanted to re-sign me. It's all hypothetical now because it didn't come off. But I wouldn't have minding being a fly on the wall during that conversation in the St James' Park boardroom. If there was an approach I never got to know about it.

The second time there was interest from Newcastle; Carver was the conduit in the story once again. He rang and asked whether I'd consider returning. I was like, "Of course, let's do it." Don't get me wrong, I was enjoying life at Craven Cottage but a chance to return and play for Sir Bobby Robson was an offer I wouldn't turn down. Fulham wanted their money back plus a little bit more, which amounted to £4.5m. But then the deal stalled and went dead because Newcastle decided to sign Christian Bassedas, instead, on the back of Mick Wadsworth's say so. Bassedas was a £1m cheaper. I'm not sure how far down the line it got and whether it was actually put to Freddy Shepherd. I don't think it did though because if it had gone to him I'm sure he would have tried to find the extra money. It was frustrating to see all of those other midfielders come in after I left. I didn't feel any of them were better than me.

I played my home-town club several times wearing the colours of Fulham but never faced Sunderland for the Cottagers. The first time I lined up against the Magpies resulted in a 3-1 home victory at Craven Cottage. Louis Saha scored an absolute beauty that day while Edwin van der Saar saved an Alan Shearer penalty. I netted the winner in a 2-1 victory the second time I faced my old club at Loftus Road. It was Chris Coleman's first game in charge. There was no celebration because that would've been disrespectful. But don't get me wrong, I was delighted to score. We could've been sucked into a relegation battle had we not won that night.

Fulham were in freefall just before that game at the time and couldn't buy a win under Tigana anywhere. Ultimately, that's why he lost his job. We played in Europe that season with a tiny squad and it killed us. The result probably scuppered United's outside chance of the league but they got in the Champions League all the same. I remember they were breaking on us with pace, as they did in those days under Sir Bobby, trying to get an equaliser. Craig Bellamy went past me and there was no way I was going to catch him so I fouled him from behind and took a yellow card for the team. The fucker jumped up and started giving it the big one. I told him in no uncertain terms to, "Do one," because I wasn't intimidated by him. It was funny because Sir Bobby and Carver both leapt out of the dugout and began giving me the verbals as well. You just fight for what's right at the time though. I give as good as I got because I was there to win the game for my team. I wasn't there to make friends and help Newcastle. I told the press after the game the three points were more important to us than United.

My first game back at St James' Park was a mid-week clash and I got an unbelievable reception from the home supporters. It was a memorable day for my son, Jak, as well because he was Fulham's mascot. As England legend Jimmy Greaves often said, football's 'a funny old game,' because we played very well and yet didn't get the rewards our play deserved. We lost 3-1. We popped the ball around brilliantly and Newcastle couldn't get anywhere near us. I think Nobby Solano opened the scoring and it was a bit of a dodgy goal. I remember things kicking off in the tunnel at half-time and Shearer was trying to calm it down. I recall being apprehensive and nervous prior to the match. It was weird going back home to play against my old team. I never ever thought it would ever happen. But when the match kicks off you're in the zone and you're a professional trying to win the game for your team.

There was another match where Saha and I put us 2-0 ahead after five minutes but, remarkably, we ended up losing 3-2. Shearer was ridiculous in the second half. He was unplayable that night and got the winner. Then there was another game we won 4-1 at St James' Park and, to this day, I don't know how. Mark Crossley, our goalkeeper, was outstanding, pulling off world class save after world class save. It was one of two of the best goalkeeping displays I've ever seen in my life (the other was Edwin van der Saar at Highbury in a 0-0 draw). I was standing watching thinking, 'How did he stop that?' or 'How did he get to that?' The scoreline flattered us, without a doubt. But that's football.

The only time I ever faced Sunderland was in the colours of Newcastle. My first game against our biggest rivals came when we recorded victory number 11 at Roker Park. A Gary Owers own goal and a Liam O'Brien free-kick was enough in a 2-1 triumph. We stopped at Linden Hall, near Morpeth, the night before the game. There was an extra bit of spice to the match because both Paul Bracewell and Barry Venison were in our ranks and they were two former Black Cats captains. It was a bit raw where Brace was concerned because he was their best player when Keegan took him from Sunderland the previous summer. We also had Wearside-born Steve Howey in our ranks. He may have been from Sunderland but grew up as a black and white.

We were playing well in the run-up to the game with ten consecutive league victories, whereas our rivals weren't in good form at all. It goes without saying that we were confident going into the game. But all of that goes out of the window in a Tyne and Wear derby. I know it's a cliché but it's true: the result was all that mattered and not a great personal showing or a fantastic team performance. I'm proud of my record against the Black Cats. I never lost a game. There aren't too many people with that achievement on their CV. We also beat them 1-0 in a rain-soaked monsoon at St James' Park that term, thanks to a Scott Sellars free-kick. It only got played because it was planned for television and a Sunday noon kick off. It wouldn't have gone ahead had it been on a Saturday afternoon at 3pm.

All the lads in Keegan's squad got what it meant playing in a Tyne-Wear derby. It doesn't seem as if a lot of foreigners get it nowadays. But all our lads understood the importance of it. We never lost any games when I played under Keegan and until I left under Dalglish. I can't imagine what it would be like losing one of those fixtures. It must have been soul-destroying. I remember how bad I felt after losing a normal league match. It seemed like it was the end of the world. Planned nights out were cancelled. You'd stop in with your wife or girlfriend. You never went to a restaurant or pub. Although we always give 100 per cent in application and effort we felt we'd let the supporters down. That's changed now because it seems managers and coaches get the blame rather than the players.

I look at my old clubs, like Newcastle and Sunderland, and you see the managers they've had down the years. They've all been experienced and successful in their careers yet they have struggled at St James' Park and the Stadium of Light. The Magpies have been up and down the leagues over the last several years, while the Black Cats are always fighting relegation. You look at the managers they've had and they're not novices, so the common denominator in this is the players. They haven't been performing to a level anywhere near what's expected. The players don't seem to get it. They're treating football like a job and that's all. It's not their life or livelihood. It was always hard for me to go food shopping with my wife to Tesco or Asda. I'd always get stopped by excited fans asking about the game I'd just played in or chatting about a forthcoming match. You don't see that anymore. The fans and players don't seem to have a relationship where they can be approached. There's a divide between the players and supporters.

Sir Alex Ferguson was a great manager over a 30-year period at Old Trafford because he was allowed to build a team in every era. He had an eye for a player and could knit them together in his sides. It's very rare you turn an average team into world beaters. My former United colleagues and the supporters always talk about Keegan's era at Newcastle. But the turnaround in players, year after year, and standard of footballer he was bringing in got higher and higher. That was down to Keegan building something. And he was allowed to do that by Sir John Hall. That is why he had the success. He inherited a few good players and bought and built on it. It's not rocket science. Me, Robbie Elliott, Howey and Steve Watson survived Keegan's first day until his last because we were good players. Mind you, KK 'got' the local side of the team and how important it was to have some Geordies in it. I don't think the clubs in the North-East get that now. You have to have those local kids coming through because they understand what it is to be a Newcastle United player. They'll let the others know what it is to play for the club, the city and its supporters. They know supporters are spending their wages on their team. It's almost like that's a thing of the past now; a bit parochial, a bit 'going to college in your home town.'

Take David Ginola for example. We were into Ginola within two weeks of his arrival at the club. We took him into the town centre. We showed him what it was to be a Geordie. We took him out for a day on the drink. He thought it was crazy. He couldn't believe the following day in training when we were at the front of the running going at it like lunatics. We would never allow a day out to affect our training sessions. But Ginola bought into it. So did Tino. Mind you, I reckon he was crazier than any of us. Rob Lee came from London and bought into it. Lee was never in a hurry to jump on a plane back to the capital. People who say he never settled were talking nonsense. He hit the ground running and loved being in Newcastle. You can see the ones who *become* Geordies – you see it on and off the pitch.

My last start for Newcastle, ironically, was at my old club Sunderland. It was Alan Shearer's last start as well. It wasn't going well at first because we were losing 1-0 after an hour. But then Glenn Roader changed it. Michael Chopra came on in place of me and scored within seconds. Then it was bang, bang, bang:

Shearer scored a penalty a minute after that, Charles N'Zogbia netted after a mazy run and, as the terrace anthem goes, "Albert Luque wrapped it up!" Prior to that, we couldn't get a foothold in the game and it was hardly a classic. The game needed changing and the manager should take credit for that. Although I was close to Roeder, he knew I wasn't performing to the high standards I'd set myself. There would've been no point leaving me on and losing the game 1-0. And I wasn't in it for personal honours, it's about the team and winning. He did what had to be done and that is why we triumphed.

I should've had a double hernia operation in the January but Emre got injured and we were short of midfield players. Prior to the pre-match meal against Sunderland, Roeder pulled me to one side and asked how I was feeling. There was no way I was going to give up the chance to play for Newcastle against Sunderland at the Stadium of Light, so I declared myself fit. I got a lovely reception from the home supporters when I went to warm up. There were several derogatory comments from those who were inside the ground early, none of which are suitable for the book or family readership. Paul Winsper, the fitness coach, put some cones at the side of the pitch so we could go through some drills. I'm sure he did it on purpose to wind up the Black Cats' fans. Supporters were running down from the back of the stand to tell me I was someone's lovechild (at which point a Geordie on the receiving end of such abuse could point out the irony) and several other stinging comments not suitable until after the watershed were hurled in my direction. Obviously there was a chorus of boos every time I touched the ball, but I just got on with things. And when I was being substituted, we were 1-0 down. The Sunderland faithful were quick to tell me about it. Obviously, I had the last laugh because we won and that's all that matters.

At half-time in the dressing room there were some heated words between the players because we weren't happy with the first half performance. It was the perfect tonic because we won the game well. I didn't care whether we played well or not, it's the result in a derby match that matters, nothing else. Win by all means necessary. The dressing room was ecstatic after the game. We were buzzing!

After the match we passed a Newcastle supporters' bus. The windows had been put out by rival fans by the looks of things. The coach was still motoring down the A1231 towards the A19 and home. United fans saw our team bus and they were nearly falling out of the coach to reach over. It was fantastic to be part of it. And when we were out having a beer after, we didn't get, "You were shite today," because we'd won 4-1. Had we lost we wouldn't have gone out. Shearer was getting a special merit award in London the following day so we didn't party too hard that night because there was a few of us going with him. But you do want to milk it and let the result soak in, so five or six of us went into Ponteland post-match for a few beers.

The game at St James' Park earlier in the season was a better spectacle to be honest. There was a fantastic atmosphere and some cracking goals. Stephen Elliott scored a worldy for them, while Liam Lawrence also netted with a good strike. Shola Ameobi got a brace and Emre curled home the winner from a free-kick.

I am a Newcastle supporter but I couldn't be a fan on the day because I would've been red carded after ten minutes. It has to be controlled aggression. There was plenty of needle on and off the pitch but nothing violent. The Sunderland players often came over to Newcastle to socialise and if we bumped into each other we'd always be winding each other up

Another proud moment, in a career full of proud moments, came when I was boss of Huddersfield and Chris Hughton brought his Newcastle team to play my young fledglings. As it happens we lost, 1-0, at the Galpharm, but that wasn't the point. I was going head-to-head with the Magpies for the first time as a manager. It was a mid-week game after United's debacle at Orient, where they crashed 6-1. There was a well-documented inquest, after the heavy defeat, between the senior professionals to find out who was in and up for the fight and who was out. Obviously the players who played for Newcastle that night were keen to show they were fully committed to the cause. It was a bit of a feisty affair and it kicked off between both sets of players.

Newcastle fans will think I fired the players up for the encounter but that wasn't the case. I told my charges to go out and be competitive. United had just been relegated and still had a squad full of Premier League players. My lads were motivated to do well against a team full of big name players and impress Hughton and Colin Calderwood. It would've been a dream for them to play for Newcastle. I think there was a bit of a spat between Coloccini and Lee Novak that kicked it all off. Novak is a Geordie boy and had a point to prove. He came into football the hard way through the non-league system. He is a strong character and a tough lad. It was a cracking game and one that wasn't played like a pre-season friendly. We got lots out of it and I'm sure Newcastle got a lot out of it too. They bounced back from relegation and got promoted as Champions that season.

We then met Newcastle in the League Cup a month or so into the new season and my Huddersfield team were very close to knocking them out. We were 3-1 up before Hughton brought on the big guns which he'd rested. The gate money from that game allowed me to pay a loan fee to bring in Danny Drinkwater from Man United. In cup games you get a percentage of the gate receipts unlike a league match where you keep your home takings. It's something like 40 per cent each while the rest goes to the FA or whoever. I'm not quite sure exactly who gets it. Most clubs don't budget for a cup run but once we'd progressed to the next stage and drawn Newcastle at St James' Park, we knew we'd get a 25,000-plus gate.

I was really proud of taking my team back to St James' Park. I wanted to show Newcastle fans I could be a manager and put a good team together and they saw that themselves on the night. I got a good reception from the supporters. I do think Geordies like seeing one of their own doing well. But the game wasn't really about me. I wanted my home city to see that I could be a manager, but at the same time it was about the team getting a result. I celebrated when we scored but tried to keep a lid on my enjoyment. You don't want to be seen giving it the big one and ending up with egg on your face. I remember acknowledging Huddersfield supporters singing, when I was Birmingham boss. I got criticised by a large section of the Blues' following. It wasn't being disrespectful to Birmingham fans I just responded to the Terriers' travelling faithful that day. I'd had three good years down there. If I didn't react positively it would have been seen as a snub. I was caught in a Catch-22 situation. I didn't want Huddersfield to win that day. It's a no win situation.

Sunderland came to Birmingham in the League Cup when I was Blues boss. I'd put on a few pounds since I was last on Wearside and Black Cats' fans let me know about it. They were calling me a, "Fat Geordie Bastard." I turned to Steve Watson in the dugout and said, "They're being a bit harsh on you there mate, you not think?" Watto just laughed. You can't take it too personally.

CHAPTER 10
GREATEST NEWCASTLE UNITED SIDE

Given

Venison   Howey   Albert   Beresford

Solano   Lee   Beardsley   Ginola

Shearer   Cole

Subs: Harper, Ferdinand, Peacock, Watson, Sellars, Batty, Gillespie

Selecting the greatest players I've ever played with at St James' Park is a tough one, quite simply because the standard of footballer was phenomenal. In all fairness, I could pick two or three teams given the quality we had in my time at Newcastle. Even in the early days of my career under Jim Smith and Ossie Ardiles when I first broke into the first team. There were top drawer players in those sides, such as Mark McGhee, Micky Quinn, Roy Aitken and John Burridge. But it'll come as no surprise to learn that ten of the 11 players I've selected come from the Entertainers' era managed by Kevin Keegan. Only one player makes the cut from the post-Keegan era.

Newcastle has had some great goalkeepers throughout its history. In the Edwardian era there was Jim Lawrence, who played more games for United than any other player in the club's history. He won league titles and the FA Cup while patrolling the Gallowgate goal area. Ronnie Simpson was a great from the famous 1950 FA Cup winning teams. He went on to become one of the Lisbon Lions when winning a European Cup medal with Celtic in 1967. Then there's Willie McFaul, the Magpies' shot-stopper in the 1969 Fairs Cup triumph. In my time there was John Burridge, Tommy Wright, Mike Hooper, Shaka Hislop, Steve Harper and Pavel Srnicek, so there were some excellent keepers in the modern era. Despite those admirable shot-stoppers, Shay Given would get the nod for me. He had great athleticism. He wasn't the tallest of goalkeepers but he was brave, agile and his distribution was superb. He was the complete goalkeeper in my opinion. He was buoyant, a good character in the dressing room and one of the best the Premier League has ever seen.

Barry Venison would be my right-back. Again, I played with some talented full-backs. Marc Hottiger and my old mate Steve Watson to name just two. But Venners was probably the most consistent player I ever played with at St James' Park. He played hard both on and off the pitch but I never saw him have a bad game, whether he played at right-back, centre-half or occupying the holding role in the middle of midfield. The ex-Liverpool defender ended up getting England caps playing in midfield. He was a leader in every sense of the word. I thoroughly enjoyed playing with him. Venners was one of the senior members of the team, a mentor and I learned a lot from him. A larger than life figure with a long blonde mane of hair and boy-band, model good looks. But he was a true inspiration to all of us youngsters coming through.

Steve Howey would be one of my two centre-backs. His emergence as a top quality centre-half was a surprise to many but not to those of us who came through the youth system. He came into his own during our promotion winning campaign of 1992-93, forcing out the more experienced Brian Kilcline. Killer was the glue that kept us together in our fight against relegation the season before. He was an FA Cup winning captain, a brilliant professional and a great man. But Howey's inclusion is justified as he went on to become an England centre-half. Ironic when you think he started out as a target man in the youth team and I played off him up front. He was one of the best ball playing centre-backs in England. He would've picked up a lot more caps had he not been crippled by so many injuries.

I'd pair Philippe Albert alongside Howey. He was just a class act. People go on about not seeing the likes of a David Ginola before, but the same can be said about our £2.7m capture from Belgian giants Anderlecht. The Belgium international could've played anywhere on the pitch. He was that good. Albert was a giant of a man in stature, maybe 6ft 4", but with the touch of an angel. He was a great fella and quickly bought into the dressing room culture. Newcastle supporters even gave the Belgian his own song. Now that is a true sign of being accepted by the Geordie nation.

John Beresford would be my left-back. The Yorkshireman was the perfect signing for Newcastle at the time. A good attack minded player who, in my opinion, was underestimated. The former Pompey full-back was the type of player Keegan liked. He had a good touch, pace and flair. Bez might have been small in stature but he had a massive heart. I think he was unlucky not to have been capped by England. He was a bubbly character around the dressing room. There was a glow of positivity that surrounded him. Bez was another who bought into the club and the camaraderie of the place. I get a bit misty-eyed when I think back to those days because we had an incredible dressing room.

Nobby Solano is the only player from the post-Keegan era to make the cut. Nobby was fantastic. He was a funny guy, a top fella and proper good egg. His one-liners had everyone in fits of laughter. But not only that, listening to him play *Oops, I did it Again* by Britney Spears on the trumpet was a life-changing experience. I can never listen to that song without thinking of the little fella. He'd also play the *Match of the Day* theme tune. Awful, but side-splittingly funny! It was obviously a wind-up on his part but great fun. Solano was one of those players who could use his eyes to pass the ball and turn his head to fool the opposition. And he could do it with headers as well. He even had a spell at right-back under Glenn Roeder where he was fantastic. He was predominantly right footed but didn't need a left foot because the outside of his right made up for that. He was never blessed with blistering pace. It was all about technique with the Peruvian. He had the whole package. You can see why the great Maradona nicknamed him 'The Little Maestro.' That is the ultimate compliment from one of the best players that ever lived. But if you saw him in training every day, you'd understand why. He scored a lot of goals but he made his fair share and I'm led to believe that he made more goals for Alan Shearer than anyone else during his time on Tyneside.

Rob Lee came to the club from Charlton as a wide man but developed into a proper box-to-box midfielder in the centre of the park. Under Sir Bobby Robson he became a holding defensive player. He was strong, powerful, could tackle, pass with both feet and score goals. The Londoner is another who loved the North-East, adopted Newcastle as his home and despite what people said I got on very well with him. And yes, the rumours are true. He does have short arms and long pockets. Lee was incredibly tight. In a former life he could've been a

19th century Dickensian character. In fact, the Charles Dickens characters, Scrooge and Marley, in *A Christmas Carol* , would have worked for him! You couldn't even get a pin up his arse with a sledgehammer, man.

Peter Beardsley, as I've already said, was my hero as I grew up. I was lucky enough to actually play alongside him and he was the best player I ever played with. Pedro was another player, like Ginola, who could do everything. He scored two goals against Tottenham at White Hart Lane, in our first season back in the big time, which took my breath away, and of those who saw it in North London. It was *Schoolboys' Own* stuff. It was like he was in the school playground and just slalomed past everyone as if they weren't there and scored. Beardsley scored goals like this in the twilight of his career. He'd net ridiculous goals and make many more for other players, such was his unselfishness. I'd play the Toon magician behind the front two in my team.

David Ginola was, unquestionably, one of the most gifted players I ever played with. In his first six months at the club he was unplayable. Ginola could do anything he wanted with a ball. He relished being man-marked and the tighter the defender, the better for him because he could manipulate the ball. He was an anachronism in a lot of ways: a wide man, who was over 6ft, built and looked like a Greek god, muscles everywhere. He used his physique to his advantage. The Frenchman was a real match-winner and had fans on the edge of their seats with his breathtaking Gallic flair. If we were drawing or losing he could produce something a little bit different to mere mortal players and get us that result. Admittedly, the former PSG man's defensive responsibilities weren't that hot. But we were prepared to do that little bit extra work off the ball because we knew if we could get the ball to him he'd produce something magical.

Choosing a couple of handy strikers from the fertile crop of goalscorers during my time is almost impossible. Throughout Newcastle's rich history there seems to have been a legendary hit man that has captured the imagination of every generation following their goalscoring exploits. From Hughie Gallagher to Jackie Milburn to Malcolm MacDonald and on to the modern era, they have all stamped their inimitable style, swagger and personality on the famous number nine shirt. There are about a dozen to select from in my time on Tyneside. Micky Quinn was up there with the best of them. And what about David 'Ned' Kelly, whose goals not only saved Newcastle from the drop but shot us into the promised land of the Premier League. In any other time, they would've been my front two pairing.

Yet Andy Cole would be my first choice and it's not because we got on as well as we did. His goalscoring record for Newcastle in a black and white shirt is phenomenal and as good as any number nine throughout our history. He netted 68 goals in 84 games for us and only Hughie Gallagher has a better strike rate. The gloss has been taken off Cole's achievements because he moved to our nearest rivals Man United and one or two other things that happened when he was at Old Trafford. This frustrates me a lot because on the pitch he did the business. He is in my team on merit and it's a tough one because I've given him the nod over Les Ferdinand, who is a true gentleman and another exceptional striker loved by all Newcastle supporters.

Obviously, you can't ignore Alan Shearer; another whose goalscoring record speaks for itself. I've spoken at length about how Keegan just kept raising the bar at St James' Park, in terms of the type of top player he signed. This was nowhere near more evident than in Shearer's signing. The club broke a world record transfer fee of £15m to capture him. He could've gone to any club in the world but he chose to sign for his home-town team. And when you looked at our squad, the one which narrowly missed out on the Premier League title, could you really improve it? Keegan went and signed the top striker at Euro 96 to make a statement of intent.

Shearer was as strong as an ox. You couldn't push him off the ball. He wasn't blessed with great pace, certainly in his later years because of injury, but he knew where the net was. You can't teach what he and Cole had. It was a natural instinct in two great strikers. Shearer and Cole were number one and number two in the greatest number of goals scored in the Premier League until Wayne Rooney moved up to second last season. Can you imagine how hard it would be for two centre-halves to pick up one of those never mind two of them?

Now, who would captain my side? That's a tough one because we have a skipper in every position. The team wouldn't need a captain or a manager because it could manage and captain itself.

With Newcastle manager Willie McFaul

Signing my first contract with Newcastle with my mam, Joyce, dad, Robert and Willie McFaul

First team pic

Young Sports Personality of the Year for Newcastle City Council as a 15-year-old

Newcastle Youth team after triumphing in the 1987 Milk Cup in Northern Ireland

With Newcastle director George Forbes and the Barclays sponsor after winning Young Player of the Month

Team photo for Newcastle School Boys circa 1982-83

In action at Old Trafford in Newcastle's first trip to Manchester United following promotion in 1993. We drew 1-1

Best man duties for Steve Watson

My dad, Robert, and sister Kerry on her wedding day

Here I am netting against Ipswich at SJP with Jason Dozzell looking on

As an 11-year-old kid visiting my brother-in-law, Paul Baker (not in pic) at Southampton. George Lawrence, Danny Wallace and Nick Holmes

The boy done goo- Me and n granddad Robe

One of my big mentors Steve Black at Jak's christening

England Schoolboys at Boston before match against Wales. Chris Makin, Gary Flitcroft and Marcus Stewart in the line up

Home from home at La Tournoi with my Newcastle teammates, Alan Shearer, David Batty and Rob Lee

On England duty at La Tournoi. Alan Shearer strangles me after he hears I've signed for Sunderland

Celebrating my first goal for Sunderland at the Stadium of Light with Niall Quinn and Kevin Phillips

Loz and I after we ran away to get married at Gretna Green

My eldest son Jak and stop for a pic at the opening of the SOL

One of my best friends in football, Andy Cole

Got the Blues at Birmingham

Me and my Sunderland teammate Alex Rae take time out for a laugh

Jollie Boys outing to Ascot races

Spot on! Here I am netting from the spot against Steve Bruce's Huddersfield to prevent Town making the play-offs.

My kids, Claudia, Jak and Bobby

Skipper for Fulham against my former team. My son Jak is Cottagers' mascot

My sisters, Kerry, Bev and nanna, Ellen

Daddy's boy. My youngest Bobby when I was at Birmingham

My son Bobby signing for Birmingham City

Special achievement award at Huddersfield for breaking the longest run of games without a defeat, which was 43 matches unbeaten

CHAPTER 11
BEST OF THE REST

Edwin van der Saar

Steve Finnan   Andy Melville   Chris Coleman Michael Gray

Steed Malbranque Papa Bouba Diop   Sean Davis   John Collins

Kevin Phillips   Louis Saha

Subs: Thomas Sorensen, Niall Quinn, Alex Rae, Martin Djetou, Michael Bridges, Alain Goma, Kevin Ball

Number one in my *best of the rest* team is an easy one because Edwin van der Sar was one of the greatest goalkeepers that ever played. You don't need to take my word for it; everyone who played with him will tell you the same. He was a world class goalkeeper. I was surprised to learn he is the second most decorated shot-stopper in the world. Apparently the first honour goes to Portuguese keeper Vitor Baia.

I was flabbergasted Fulham signed a player of the Dutchman's stature and even more surprised at how long we kept him. Although, to be fair, Fulham were signing players of van der Saar's calibre in my time at Craven Cottage. His distribution, handling and touch on the ball was like an outfield player. We signed him from Italian giants Juventus and he had an abundance of experience. When you sign, so called, superstar footballers you generally expect them to come with some baggage. But van der Saar was a top guy, humble and he certainly wasn't a big-time Charlie. He's as close to the complete goalkeeper you'll ever come across. It was no surprise he went to Man United. It was more of a surprise it hadn't happened earlier really.

Steve Finnan was an accomplished right back and a Republic of Ireland international. He went on to play for Liverpool and win the Champions League with them. Finnan also holds something of a unique record. He's the only player to have played in all four levels of the English Football Leagues, the Football Conference, appear in a World Cup, European Champions League, UEFA Cup and Intertoto Cup. That is some roll of honour. He had great athleticism and got up and down the right flank like a wingback at times. And his delivery was as good as a natural winger.

Micky Gray played at Sunderland with me. He's like marmite isn't he? You either loved him or you didn't. He was told, "Don't do anything too extravagant or ostentatious with your money because people are losing their jobs at Sunderland." The day after that he turned up to training in a Ferrari. Mick McCarthy fined him two weeks' wages and stripped him of the captaincy. That says it all about how daft he is. There must've been no hard feelings from McCarthy though, because he took him to Wolves a few years later. But he was a great lad underneath it all. I didn't realise how good a player he was until I arrived on Wearside. He won his three England caps while at the Stadium of Light. He was good on the ball, could deliver telling crosses and another blessed with good athleticism.

I played with Andy Melville at both Sunderland and Fulham. Melville wasn't the quickest of centre backs but could read the game really well. He was aggressive and comfortable on the ball. He went on to be capped 67 times by Wales and was an underrated defender. The Welshman knocked about the lower leagues early in his career but went on to establish himself as a fine Premier League player.

Chris Coleman was a class act. Unfortunately, I didn't get to spend much time on the pitch with the Welshman due to injury. A car accident robbed him of his football career and nearly took his life. But he's established himself as a top manager subsequently and no one is more pleased for my old teammate than me. It gave me an enormous amount of pleasure to see him lead Wales to the semi-finals of Euro 2016. Who knows, Wales could have won it if it wasn't for losing Aaron Ramsey to suspension.

Coleman was a bit different to most in the heart of defence because he was a left-footed, ball playing, centre-half. He had a lot of finesse but was powerful and aggressive at the same time. He was a great leader and captain in every sense of the word.

Steed Malbranque was another superb signing for my old team Fulham. Jean Tigana signed the Belgian-born playmaker from Lyon for £4.5m. He was a bit of an unknown quantity when he arrived at Craven Cottage. But it didn't take long for him to settle in and for people to sit up and take notice. He hit the ground running in no time and became a firm fans' favourite. He was never capped at full international level despite playing at every youth stage. Belgium offered him a chance to play but he refused, hoping to play for Les Bleus. It just goes to show how strong the France side was at the time, that he couldn't get in the squad. He was a quiet boy and didn't really mix a lot socially but a good lad all the same. He had terrific technical ability to open up play and score goals or make them for other players.

John Collins was in the twilight of his career when he turned up at SW6. He was well known to our manager, Tigana, who had him at Monaco a few years earlier. I played with the cultured midfielder in our promotion season. When you look at left-footed players, they seem to have an extra bit of finesse on the ball and the Scotland international had that in abundance. I would play him on the left but tucked in as a narrow midfielder rather than a winger. He was more a central midfielder and wasn't blessed with a lot of pace, despite being a bit of a fitness fanatic. But it goes without saying; he was a class act on the ball.

I actually signed Papa Bouba Diop when I was Birmingham manager. I would have loved to have kept him longer but the financial state of the club meant I couldn't. Papa was another at Fulham who turned out to be a real favourite of the supporters. They nicknamed him 'The Wardrobe' of all things because of his height and stature. He was a 6ft 5" powerhouse but had an unbelievable touch. He could score thunderous goals with both head and feet. Ironically, I remember him scoring a bullet of a header at St Andrews for Fulham. A 35-yard half-volley at Old Trafford also stands out. He was a no nonsense central midfielder and a good lad to have on your side.

Sean Davis was just a young lad when I played at Craven Cottage and played an important part in our promotion to the Premier League. Like Finnan, Davis is one of the few players in England to have played at all four professional levels of football. But, unlike Finnan, he did it all with Fulham. He is the only player from Craven Cottage to achieve this.

It always tickles me every time I think of Davis. His line, "I don't want to get involved in that entire circus that follows you around," after David Beckham jumped up, not happy with one of his tackles. He was a tremendous player and has gone on to have a great career. He moved to Tottenham and then enjoyed success at Portsmouth when they were in the top flight. Injury curtailed his career and robbed him of fulfilling his ambitions.

I've been lucky to have played behind some great strikers and Kevin Phillips was no different. He arrived on Wearside as a bit of an unknown from Watford, but he must have been one of Peter Reid's best signings and was a snip at £325,000. He went on to break several goalscoring records in his time at the Stadium of Light. He won the Premier League Golden Boot and also the European Golden Shoe. No English striker had won the award before and no one has claimed it since.

Phillips wasn't as prolific at other clubs but he was a terrific finisher with both feet. He was very good in the air for his size and it is tough to leave Niall Quinn out of my team because they paired up well together during my time at Sunderland. Quinny had an unbelievable first touch to bring players into play, something often dismissed about him.

Louis Saha arrived at Fulham in a £2.1m deal from Metz. Newcastle supporters would've raised their eyebrows at that one because he hardly pulled up any trees during his loan spell under Ruud Gullit. But, in all fairness, he was a very young striker learning his trade and I'm sure the experience of playing alongside Alan Shearer did him the world of good. He was worth every penny of his transfer fee and paid it back sevenfold when he left.

Saha played the striker role up front and on his own. I felt that was when he was at his best. The Frenchman was an unbelievable athlete. He had a change of pace, skill, could manipulate the ball, power in his shots and what a leap. He was a little bit different to the little and large type of strikers we've come to know in the top flight of the British game, as in he didn't need to play off anyone. Fulham sold him to Man United when we were third or fourth in the Premier League. We got mega money for his signature. We finished in the top ten that season but who knows what would have happened or where we would have finished had we kept him. Saha was a phenomenal player for Fulham.

CHAPTER 12
FLYING THE NEST

The call from Glenn Roeder came out of the blue. It was a big surprise. There was never a conversation or hint, when I worked under Roeder at Newcastle, that he would take me with him if he got sacked, moved on or took another managerial position. We did have a good relationship before I became a coach, when he was United's club captain and I was a schoolboy back in the 1980s. He was always great with me, taking time out to offer advice when I was a kid coming through the ranks so there's always been a connection between us. It goes without saying I was flattered when he wanted me to join him. In some cases, managers take a number two out of nepotism and employ their best mate. But this wasn't like that. We were never former teammates on the pitch or best friends. Roeder asked me to be his number two because he'd witnessed my development as a coach and believed I was ready to become a number two.

The decision to leave St James' Park for Carrow Road was a tough one to make. I'd cut my coaching teeth at the football team I've loved and supported all of my life. It's difficult to get on the staff with any club never mind a Premier League outfit the size of Newcastle. And then I had a dilemma of whether to leave the North-East for East Anglia. It was as tough as swapping Tyneside for Wearside back in the 1990s.

I sat down with Sam Allardyce and talked about my predicament. He didn't want me to leave and set out a plan of progress for me to follow. But I was impatient. I didn't want to wait because there were two good coaches preventing me from climbing the ladder quicker than I wanted. I knew they weren't going anywhere. The only way I'd progress before my time would be if they were sacked or got better job offers elsewhere.

Then again, had there been any inkling Allardyce would be sacked a few months later, Nigel Pearson would move on and Kevin Keegan would be returning, I would've stayed put. Instead Chris Hughton came in as coach. Who knows how things would've worked out had I stopped? Sometimes fate gets in the way and takes it out of your hands.

I never regretted joining Norwich City for a minute. I relished my time there. It is a great club with fantastic facilities, terrific support and an excellent stadium. The remit in our first season was to keep the club in the Championship because they were struggling at that time. We managed to fulfil that task with about three or four games to go.

Roeder recruited Paul Stephenson from Hartlepool and Tommy Wright as a goalkeeping coach and we had our own Geordie back room staff if you like. I grew up with Stephenson as we're both from Walker. He was unearthed by Brian Clark, just like me, Jeff Wrightson and Ian Bogie. He was a bit older than me and part of the famous Wallsend Boys Club when I first went along. Stevers made just as much an impact at Newcastle as Gazza, when he broke into the side. Unfortunately for him, after a run of first team games, he was called upon to play for the juniors in the Northumberland Senior Cup Final. Consequently, he injured his ankle ligaments. Stephenson was out of action for a long time and when he returned to full fitness he was never quite the same. He was a speedy winger with a quick burst of pace. Stevers also had two good feet, an excellent crosser of the ball, could twist and turn and beat the full back with ease. He lost that, however, and had to change his game. It still frustrates him to this day. Despite that he had quite a successful playing career at Millwall, Brentford and Gillingham, where, ironically, he played for Roeder in his first managerial post.

The former Magpies boss had kept an eye on Stevers' coaching career at Hartlepool, where he also enjoyed a brief spell as manager. He was impressed enough to recruit him to look after the kids. He was highly thought of and we both felt he could work with us. Stephenson is a very enthusiastic and positive coach, which is a great quality to have when things aren't going as well as you want them to go. The same went for Wright. We both knew the Northern Ireland international from his time on Tyneside with us and he was looking to get back in to the game. Later on Adam Sadler joined us; another with a black and white link. He had worked at the Newcastle Academy. I enjoyed coaching the Norwich team. I would take the lads and put them through their paces. As the days progressed towards the end of the week, and the game, the manager became more involved with the tactics. It was a tight-knit football club with really good people running it behind the scenes. I thoroughly enjoyed my time there and it wasn't without incident.

I managed to get an invite to the FA headquarters for a disciplinary reason. I got sent to the stand by referee Andy D'Urso, at Ashton Road, after I disputed a decision, or rather a non decision, with more colourful language than I normally would have used. Lee Croft got fouled, although the match official had an alternative view to mine. As a result, Bristol City scored and went on to win the game. We felt as if we should have had a point from the fixture. A couple of weeks later I stood in front of an FA panel and received a fine. It's the only time it has happened in my career. The boss got in bother after the game because he had a pop at D'Urso after the final whistle. The deal we were trying to broker was that Roeder would get a fine and a suspended sentence and I would get a rap across the knuckles. But my PFA rep, Mick McGuire, must have done a deal for Roeder, the swine, because it flipped on its head. It was me who got the fine and suspended sentence while the Canaries chief got a rap on the knuckles. Ironically, Gordon Milne was on the panel. Milne ended up working at Newcastle under Sir Bobby Robson and Charlie Woods. I thought it would've worked in my favour but did it bollocks! It was a lesson learned. We had Ched Evans at Norwich on loan from Manchester City. He scored a lot of goals for us and was a top young striker. Evans was a pleasure to work with and it's sad and unfortunate the way his career has turned out. We had a lot of good young players on loan at the time: Ryan Bertrand and Kieran Gibbs, who both went on to be capped by England, and have had flourishing careers. We also took Jonathan Grounds from Middlesbrough and Matty Pattison from Newcastle.

Foolishly, Pattison got done for drink-driving on his way to training one morning after over indulging the night before. He mustn't have been thinking straight because it was his day off! I was down at Great Yarmouth with the kids when I got the call. A receptionist, at the hotel he was staying in, notified the police after seeing him climb into his car a bit worse for wear. It was an idiotic thing to do. The South African let down the club, its supporters and the manager, who had shown a lot of faith in him. There could have been serious repercussions and someone's life could've been at risk. Fortunately, no one was physically hurt by his actions. In this situation Pattison was punished financially and we didn't select him for a couple of games.

If this was a punishment for some indiscretion I'd made in my playing days, it would have killed me. Nothing is worse than training from Monday to Friday without the reward of a game on a Saturday. Does this hurt today's modern player with all the riches he has? Probably not. I doubt it would make much difference to the pocket of a top player. But any player worth his salt, you would like to think it would hurt him not playing.

Ideally, I would have liked to play for another year but there wasn't an offer on the table to do that from Newcastle after my first season back. But there was a deal from Roeder and the club to take sole charge of the reserves. I'm guessing that was when the boss saw my potential in the game as a coach. My dilemma was, do I want to try and find another club and play for another year, or take the coaching job offered by my home-town club. Invitations to coach in the Premier League don't come around very often so it was a no-brainer in the end.

I wanted to get on the coaching ladder and eventually become a manager. I knew the process. I'm glad I didn't go straight into a manager's position from being a player and took the route I did. I learned a lot from my mistakes at that level, and got to work with some very good young players at Newcastle: Andy Carroll, Tim Krul and Fraser Forster to name just three. Carroll and Forster went on to command massive transfer fees and have successful careers.

I was always interested in coaching and started my badges at Walker Central Boys Club under Brian Clark, as a teenager. I'd coach one of the teams twice a week and go down and watch them in action on a Sunday, games permitting. I really enjoyed it. The process continued when I was at Fulham and the Scottish FA came down to assess several of us doing our UEFA B Licence, such as Gary McAllister, Chris Coleman and Gary Mills. The UEFA A and B Licences are mainly practical although there are some written assessments that have to be completed. I completed my UEFA A Licence in Belfast, which was a two-year course.

There are more written assignments when you take your UEFA Pro Licence, the final coaching badge which allows you to become a manager. Bizarrely, you have to act out negotiations in the boardroom and transfer dealings with agents and other managers. It's all good practice but it doesn't really prepare you for the reality of the situation when you become the boss. I started the UEFA Pro Licence while at Newcastle and finished while assistant manager at Norwich.

There's no script about dealing with players' personal problems while doing your coaching badges. But it is one of the many real life issues you have to try and resolve as a manager and coach. A player needs to be happy to get the best out of him, so if he's got problems off the pitch it'll be hard to get him to focus and perform to the best of his ability. As a manager you have to help, no matter how trivial or whether it is a domestic problem.

There are several different types of players you're dealing with and you have to resolve their problems and treat them differently. You have regular players in the first team; players with long-term injuries and have psychological problems because of it; players who aren't in the team and have insecurity issues over whether the manager and coaches rate them. Then there are players who have been told they're surplus to requirements and you wonder if they're going to disrupt sessions and corrupt other players' thinking. So, in essence, you have a broad number of players with different issues.

The players with long-term injuries always feel left out. They come into the gym and go through the laborious process of fitness centre work. It is soul destroying when you can see your mates out on the training pitch enjoying themselves. So sometimes you'll tell them to come in when the lads aren't training and stagger their times. Alternatively, a change of environment is needed so you'll send them away on holiday for a week or two to recharge their batteries. But at the same time these players have to have the desire, strength of character and attitude to get through this tough period. They're no good to you if they can't.

Sometimes first team players have friends not in the first team and, subconsciously, is feeling the hurt of his colleague. This happened when I was sent to play for the reserves after reacting badly to being substituted at Southampton under Kevin Keegan. Andy Cole thought my punishment was too severe. This can create a bad atmosphere in the dressing room. Other times a player might just have a disruptive personality and will blame anyone but himself. He'll blame the training, teammates and the manager. They'll go through a check list of about 20 reasons and then finally realise 'well, I'm not playing very well either'. And if there are some weak characters in the dressing room they will follow that. That is why recruitment is important. You not only have to get good players you have to get good characters, good leaders and set good examples. This helps when footballers go through adversity. And they all do, it's just that the first-class characters deal with it better.

You witness this all the time, as well as other problems. You can see a slow change with some players and this gradually starts to deteriorate. One player, for example, found a lump in his testicles. Others have had marital problems or difficulties with their children; pregnancies and players' parents splitting up. You become a part-time marriage guidance councillor and social worker at times. But I tell players that my door is always open. I don't always have the answer myself but I can generally resolve them by putting players in touch with those who can, thanks to the contacts I've made over the years.

Footballers are no different to the average man on the street. They still suffer from the same social problems. A painter and decorator can do a bad job. When he does that he usually just upsets the people who employed him to do that particular job. However, the man on the street isn't performing in front of thousands of people every week and getting his performance scrutinised by the public, press and social media, and that sort of thing can affect you. And as a manager I have to protect my player. I can't come out and say, "Back off, he's just had one of his testicles lobbed off," or "His wife's ran away with the physio." I have to honour their confidence. You try to be as transparent as you can but supporters and the press have to understand it's not possible all of the time.

You're continually assessing players. Do they respond to a group telling off in front of their teammates? Will you lose the player if you do that? Belittling a player in front of his colleagues knocks confidence with some. Other times you can bollock a player in the manager's office. Some players can't even take that. Then there is the arm around the shoulder and you sugar-coat it. You're dealing with 25 to 30 players; even more at a bigger club. It's not an exact science. Every player is different.

I always tell the squad the most important players are the ones not in the starting eleven. The staff are told to watch them. If they're training right they're pushing the players in the first team. These lads will get a chance if someone isn't performing. Successful teams are judged on the strength of their squad or the players on the bench. Those on the outside of the team are pushing those on the bench and those on the bench are pushing those in the starting eleven. And the lads who have the shirt know they have to perform otherwise they're out.

On the other hand, I've had a player knock on my door with a face as white as a sheet, saying, "Gaffer, I've got a big, big, problem." I'm thinking, 'What's he going to say?' I've been worried sick that it's going to be something life-threatening. 'Is it his health, drugs, alcohol or marital problems?' Then it turns out the player's dish washer isn't working! The relief is tangible. I told him I was many things, a plumber isn't one of them, but I'll find one in the yellow pages. I took a call from an academy player's aunty one time, saying the player in question had chinned one of his cousins at a family party and is demanding an apology otherwise she is going to the papers. This is the weird and wonderful world of being a coach and a manager. Everything is chucked at you, including the dishwasher!

There wasn't a lot of money around at Norwich so we had to use the loan market quite often; maybe too much. But we had high hopes for our second season in charge. We certainly didn't envisage being bottom of the table or fighting relegation again. Unfortunately, a lot of our signings were loans again. We didn't want to go down that route all of the time. We wanted to own our players. You want footballers to have an affinity and fall in love with the club and you're less likely to get that with lads who know they're only going to be there for a few months. Saying that, the loan players we brought in, in our first season, ultimately did well and kept us in the Championship.

David Marshall was an exceptional goalkeeper for us. Dion Dublin was still a fantastic player despite coming to the end of his career. The former Man United, Coventry and Aston Villa striker is an unbelievable man and a great role model to everyone on and off the field. I loved working with him for the five or six months he was with us at Carrow Road. He was enthusiastic every day and a pleasure to coach. I can't emphasise enough how important a player he was for the Canaries. The manager played him up front but sometimes when we wanted to protect a lead we'd drag him back into the centre of defence and he'd do the business for us there.

I felt honoured to be involved or play a part in Dublin's last game for Norwich at Sheffield Wednesday. Unfortunately, we lost the game despite playing well. We found it difficult to replace him when he retired. He could have played on for another season or two in the Championship; I have no doubts about that. But the former England striker decided to call it a day and we had to respect his wishes.

Darren Huckerby was another one who became a fans' favourite in East Anglia. Huckerby made Norwich his home and was loved by the supporters. I got to know him at Newcastle after he arrived from Lincoln. Maybe the fleet-footed front man wasn't the success at St James' Park he was elsewhere because he turned up at the wrong time. We had so many good players that he couldn't get in the starting eleven. It was the same for me. I had to move on to get a game. Had he stayed another season there might have been a better chance of establishing himself. He went on to have a successful career after that at Coventry City and Manchester City.

I can't talk about Norwich City without discussing Delia Smith. The famous TV chef was an incredible woman. She made my family and I very welcome at Carrow Road. Delia loved my wife, Lorraine, and, daughter, Claudia. Claudia was very young at the time. Delia and her husband, Michael, were proper fans and had an abundance of enthusiasm for the club. You could tell because when we lost it hurt them. That's what being a proper supporter is about. Norwich wasn't a rich club but Delia and Michael tried to finance City the best they could from their business. They put a lot of personal wealth into the Canaries' pot and actually saved the club from bankruptcy. They were, and are, desperate for Norwich to do well and travelled home and away to watch their beloved team. The now famous footage of Delia trying to whip the crowd into a frenzy at half-time is typical of the woman. She wore a heart on her sleeve. It was hurting to see her team losing at home to Man City and she wanted the supporters to get behind them and become, in her words, "a twelfth man."

The award-winning celebrity chef has been a majority shareholder since about 2005 and despite that she can't escape the fact that she's a supporter first and foremost. An incredibly passionate woman who loves her football. And I have to say the sausage rolls she left for us in the manager's office were to die for! They weren't too good for my figure, mind you, but they were delicious. She and Michael would often come down into the manager's office with the directors to talk about the game and share a drink with us. Delia was aware she couldn't do it all by herself so got people in to help out. But the TV chef was careful about who she employed. She insisted all of those involved had to have an affinity with the club. I wholeheartedly agreed with what she was doing.

Delia wrote a beautiful letter to me when I left to go to Huddersfield. I still keep in touch with her and whenever I'm in Norwich I always go to see her. She's a special person. You just wish every club in the land was owned or run by someone similar and the game would be a better place to play, watch and manage. I was only at Norwich for a short period of time but I felt something for the club. I moved my family down to the area because it was too far to commute. My two eldest children went to school down there and my wife and I became good friends with Bryan Gunn and his wife Susan.

Gunn was a former City goalkeeper and head of club recruitment. My son Jak became good friends with their son Angus, who is a goalkeeper for Man City and England. He is going to be a big player in the future. Gunny is now working for my management and agency team Triple S Sports and Entertainment Management and our relationship has evolved because of that.

Norwich was a brilliant city to live in. There was never an empty seat in a home game and the fans are really passionate about their team. I remember when we secured our Championship status against QPR following a 3-0 victory. Delia came down to the manager's office and brought about 12 crates of champagne with her. Next thing I see is my ten-year-old daughter with a glass of bubbly in her hand! What a fantastic, infectious and ebullient woman.

A year after I arrived at Carrow Road, a call came asking whether I'd be interested in the Huddersfield job and I left the Canaries in the December. It was another season of struggle for Norwich, and, unfortunately, it culminated with my old boss being dismissed three months later. My relationship with Roeder was good but he was disappointed and frustrated I decided to leave. It is fair to say our friendship cooled for a few years and we weren't in touch as often as we were. I think he took it personally when I left and he shouldn't have done. Maybe he thought I should've stayed with him longer. We've since spoken and everything is fine with us now.

We worked well together and I left when Norwich were in the bottom half of the table. I was always up front with him and everyone I've worked with. Being a coach was a step to becoming a number two, while being a number two was a stepping stone into management and being a number one. I never hid that from anyone. In Roeder's heart of hearts he knew I'd be moving on. I think my ambition was one of the reasons he took me to City in the first place. I didn't want to stay assistant manager at Norwich or reserve team coach at Newcastle; I wanted to be the boss. I was grateful to my old gaffer and Norwich for helping me take the next step up. I have nothing but fond, fond memories of my time as one of the Canaries. But becoming manager of Huddersfield was an offer I couldn't refuse. It was about to become the biggest challenge in my coaching career and I was relishing the opportunity.

CHAPTER 13
THE BOSS

I got a good impression about Huddersfield Town almost immediately. It was a club rich in heritage, history and culture. The Terriers won the old First Division title three years on the bounce in the 1920s. Only three other clubs have equalled that feat and none have ever beaten it. Illustrious names from football's past such as Herbert Chapman, Bill Shankly, Denis Law and Ray Wilson have graced the club with their presence. But you don't know how great a club is until you engross yourself and embrace what it is to be part of a community. I did exactly that. I got a flat in the area, ate and went for a drink in the town centre.

I read about the history of the town and found the surrounding areas, also rich in culture. People might think I'm being patronising but, I'm not, it is true. I know a little about the Industrial Revolution and architecture because I come from a city, Newcastle, which is steeped in its development. The architecture around the town is beautiful. Huddersfield Railway station is a Grade 1 listed building. I've been told it was described by the poet Sir John Betjeman as "the most splendid station façade in England" second only to St Pancras in London. Huddersfield was also the birthplace of rugby league and gave the country two Prime Ministers: Harold Wilson and Herbert Asquith. You have to develop affection for a club, a connection and fall in love with the place. And that's what I did with the West Yorkshire outfit. I also did this at Birmingham. It's like falling in love with a girlfriend for the first time. It might be a clichéd analogy, but it's true. Yet it was something I could never do at Blackpool. Blackpool was like meeting a girl on the rebound.

I felt after my time as reserves team boss at Newcastle and assistant manager at Norwich I was ready to move into management. My agent alerted Huddersfield that I was interested in the vacant position at the Galpharm Stadium. Dean Hoyle was a young, hungry, ambitious new owner and chairman of the Terriers. He wanted to meet up without being committed to taking me on. I was just as curious about the owner as he was about me. I wanted to know whether he was as ambitious as I was. If he wasn't, it wouldn't have worked.

The call to meet my future boss came when I was across at Everton with David Moyes, as part of my UEFA Pro Licence, which was brilliant, exceptional even. Hoyle may have been the new owner but he hadn't been involved with the football side of things until now. The young businessman had left that to other people. They had brought in Stan Ternent and it hadn't worked out. The next manager was to be his appointment. He must have been impressed with what I'd said because he asked me back for a second interview.

I met with Hoyle and the chief executive, Nigel Clibbins, to talk further. I brought Steve Black with me to the second meeting to put our philosophy forward on how we could turn the club around. I later learned Nigel Adkins was favourite for the position. He'd done an excellent job at Scunthorpe so it was understandable he would have been interviewed. There were dozens of more experienced applicants who were, arguably, much more suitable than me. But the owner was impressed with what I had to say and offered me the job. I brought in Paul Stephenson to look after the youth team set up and Derek Fazackerley as a coach, while Terry McDermott came in as my assistant. It was a large backroom staff for a club in the third tier of English football but the owner allowed us to do that.

Hoyle was very much like Delia Smith in many ways because he was a huge fan and a successful businessman. There are photos of him standing on the terraces with his mates at the old Leeds Road Football Ground. We were both around the same age, came from a similar era and had an identical work ethic and mentality. And when I spoke with Hoyle I felt a connection. He wanted what I wanted. The manager got what he was looking for in me and the type of owner I coveted was him. The bond got stronger as we worked together. We had dialogue every time he was at the football club, even if it was just for a cup of tea. We'd also talk on the phone if he was out of the country on business. I wanted that open relationship. I encouraged him to tell me if he wasn't happy with the way the team played or something else was bothering him. We were constantly trying to improve the club.

There was a lot of work to do at Huddersfield on and off the pitch and I set about revolutionising the Galpharm. The manager's office was bare, other than a shabby old fridge which housed a desperately lonely bottle of Yorkshire bitter. We started right at the bottom as if it was a new football club. We didn't own our own training ground at the time and had to train at the university. There were a couple of Portakabin type 'buildings' on the site belonging to us that were so old it looked as if they were from the Edwardian era. There were all sorts of unknown vegetation growing inside. And it was so dirty that even the mice were wearing overalls.

My staff and I went about changing the mentality and philosophy of the club. I couldn't have done this without the help of the owner because he had to finance it. He allowed me to bring in Prozone, which in essence, is a pioneer of performance analysis. I was given the go-ahead to put in place a scouting and recruitment system; while over the space of two to three transfer windows we overhauled the squad. And while that was going on a permanent place to build a training academy was sought after.

The squad didn't have much value in monetary terms and there were several ageing players that weren't bringing much on to the pitch. We had one player, Gary Roberts, who was arguably our only saleable asset. The club paid a decent transfer fee to bring him from Ipswich. On the youth side there were a few players coming through, such as Alex Smithies, but not that many. That is why in the first two transfer windows we targeted young, hungry and ambitious players, who would bring quality to both the squad and value in monetary terms to sell on. They had to play at a high-tempo, with or without the ball. The squad I'd inherited were the complete opposite to that, although you do need experienced players as well. I have nothing against the odd veteran but they have to make a contribution. We couldn't afford to have mercenaries there for one last pay day. Out of the squad I inherited, about six or seven players stayed with me.

I made an immediate impact with the type of players brought in. We made some outstanding signings, such as: Jordan Rhodes, Anthony Pilkington, Lee Peltier and Lee Novak. We loaned players such as Danny Drinkwater and Benik Afobe, while bringing through youngsters from the academy like Jack Hunt, who was eventually transferred for a seven figure fee. The same happened with goalkeeper Smithies, who became a regular in the side under me. Roberts' game improved under my wing as did Scotty Arfield, who went on to be a fantastic servant for Burnley. I also wanted a relationship and link to the past so I brought back Mark Lillis to become the club's academy director. He had been an important player in Huddersfield's past.

Andy Booth was at the club when I arrived. He is a Town legend, and rightly so. I was pleased to play a part in his last ever game against Leyton Orient, where he scored in a 1-1 draw. It was a fitting way for him to sign off. He netted 150 goals which put him third in Huddersfield's all-time goalscorer's chart. The owner and I agreed to keep him on as an ambassador for the club when he retired. It was the first time this had happened at Huddersfield. He was a fantastic lad and great example to everyone. He started his career as a Terrier and finished as a Terrier. He had a spell at Sheffield Wednesday and also had a month's loan at Tottenham, where he wasn't treated very well by Spurs' so-called superstars. He told me he'd rock up to training in his Ford Fiesta while all the Spurs lads had flash sports cars. This tells you all you need to know about how modest a lad he was.

We got off to a great start under my managerial umbrella, recording a 2-0 victory over Hereford at the Galpharm. The result won't erase what the Bulls did to my home team favourites, Newcastle, in the 1972 FA Cup but it was satisfying all the same. Only joking lads. I was brought back down to earth in my second game, a 3-0 defeat at Carlisle on Boxing Day, but after that it was a reasonably satisfying baptism into management. We finished ninth, remained unbeaten in our last five fixtures and did the double over Leeds United for the first time in 78 years. I never lost a West Yorkshire derby in my time as Town boss.

It would've been nice to finish higher in my first campaign but coming in when I did made it difficult. I was fairly satisfied. The season was used to get my ideas across and build for the following campaign. I don't think the club was in any danger of going down and we weren't going to scare the play-off teams. But it gave me a chance to assess the squad and what I needed to do to make progress.

The owner and I didn't sit down at the beginning of my first full season and set any targets but we were putting a good squad together. But the least I expected was making the play-offs. Only champions Norwich scored more goals than us overall and we netted more times away from home than any other team in the league. We secured our place in the play-offs with a resounding 6-0 triumph over Stockport on their home patch. We also put six past Dagenham and Redbridge in the FA Cup and netted six times against Wycombe Wanderers, while putting seven past Brighton that term. We scored a lot of goals breaking on the counterattack from set plays. We had an excellent young keeper in Smithies, who could take crosses in the penalty box and set us off. The team had three or four players breaking at pace and within three to four passes; it was in the back of the net. This happened when we played Wycombe at the Galpharm. This was the benchmark of what I was trying to do with the team: fast, attractive, football. They all bought into what I was trying to do.

The next challenge, arguably, was to get the older heads to make a contribution. Peter Clark was that player. He was about 26-years-old, so not young but not too old either. I made him my captain. My skipper was a born leader and went on to be a terrific servant to Huddersfield. He arrived on a free transfer from Southend and I instantly knew we'd pulled off a coup. Clark was someone I could rely on to be an extension of myself in the dressing room, getting my message across.

A football club dressing room is a complicated and intricate place. There are strong, loud personalities in there mixed with some weak characters. I needed someone to set the tone; tell players what I was about and how high my standards were. A strong captain can do that without running back and forwards to see the manager and staff. This is where Clark came into his own. Obviously there is the odd occasion a captain can't keep on top of everything, that is when I came in.

If you have a player in your dressing room that is angry or there is a bit of negativity that can override all of the positivity you have created. You have to have a strong dressing room to prevent that happening and dismiss that player. They always have their reasons for being unhappy: whether they're not in the team, don't like the manager, coach or training regime. It's very rare the player will blame himself and the fact he's not playing well is the reason he's been left out. He'll go through all of these excuses before there's a realisation that he's the problem.

There is a general myth you have to kick your way out of the second and third tier of football. It's not all kick and rush from the schoolyard or playground. Teams are trying to do the right things. You have to understand League One and League Two outfits have a limited budget and that determines what type of player a team can bring in. The player you recruit rarely goes on to be a top Premier League footballer. Some of them do but in most cases you have to bring the best out of them and make sure they can compete athletically. I watched all levels of football as part of my recruitment, when I was managing in League One, and when we came up against League Two or non league teams, there were some good players at those clubs. Sometimes a talented footballer gets overlooked because of the standard of player around them.

I like to think I created a bond with all of our players and that won us several matches when we weren't on our A game. We played exciting football. And the fact Sky TV picked us for a lot of games was quite a compliment. Being the manager I took a lot of credit for all of this but I wouldn't have been able to do it without my staff. And none was more important to me than my assistant, Terry Mac. He'd been there, done it and got the proverbial t-shirt.

Terry Mac never talks about his past when, in my opinion, he should let more people know about what he has achieved in the game. He won three big ones, as in the European Cup, as well as several top flight titles and England caps. The ex-Newcastle number two is a good family friend of mine and whenever I'm over at his house and see his medal collection, I go, *wow*! I remember Darron McDonough getting a bit lairy in training one time at Newcastle in the early days of Kevin Keegan and Terry Mac. I don't know why, he was duck-toed and couldn't pass water. In fact, I nearly got hit in the stand by one of his passes at Grimsby one day. To shut him up, Keegan said if he had a spare five or six hours he was welcome to go around to his house and look at his medal collection. McDonough quickly got the message and spent the rest of training with a tail between his legs. Terry Mac was never one for boasting and KK only did it in jest.

At Huddersfield there was quite an age gap between the players, Terry Mac and I. I had to explain who he was. Rhodes is a good example of this. Our young striker was one of the best professional footballers I've ever come across. He is a diamond of a guy: pleasant, polite and respectful. He is someone you would give your blessing too if he wanted to date your daughter. Terry Mac and I did an extra session with him after training one day. My number two mentioned Kenny Dalglish, as an example, in the exercise. After we'd finished the drill, Rhodes approached and thanked us for the work out. He let us know how he enjoyed it before asking, "Just one thing boss, who is Kenny Dalglish?"

You might laugh reading that and ask how a current professional footballer is unaware of one of the game's modern greats. I suppose Rhodes' generation had more options than us to occupy their spare time. We only had football really. There wasn't much in terms of computer games when I was a lad. I had the same thing with Ravel Morrison at Birmingham City. He didn't know who Paul Gascoigne was. Rhodes wasn't being disrespectful; after all, he's been brought up in a footballing family. His father was a goalkeeper. His uncle is Steve Agnew, who played for Barnsley, Leicester and Sunderland, among other clubs. It made us chuckle, yes, but he was born in the 1990s and Dalglish's career was over by that stage. He was at an age where he hadn't discovered any footage of the Liverpool legend or any other football greats.

How would I explain Terry Mac to players today? I'd say he was the 1970s equivalent of Frank Lampard. He had a phenomenal goalscoring record, and was without question one of the best midfielders of his generation. His trophy collection backs that up. He was part of that unbelievable Liverpool team, and era, when they had three European Cup triumphs in five years. He left Newcastle in 1974 and returned to St James' Park in 1982. He survived, competed and kept his place in an extraordinary side for eight years. Terry Mac could do this because he was the best in his position in the UK and, arguably, Europe. Even when he returned to the North-East at the end of his career he was still a cut above. In fact, he was probably too intelligent for most of the players in Arthur Cox's team at that time. Did we have any players that could pick him out when he made those blind side runs? Probably not as many as the Liverpool teams he played in. We had Keegan, Peter Beardsley and Chris Waddle on that wavelength. But at Anfield he had Graeme Souness, Ray Kennedy, Dalglish, Alan Hansen, Mark Lawrenson, Alan Kennedy and others.

Terry Mac's personality changed when he joined Keegan in the management side of things at Newcastle. In his playing days he played hard on and off the pitch like a lot of professional footballers. He and his colleagues liked a day at the races and a good drink, like we did in my playing days. But that changed when he became KK's number two and he continued that professionalism when he was with me. The Scouser had no interest in taking coaching sessions or becoming a manager. The former Reds midfielder's strength was his social and personal skills around the players. He could motivate and lift a dressing room, if it was needed, and resolve any problems players might have without me getting involved. He lifted a burden off my shoulders and he was very popular with players and staff.

This dynamic worked perfectly at Newcastle with Terry Mac, Keegan and Derek Fazackerley. Faz was a very good coach, loved being on the grass and taking sessions. Keegan was the motivation and inspiration for us all. He gave sound bites, spoke to individuals from time to time and set an unbelievable example when joining in the sessions. Terry Mac was the glue that bonded everything together and the link between the manager and players. And that is what I wanted from him when I took him to Huddersfield and Birmingham. He delivered it brilliantly. I've heard the odd snide comment saying he was only there to put bets on for the lads and that is an outrageous slur. He was an important member of our team and played a big part in our recruitment process as well. We had a chief scout, Brian Young, who was a terrific guy. He had a full-time job out of football and worked for us part-time. Terry Mac would ask what type of player I was looking for and then he liaised with Young. Between them they would deploy our scouts to find that player. Those identified would go into our database for future reference. Terry Mac was very knowledgeable and had a good eye for a player. He could tell very quickly whether he was good enough. My former associate was also good when I was under pressure; certainly at Birmingham. His experience helped get me through some tough times in the Midlands.

Talking of experience, I didn't have much in a managerial position but I was learning on my feet all of the time and putting a stamp on things. I like all players to be dressed the same, so I made sure they were all in a club tracksuit around the training ground, while on match days they wore a suit with the club's emblem on the breast. Man United still do that and if it's good enough for them it is good enough for my clubs. This is just a small thing but it sends out a statement of intent. Then there was the discipline side of management. It was all brand new to me but I grew into it quite naturally.

I don't like players being late. I find it disrespectful. Not so much to me but their fellow professionals who have turned up on time for training, team meetings and bus departures. In the winter this was tough because the Pennines was horrendous for snow and ice. There was the odd time when there'd been an atrocious road accident. We were flexible in those instances. In those cases, we'd tell the player to come in when he could and we'd put training back. But pure laziness or they've slept in because they've been on a PlayStation until yon time in the morning is not good enough. I've had my PA come in with print outs of Facebook and Twitter accounts where players have been posting stuff at 1am in the morning. No wonder they've slept in.

I didn't like mobile phones brought into a team meeting. You need your players fully focused not worrying about what their girlfriend might want for her tea or whether he likes her new earrings. One player said he needing his phone to distribute match day tickets. In cases like that there is a bit of leeway, so I you allow them cut off time.

The fines I introduced varied between £10-£100. The lowest was for smaller indiscretions and increased when players were booked for dissent and sent off for foul and abusive language, which could be up to a week's wages. The same goes for throwing a punch off the ball. That is extremely ultra unprofessional. There'd be fines for players trailing muddy boots into the dressing room. Why can't they clean and hang them up? I would never let the club fine a player for receiving a yellow card for a challenge. They wouldn't want to tackle if we did that. I even introduced fines for leaving water bottles or kit on the training ground. Why should I, my staff or one of the other players have to bring in someone else's kit because they've been lazy? Also, players have to put dirty kit in baskets provided in the changing rooms. I remember at Newcastle, the reserves had a kit man, old Geordie, and he complained that the players never picked up their kit and put it in the baskets provided. Reserves team boss, Tommy Craig, told him to leave it and those guilty would have to play in their unlaundered kit full of sweat and muck. You always found out who they were because training gear is numbered. Players quickly learned not to do it again.

I never got involved in wage negotiations. I left all of that up to the owner and his staff. I didn't get roped in quite simply because I didn't want any player thinking one player was valued more than another. The wage structure is different at every club, as are the bonuses put in place. I didn't know what most players were getting although a goalscorer generally gets more money than a centre half. There were players at Birmingham City on £5m a year because they were still on a Premier League salary after being relegated. But I think most were on about £5,000 a week when I was in charge.

The only time I got involved in negotiations was if a player was asking for more money than the club offered. In that scenario the owner and chief executive would bring me in to ask whether the player was worth it. As for scouting players, obviously I watch a lot of games myself but I also have a network of scouts. That's been built up over the years. Now I have a big database of players I keep an eye on. There has been the odd time when I've gone to see one player and ended up signing another. This happened when I went to see a centre half called Murray Wallace in a Scottish Cup semi-final. I ended up signing Kallum Higginbotham, as well, who I had at Kilmarnock.

Anthony Pilkington is arguably my best ever signing. I sold him to Norwich with a broken ankle. He broke it in the February and we sold him to the Canaries for £2.5m plus add-ons. We would have got £5m if it wasn't for the injury. I got a tip off about a player at Stockport County. I went to see him a few times and knew Cardiff, who were a league above us, were in for him as well. Ironically, he eventually went to the Bluebirds later on in his career. We were a bit cute with Pilkington. We told him to turn his phone off in the boardroom, because we knew Cardiff boss Dave Jones was desperate and ready to pounce. We agreed terms and got him to sign a contract before he left the room. Pilkington probably wasn't aware of that but we wanted him that badly. Then again, his agent knew it would be a better career move for him at the Galpharm Stadium. Recruitment is a huge thing for a manager.

I've heard and read it several times that it came as a surprise when I became a manager. Others didn't think I was management material. That seems to be the perception of supporters from clubs I've played for. I liked a laugh and a joke and was a bit of a prankster. This is true in many respects because I love a laugh as much as anyone. But when it came down to the nitty-gritty there was no one more committed to winning than me. You ask any of the lads who played with me and they'll tell you that. I used to room with Steve Watson on away trips quite a bit. He was never a great sleeper and wanted to be up until late watching that WWF. But I'd be doing sit ups and press ups before bed and wanted the light out at 10pm.

Becoming a manager was a natural progression for me. I generally captained most sides I played for; right from when I was a kid. I like to think I'm a leader and thrive on the responsibility. I am what I am. I'm from the east end of Newcastle. I'm not going to pretend to be someone I'm not. I've been lucky to have made a few quid from a game I love playing. It's also allowed me to have unbelievable commodities: like a lovely home, cars, holidays abroad and nice things for my wife and children. It doesn't change me from being Lee Clark from

Pottery Bank. There is a time for a laugh and a joke and there's a time when you need to be serious and I believe I get the balance right.

I've always been completely focused in football whether I've been a player, coach or a manager. I'm like that before and during every game. It doesn't matter whether you're playing against a former team, colleague or friend. For 90 minutes I'm determined to win the game I'm involved in. I remember seeing Duncan Ferguson in the tunnel at Goodison Park when he was playing for Everton and I was at Fulham. I tried to catch his attention for a moment but he was fully focused and blanked me. I didn't want a conversation, just an acknowledgement, but I didn't get one. He apologised after the game saying, "I heard you wee man, but at that point I just wanted to fucking kill you." I totally understood where he was coming from. You have no mates for 90 minutes when a game is being played.

Ferguson and I became good friends. He rented my house while he was playing for Newcastle and I was at Fulham. In fact, the Scot and my old man got along famously because they're both pigeon fanciers. My dad informed me this day that the ex-Scotland striker wanted to keep pigeons in my garden. I told him to, "Fuck off. I don't want birds shitting all over the gardens." He was very insistent, saying he'd make sure everything was OK, to which I replied, "So you're going to stop the birds shitting all over the place, are you? How do you intend to do that?" He finally got the message. Sorry Duncan, I'm sure you understood, even if you didn't at the time and wanted to kill me!

Generally, when you come off the pitch, the aggression, intensity and competiveness is all over with. But sometimes it spills over down the tunnel after the final whistle. There's been the odd time when a few of my players have swapped a few punches in the dressing room. Then there are times when unsavoury words are exchanged between opposing dugouts. I don't get involved with the opposition dugout unless they've been disrespectful to me or my staff. Overall I don't get it. As a player you might be upset if someone has done you in a late tackle or left an elbow in your face and there's a flare up because of it. But managers aren't two-footing each other in the technical area or head butting someone, unless you're Alan Pardew that is.

There are managers who try to wind you up or inflame a situation. Neil Warnock tried this on after we'd beaten his Sheffield United team, 2-1, at Bramall Lane. Warnock went to shake Glenn Roeder's hand and said to him and our staff, which included me, Terry Mac, Nigel Pearson, "Why couldn't you fucking play like that against Charlton?" We'd lost 2-0 at the Valley prior to this fixture. I'm thinking, 'Hang on, how we do is none of your fucking business, Warnock.'

I remember taking my team to play Peter Reid's Plymouth. I have an unbelievable amount of respect for the man and love him to bits. He had a player called James Noon, a Scouser and an exciting player. He went past two of my players; put the ball between their legs and starts taking the piss by shouting, "Whey, whey!" I'm furious by this and shout at Reidy, "Have a word with him, gaffer. He's taking the piss." My old boss responds with, "Fuck off, you. You're always moaning." He was the worst one I could have had a pop at because he knew what I was like. We had a drink after the game and that was that.

Graham Westley, who was Stevenage manager, tried to prevent one of my players take a throw in. We were 2-1 up, they'd missed a penalty and I celebrated a little over zealously. Westley shook my hand but things got a little heated straight after the game with his assistant and it kicked off. My kit man, goalkeeper coach and several others were all caught up in the flare-up. But despite my earlier celebration causing the commotion I was half way down the tunnel before it fully exploded into a full scale brawl. It was like I'd chucked a hand grenade into a crowd and watched it explode as I disappeared. I laughed to myself as I turned away.

Football is an incredibly emotional game. I am representing the club, its fans and city or town. It's easy to get involved or wrapped up in it. I like to get a feel for a club and immerse myself in its culture and history. I don't think you can do the job properly unless you do that.

Early in my managerial career at Huddersfield a story got back to me from our chief executive, who was at a house party with Dave Penney. Penney appeared to have been disgruntled about my appointment. He asked our chief executive how long the club were going to give me. The owner made me and my staff aware of what was said prior to our game against his Oldham Athletic, where he was the manager. My number two, Terry Mac, was furious. We beat Oldham and I shook Penney's hand, as you do traditionally, after the game. I never made a mention of what was said but Terry Mac did. He was very loyal to me. My assistant told him in no uncertain terms he was out of order and it was something we wouldn't do. Penney reckoned it had been taken out of context but we knew it hadn't.

Ironically, I met Penney when he was manager of Doncaster when I returned to Newcastle for my second spell and we talked about me going there as a player coach. I found him good company. That's what makes it disappointing. There is also an unwritten rule where you don't bad mouth a fellow manager and say something like that. The job is difficult enough as it is. In general, we always support each other in good, bad or indifferent times.

When I look back on my first full season in charge at the Galpharm it was fulfilling yet disappointing at the same time. The club had made great progress both on and off the pitch. We improved three places on the previous campaign by finishing sixth and securing a place in the play-offs. But ultimately we lost and had to spend another season in League One. The only thing we lacked was a bit of experience. This was evident when we were defeated, in the second leg of our play-off semi against Millwall. Kenny Jacket's side were big, strong and their physicality overrun us.

The owner and I discussed the type of player we required and identified where we wanted the team to be after two to three transfer windows. We decided on youth over experience and both accepted there would be issues to overcome because of this. This was evident against Millwall. We knew it would be tough going to the New Den after the first leg finished 0-0. It is an intimidating place and we knew we'd be up against it. Subsequently, we lost the game and tie 2-0. The staff and I were despondent but we were ready to put the setback behind us and go again. We were building something special and determined to go one better next season. We knew we weren't quite good enough at that stage. Don't get me wrong, it was awful, because we'd got so close. But I sat down with the owner and we set about improving the team further to take the next step and he backed me all of the way.

CHAPTER 14
TERRIERS IN THE DOGHOUSE

Devastation wasn't the word. It's difficult to describe the feeling. Emotional is an understatement. It was like having an out-of-body experience in one respect. Moments after the referee blew the final whistle to confirm our play-off defeat to Peterborough, autopilot kicked in. The excruciating pain and hurting had to be put to one side. I congratulated or commiserated with everyone in the Huddersfield and Peterborough squads. I applauded our fans then disappeared down an extremely dark tunnel to the dressing room to reflect on a highly charged, poignant game. I couldn't face any presentation. Dean Hoyle came looking for me, told me to keep my head up and said, "Let's go again next season," which was a reassuring gesture. That tells you all you need to know about the relationship I enjoyed with the owner. It didn't soften the blow or erase any pain but when you get that support from your leader it encourages you to go the extra mile.

Never thought I'd feel as gut-wrenchingly shattered as I did after Sunderland's play-off defeat to Charlton, but this was worse. When you're a manager you feel responsible for everything and everyone. I was hurting for not only myself but for the players and staff as well. A 3-0 result looks as if it was a walk in the park for Posh. It wasn't. The score flattered them but, to be fair, on the balance of play they deserved it. We started quite brightly and hit the bar before two quick goals, one of them a deflection, killed us. We were a team worthy of going up and challenging for promotion again. The players had given me so much over the course of the season and they were devastated. It was tangible; and a lot of tears were shed that day.

A gathering was arranged at the Galpharm Stadium after the game. It would have been a party had we won of course. It was flat. The families of the players were gutted as well. It was tough but I managed to regroup, gather my thoughts and give some comforting words to the players. On the coach back to Huddersfield, from Manchester, I told the lads to hold their heads high. They had nothing to be ashamed of. They'd had a terrific season and fell at the final hurdle. A little bit of luck had escaped us on the day. In the build up to the first goal, there was a player offside. And was it a free-kick from where Peterborough netted the opener? I think it was. The second goal was deflected. But I was a proud manager and told them so.

It took about a week to get over it. I came home and Lorraine and the kids were walking around me on eggshells. I was oblivious to anything that was happening anywhere else in the world. There was a lot of staring at the TV, the wall and into space. It was like going through a grieving process. It was quite an introspective period of my life. I was asking whether there was anything I could have done differently. Was it my fault? Without realising, looking back, this is probably what Kevin Keegan was going through in 1996 when we finished second to Man United and Peter Reid when Sunderland lost to Charlton in the 1998 play-off final.

There was criticism from a few over my team selection for the final because I didn't start with Jordan Rhodes. The reason behind that was simple. I played a different system when we were away from home. It had been very successful during our unbeaten run. We did the double over Brighton that season and they went on to win the league comfortably. I went for this away mind set at Old Trafford, which meant Rhodes didn't play. Instead I selected 18-year-old Benik Afobe, who got transferred to Bournemouth for £10m in 2016.

I was open for criticism after the game because Rhodes was our top goalscorer. Had we won, it wouldn't have been mentioned. No one complained when the system was previously successful on our travels. It wasn't as if I went out to play defensively, I didn't. I played three attackers but two of them were wide men. This was one of the decisions I tortured myself with. Rhodes was on the verge of making an appearance as a substitute when Peterborough scored a second goal, which made it look even worse for me.

Darren Ferguson was the Posh manager and I got on with him very well. He's a nice guy. It must have been tough for him in his career. His dad was manager of Man United but he's carved out quite a niche for himself as a boss in his father's shadow. He had an exciting Peterborough team with George Boyd and Craig Mackail-Smith and they were a high-scoring team.

Southampton went up that term automatically with Brighton. They had a fine team with Ricky Lambert, Adam Lallana and Alex Oxlade-Chamberlain in the side. I tried to sign Lambert from Bristol Rovers to pair with Rhodes but the deal never went through for whatever reason. They had strong backing; a good stadium at St Mary's and Southampton was always going to be too good for the league. We beat Saints at home but lost quite heavily away despite being seen as a big threat.

I still maintain to this day that had Anthony Pilkington been fit, we would have achieved automatic promotion. A play-off defeat to Peterborough and heartache would have been avoided. He was the best player in League One and we didn't have him for the final three months of the campaign. Our talisman was that good, a Premier League team was prepared to take him despite recovering from a dislocated ankle and broken fibula bone above the ankle. The injury was horrific. He suffered it at Rochdale. It wasn't a bad tackle. It was two players fully committed to the challenge. I have to say, Keith Hill, his staff and players were as distraught as we were. In fact this spread to the terraces and for the last 20 minutes of the game you could hear a pin drop. Some players were crying and wanted to come off. I got the lads in a huddle and said, "Run through a brick wall for the last 20 minutes and win this for Anthony." The relief in the dressing room was substantial. There was no celebration that we'd won. Obviously, I didn't know it at the time but that was the last game he played for me. Rochdale was phenomenal throughout this and showed a lot of class.

Putting the play-off defeat to one side, we had a reasonably successful campaign. We gave a good account of ourselves in the FA Cup at Arsenal. We got done by a late penalty in the fourth round tie. Mark Clattenburg, a fellow Geordie, was the referee. He didn't do me any favours there. We played exceptionally well at the Emirates. It would've been nice to get them back to the Galpharm. My League One boys were facing some world class players but were fantastic in front of 5,000 of our own supporters. There were close to 60,000 fans inside the stadium.

Arsene Wenger and his staff were brilliant. I went into his office after the game for a chat and a drink. You don't get the opportunity to speak to a manager of his stature very often so I made the most of picking his brains. You usually only get ten minutes but I was there a lot longer, like a sponge taking it all in. The Frenchman loaned me Afobe. He was a powerhouse as an 18-year-old. It makes me enormously proud that I gave these guys their debuts, some of them have played for England, like Danny Drinkwater. You'd like to think you've played a small part in their development and success.

The Football League Trophy Northern Final was another blow. We lost the first leg at Carlisle, 4-0 and then won the return 3-0. We battered United in the second leg. Alan Lee missed a sitter in the last minute which would've taken it to extra-time. We tried to play our strongest team in every round and gave it a right go because we wanted to play at Wembley. But it wasn't to be.

I received loads of good wishes from managers at the top and bottom of the pyramid when I landed the Huddersfield job. I even got a Christmas card from Sir Alex Ferguson, which was nice. I became good friends with Steve Bruce, while Mick McCarthy became somewhat of a mentor to me. The ex-Republic of Ireland boss and captain is a man I look up too with enormous respect. I didn't really know him that well before I became a manager but when our paths crossed he'd spend an enormous amount of time with me. I've always picked his brains whenever we've bumped into each other. Brendan Rodgers and David Moyes are others I've got a lot of time for.

Football managers are part of a very close-knit family. They're always there for you in times of trouble, like losing your job. Your peers will try and help you if they can. There is a general perception that it's dog-eat-dog, and it is to a certain extent, but that's because we all want to be the best. Of course there are exceptions to the rule. Jose Mourinho, Wenger and Sir Alex have had the odd spat but, in general, there is a healthy respect for each other. In my experience, Premier League managers have been very helpful to me. The big guys with the big resources, at the higher level, do help you as often as they can.

Sir Alex dealt with the Drinkwater loan for me at Huddersfield from start to finish. I'm sure he had several dozen other more important things to do but that is the measure of the man. He even gave me a bit of a bollocking at first because he thought I'd gone directly to the player without getting his permission. He called on my car phone while I was driving. My son, Jak, was in the car at the time. Sir Alex gave me a proper telling off before telling me the deal was off. As the phone went dead, Jak said, "Got a bit of a bollocking there, didn't you dad?" A *bit* of a bollocking? You've got no idea what a bollocking is until something like that happens to you! I chased it back up and told Fergie there'd been a misunderstanding. He was happy to resurrect the deal after I had cleared the air. I certainly didn't want to upset the best manager there's ever been. As a lower league boss I wanted to build relationships with the big clubs not destroy them. Such was my appreciation I always informed parent clubs how their players were or weren't progressing.

When you take a player you have to treat them right, do things correctly and develop them. And I got other players as a consequence of that. I've done the same with players from: Chelsea, Arsenal, Man City and Newcastle.

I can't emphasise enough how helpful Sir Alex was with young managers like myself. He would go out of his way to give advice. You would think the job of loaning players out was delegated further down the chain, but it wasn't. Ferguson dealt with everything. He knew about every player at Old Trafford. The former Red Devils chief was modest with it and showed humility when he'd made a mistake. And when I think back to my time when I was an apprentice and remember the behaviour of John Gallagher and Scott Sloan, it made me shudder. These were two players who thought they'd made it. They played in a side that made the play-offs in the second tier of English football. We weren't a great team at the time and they weren't good players. You think if Ferguson, one of the greatest managers that's ever lived, can show some respect, compassion and humility, why couldn't they? Paul Gascoigne didn't treat us badly and neither did Peter Beardsley, two world class footballers. Club captain Glenn Roeder, Kevin Keegan and Terry McDermott were the same when they were players.

One of Sir Alex's greatest signings, Roy Keane, was the same. He was unbelievably humble for what he'd achieved in the game as a player. Keane doesn't seem to get the credit he deserves for what he did at Sunderland. By the time he'd moved on to Ipswich he'd already had some success; getting the Black Cats into the Premier League and establishing them. Every time I rang him, he'd answer the phone, "Roy Keane, Ipswich Town." It was as if you didn't know where Roy Keane was. All joking aside, it was a statement of intent. He was proud to be the Tractor Boys' manager. For me that was a man who was respectful and humble as well. It was as if his illustrious playing career had never happened and he was starting afresh; proving and testing himself with another challenge.

I played against Keane many times and I believe he was one of the finest, if not the best players of his generation. He was an unbelievable leader. He was also very respectful to his fellow managers and peers. I got to know the former Man United midfielder when I was trying to sign Rhodes. I'd seen him play for the youth team when I was at Norwich. I'd followed his loan spells at Rochdale and Brentford and he had a good-goals-to-games ratio. To be honest I never thought Keane would sell him to us. But, as they say, 'Shy bairns get nowt,' and, I asked the question. I also knew they had Connor Whickham, who was a similar young, up and coming striker. I thought I might have a chance. The Ipswich chief made it known a deal might be possible and told me to keep in touch. And over the course of the summer and lead up to pre-season training he agreed to sell him to me.

I've heard Keane eulogise about Brian Clough, and rightly so because he was one of the best managers the UK has ever had. Mark Crossley relayed a funny Cloughy story that Keane must've told him. Keane went to Clough's office after a game to get some time off at home in Cork. When the midfielder arrived, he knocked, entered and the room is in complete darkness. He's wondering where he is because the game has just finished. Then he heard a voice from under the desk, "Irishman, you're off until Thursday. If you see that Graham Taylor, tell him I'm not here. I fucking hate him." As Keane was walking down the stairs he bumped into Taylor and asked whether he was on his way to see Clough. Taylor acknowledged he was. Keane told him not to bother as he'd just been up to his office and it was in darkness. Taylor responds, "OK, son. Tell him I tried to see him." I've never had any personal dealings with Cloughy, but he was a legend. There was a chance when I was a kid, however, Forest were one of the clubs trying to sign me as a 14-year-old.

In the short-term Loraine and my close family were there and helped pick me up when I was feeling down. They are very good and understand how emotional it all is. But I couldn't feel sorry for myself for too long because I had to get myself ready for the new campaign. Plans had to be put in place for new players. We'd made a play-off semi-final, a play-off final and now the push was on to get automatic promotion.

Opposition managers, press and supporters were saying nice things about us and scouts from the Premier League and Championship were regulars at our games. And we knew why they were there. But I'd rather have that than no scouts at all. Their presence meant we had good players. There were bids for various members of our squad. But because of the owner's wealth, we didn't need to sell. In fact, the longer we kept them, the more their value would go up. We weren't in debt but at the same time we couldn't or didn't want to solely rely on the owner's affluence. Huddersfield had to finance itself and be self sufficient. So players were sold if we were offered substantial fees and this was reinvested in the team. The only exception to this rule was Pilkington, and that was because he had a broken ankle. We could have got double the money for him fully fit.

But that wasn't going to happen for damaged goods. I could've said no, let's get him fit, but Norwich were a Premier League club and I didn't want to deny him the opportunity to play in the biggest and best league in the world. That's every footballer's dream. He would have stopped if I told him it was in his best interests. Pilkington loved playing for Huddersfield but he asked to go when he heard of their interest. Canaries boss Paul Lambert was a fan of his and he wasn't going there to be a squad player. This is one of the many problems or difficult decisions you have to make as a manager.

The team is obviously very important but the club was changing enormously as well. The commercial side was growing and that allowed us to progress on and off the field. New sponsorship meant we were on fast forward. Hoyle brought the standards he set from his business into the football club, and it worked. Maybe it was growing too fast and it was hard to keep on top of everything. But the owner employed a lot of experts in their fields so it was understandable it was like a runaway train.

As a manager you rarely have time to switch off so I had to snap out of feeling sorry for myself after the Peterborough defeat. My phone is always switched on: replying to emails, texts and calls, trying to broker deals. You have to get good players before someone else does because you're not the only one after them. There's been a few times when I've been on holiday, had one of the bairns in a pram while trying to do a deal over the phone; it's crazy the things you do to get a player over the line.

We started the new campaign as we finished the old one, unbeaten. We extended that run in the league to a record-breaking 43 games before suffering a 2-0 reversal at The Valley to promotion rivals Charlton Athletic. We'd been knocked out of all cup competitions in the early rounds but no one had managed to beat us in the league in eleven months of that calendar year. We were in and out of the top two automatic promotion places with Chris Powell's Addicks, who were flying as well. Everything was geared up to swap League One for the Championship when I took a call from our chairman to say he was relieving me of my duties following a 1-0 home defeat to Sheffield United. Shocked wasn't the word. It was a hammer blow. The conflicting emotions were coursing through my veins. It was: who, what, why, where, when, how? It was all questions and I didn't have any answers. We'd beaten the Blades, quite convincingly, 3-0, at Bramall Lane earlier in the season and that defeat was only our third loss of the new term.

There was a lot of speculation linking me to various jobs: Burnley, Leicester City, Leeds United and Wolves, prior to my dismissal. My agent actually rang after we'd lost to the Blades and informed me Mick McCarthy had been dismissed at Molineux, and their chief executive, Jez Moxey, was asking whether he could speak to me. Wolves were still in the Premier League at the time. I had to get permission from Huddersfield. I was going to call Hoyle the following day but before I could, he rang out of the blue, at the office, at 9am, saying he wanted to make a change and that I was being relieved of my duties.

I was astonished. The staff saw my reaction after I put the phone down. They couldn't believe it. I had my youngest, Bobby, with me the day I got sacked. He was in the office playing with his football. That must be quite unique, a little lad of seven, seeing his dad get peddled. I called a lunch meeting with the players and all of the staff to talk about the game because I didn't want to make them aware of what had just happened at first. But you know how it is in football and it wasn't long before the story had been leaked in the media. Soon after, I started to take legal advice through my agent and the LMA.

England's greatest ever goalscorer, Wayne Rooney, tweeted something along the lines that most managers must be under pressure if Lee Clark has been sacked after that record-breaking run. It was quite a compliment that a player of his magnitude and stature was keeping an eye on a team two leagues below his. The meeting with the players was quite an emotional one because I'd created a close bond with everyone during my time at the Galpharm. I went back to the office and within minutes there were knocks on the door as players came in to express their feelings and a few tears were shed. Then as the news broke I started to get calls from several managers. Mick McCarthy phoned and said, "I heard some crazy news that you've lost your job, is it right?" I said it was. He couldn't believe it. He asked what my record was. I said, "Unbeaten in 43 games but I've lost three out of the last 55." McCarthy's response was great, "Bloody hell, I haven't even won three out of my last 55." I have the utmost respect for the ex-Black Cats boss. I got calls from Sam Allardyce and Steve Bruce as well. They said a collective, "Welcome to management, this is your first sacking and now you've got to bounce back." It was really tough to take but I appreciated their calls.

Once the dust settled a few unsavoury stories appeared in the written press. One stating I'd lost the dressing room, when it couldn't have been further from the truth. There were around 30 knocks on my door from players gutted I was leaving. There were no celebratory songs or flicking the V-sign. It was hugs with tears in their eyes. Pity the journalists who wrote that crap hadn't been there to witness it.

The owner called a meeting with the staff when he got back from being abroad and admitted he didn't particularly enjoy pulling the trigger on my tenure. Hoyle confessed he found it really difficult. The Huddersfield chief felt he had to make this decision to move the club forward. Our relationship never deteriorated in all my time at the West Yorkshire outfit. Obviously I was disappointed and angry for a few months after.

I disagreed with the reasons why he let me go. But when I return to the Galpharm now, I'm a guest of his, and we still speak regularly. Hoyle often calls asking my opinion on different players. I know he's recommended me for other jobs and given me a glowing reference. He'll always be a man I'll have the utmost respect for. He's often told me that his biggest regret was not making the leap into the Championship together. We would have kicked on even further because we'd built this momentum and it would've carried on. We could have heated debates without falling out. That is how strong our relationship was.

Regularly the press asked whether I was interested in this job and that job. In fact the day before I was sacked a question was asked whether the Leeds United position appealed to me. I said, "No comment. The game against Sheffield United is too important to be talking about such things." The reply seemed to suggest I was courting other clubs. Whether that was one of the reasons I got sacked I don't know. Leeds is Huddersfield's biggest rivals. Speculation raged because I was a good young manager getting results. Not only that but I was bringing through good young players thanks to my excellent recruitment policy. However clubs do notice those qualities so it was only natural I was drawing interest from outside of Huddersfield. If I wasn't good at my job there wouldn't have been any interest. You can't win in these situations. Was I getting tapped? Not personally, but clubs did speak to my agent. I never spoke to any clubs while I was Huddersfield manager. Was it in Hoyle's mind before he sacked me? I don't know. Maybe one day in the future, when we're having a beer, that might come out. He didn't say that to the club staff.

I spoke to Moxey and Steve Morgan at Wolves in a hotel in the North West. But that was because I was sacked by Huddersfield and I was an out of work manager. They turned down Steve Bruce at the time, as well as myself, for whatever reason, and give it to Terry Connor. There was a press conference where I replied to a question of outside interest. I said I could understand it because of what I'd achieved in a short period of time. But as these things go, the written press didn't write it in the context it was meant. It was spun faster than an industrial loom.

It was a tough time for me personally. We'd lost a play-off semi-final; a play-off final; we were third in the league and in a great position to go up automatically. We'd had a terrific run; good young players and supporters were asking why the manager has gone. Then people were guessing something untoward must have happened. But there was nothing.

Simon Grayson came in and managed to get Huddersfield up after beating Danny Wilson's Sheffield United 7-6 on penalties, following 90 minutes and extra-time without a breakthrough by either side. Ultimately, you could say the owner was proved right because they went up. I watched the final in a hotel in Barbados with referees Chris Foy and Mike Dean. I was out there to play in a senior's competition for Newcastle.

Grayson had a bit of a wobble when Town lost four in five games towards the end of the season but he got the Terriers up. I got to know the former Leeds boss really well and got on with him. There was never animosity towards him or any other manager, unless someone was doing the naughty and touting himself for the job. There was a vacancy and Grayson got approached. He was an out of work manager. We spoke to each other when he got the job. He asked about some of the players, I tried to help him and wished him all the best. It was my squad. I wanted them to go up. I wasn't being sarcastic; it was genuine. Every time I came across Grayson he was a nice bloke. I didn't want him to fail. He had a good group of lads and it was a fantastic club.

I have a great relationship with Huddersfield supporters and I'm generally well received when I go back. Obviously there's always one or two who think you can do better things. There is a myth circulating about our 43 unbeaten run, suggesting we had too many draws. But if you take those games and the points together you'll find we had 92 points and would have won promotion with that amount. I was pushing a 50 per cent win ratio yet some people labelled us draw specialists. You would have to go back to in between the wars with the legendary Herbert Chapman to find a better win ratio with a similar amount of games in charge.

CHAPTER 15
FEELING BLUE

At times I've wondered whether I've been part of some elaborate Alfred Hitchcock thriller or a *Truman Show* type hoax, given the drama, tension and suspense that has enveloped every club I've been involved with. This was nowhere more apparent than at Birmingham City. The culmination of this manifested itself in our incredibly tense, cliffhanging fixture at Bolton Wanderers, on the last day of the 2014 season, where we survived relegation by the skin of our teeth.

I went through a whole range of emotions: fear, anger, shame, pity, indignation, sadness, confusion and also courage, because you need that more than anything else to get you through it all. Add that list of emotions to a constitution wreaking havoc within you, a scrambled brain and you're on a fast track to a cardiac arrest and a visit from the Grim Reaper. And yet somehow, from somewhere, I managed to pull myself together, gather clarity and see it through; with help from both the Blues fans and players.

Leading up to the fixture, Nigel Pearson rang and informed me that his Leicester City side were going to try their very best to beat Doncaster, our nearest rivals for the drop, even though his Foxes team had already claimed the Championship title. He did the same to Rovers' manager, Paul Dickov, as far as I know. Pearson is a friend to both of us. That's the type of genuine guy he is. Both Dickov and I wouldn't have expected anything else from a man of incredible honesty and integrity.

Just before the kick off at the Reebok Stadium I enjoyed a moment of solitude in the changing room and gathered my thoughts, while the lads went out on to the pitch to warm up. I sent Lorraine and the three kids a text, thanking them for their support and told them I'd be fighting until the end. It's times like this when you realise how much your family means to you. How they're always there in times of adversity. They go through everything I do and kick every ball.

Even when we went 2-0 down I had a surreal feeling we would get back into the game. Leicester, funnily enough, had gone 1-0 up against Doncaster, just as Bolton netted a second goal against us. We were playing well so I wasn't too worried. I was still confident of getting back into the game and getting a result. The lads kept fighting and plugging away and the vociferous support from our fans on the terraces was nothing short of magnificent. It certainly gave the team a huge boost. Then Nikola Zigic pulled a goal back with 12 minutes remaining and we were back in it. The clock was ticking and it was all us. We were all over Wanderers like a plague of locusts but couldn't find a breakthrough. But just as life in the third tier of English football beckoned, Paul Caddis headed in an equaliser three minutes into stoppage time after Jordan Ibe and Zigic combined to fashion a last-gasp chance. Caddis must have been the smallest player on the pitch. But it didn't matter because he got his beautiful head on to the ball and steered it home. Cue bedlam! We all went crazy. It might not have been a Champions League or FA Cup winning goal but it meant just as much. That act wrote Caddis's name into the annals of Birmingham City Football Club history. He instantly became a legend in the eyes of the fans. I think my overzealous celebration said it all. The outpour of relief, joy and emotion was overwhelming.

There were about 4,000 of our supporters inside the Reebok that day. The support was phenomenal. Some were in fancy dress. I was thinking about them all the way through the torturous contest. They'd seen their club go through, what seemed like, perpetual turmoil. To get relegated again would've been unthinkable. It was such a relief. I told the lads after the game I was proud of them. But I emphasised we mustn't slip into this precarious position ever again. I wouldn't say we celebrated on the coach back to the Midlands but a few beers were enjoyed on the trip home.

Me, Lorraine, the kids went out and enjoyed a meal in the Punchbowl when we got back to Birmingham. It was a local restaurant where we lived in Dorridge, which is part of Solihull. Halfway through the dinner I crashed and burned; shattered. It was a culmination of all the stress and anxiety I'd put myself through. I was physically drained and mentally exhausted. Some might have thought there were wild celebrations after the game. It couldn't have been further from the truth. I'd been reprieved and was determined not to let it happen again.

I was out of work for a little over three months before being appointed as Birmingham boss. I met Blues chairman Peter Pannu and Roger Lloyd in the Radisson Hotel, in the city centre, and must have made an impression because I was offered the job. Outgoing manager, Chris Hughton, put in a good word and I felt it was a great opportunity. I'm not sure whether Hughton knew anything about the political problems about to manifest themselves, although he certainly didn't leave the club because of that. He was offered a position in the Premier League with Norwich because of the good work he'd done in the Midlands. The ex-Newcastle boss had managed to steer the Blues into the play-offs after a good run in the Europa League, a competition they qualified for after winning the Carling Cup the previous year. Birmingham played a hell of a lot of games the season before I arrived and can count themselves unlucky not to immediately bounce back from relegation.

I knew Birmingham was a big club but didn't realise how huge until I started working there. The initial signs were good and I wanted to build on the momentum Hughton had created.

The group of players the former Magpies manager had left me wanted to go again and kick on. City had some good young players and I thought it would be a good opportunity to build on my burgeoning career at Huddersfield. I was excited at the prospect of managing the Blues. They were one of the biggest clubs outside of the Premier League and should be a top flight outfit.

Pannu allowed me to bring in Terry McDermott as my assistant and Steve Watson and Derek Fazackerley as part of the coaching staff. The only one I couldn't bring in was Steve Black, which was a blow. He has been a big influence in my career and life. The club said they couldn't afford to bring him in so I had to accept it.

I'd hardly been there five minutes when I had to slap the hands and fingers of thieves circling our cookie jar. There was a big offer for Jack Butland from Stoke City. He hadn't made his debut for City at this point but I'd seen quite a bit of Butland when he was on loan at Cheltenham. I knew he was going to be a top keeper. He got selected for the full England team before he played for the first team at St Andrew's, which must have set some precedent in itself. He also became his country's youngest ever international goalkeeper, at 19 years and 158 days, when playing for Roy Hodgson's side against Italy. The previous holder of that record was Billy Moon, who was 64 days older when he first made his debut for England in 1888. He also played for Stuart Pearce's Great Britain team in the 2012 Olympics. Ben Foster was the club's number one keeper but had moved to West Brom on loan the previous season after Birmingham had been relegated. That loan became permanent with a £5m switch and that opened the door for young Butland. Butland showed incredible maturity for a young man and refused to go to a club where he wouldn't be playing regularly. We turned down Southampton's £6m offer, while he refused to even speak to Chelsea. But the Blues were struggling financially and we reluctantly had to sell our precocious keeper in the January transfer window for £3.5m plus add-ons to Stoke. It was less money than Southampton offered the previous summer but we had no option but to accept it. It was a bonus that Butland was loaned back to us for the rest of the season.

What I didn't realise when I joined Birmingham was that the club were trying to balance the books. Yet the biggest bombshell was the owner, Carson Yeung, being put under house arrest in Hong Kong and having his assets frozen. This totally changed the landscape of the football club and my hands were now tied. I could only bring in someone who had 75 per cent of the value of the player I'd just sold. I tried for a while to get James Vaughan to sign for the club. He and his father were big Birmingham City fans. It fell down because we couldn't budget for his salary.

We tried to offload Zigic, who was a big earner at the club. He would've commanded a big fee, which would have helped us enormously but we couldn't get him off the books. I was criticised by some sections of the media following an incident in training with the big Serbian striker. I named Zigic in the starting XI for a forthcoming game, but his application in training the day before the match was disrespectful to the badge, club and group that had trained hard that day. And this wasn't the first occasion it had happened.

Zigic's attitude was that of a disgruntled player who wasn't getting picked. But this certainly wasn't the case because he was in the side. I spoke with some of the senior players that I planned to raise the ugly matter in the press and asked for their feelings on the matter. It was tough on them because they were his team mates. Despite this they agreed with my conclusion. I made the executive decision and talked about it in the public domain. I got praised in certain quarters yet criticised by others. The criticism was that you shouldn't wash your dirty laundry in public. I could see that point of view but this was pretty much a last throw of the dice. I'd tried everything I could to motivate Zigic without much success. I felt it was the right thing to do at the time. I made a stand. I was telling players it wouldn't be allowed to happen by any player while I was manager. The Serbian was popular with the fans and I liked him as well. There were people who thought there was a constant battle going on between us but there wasn't. I was a big fan of the Serbian international. He gave us an alternative option up front. He was good in the air and could score and create goals.

You can't turn it on and off in training and in a game. The best or more successful players can't switch it on and off so why would this be the case for those who aren't top class footballers? The fierce competitiveness, drive and motivation to win are there all of the time. There has been a time when I've had a bad training day and it has affected me. But it wasn't down to a lack of application or effort. I always gave 100 per cent but sometimes things don't go for you. When this happens you worry whether you'll be picked for the team.

This is always a bone of contention for the average football fan who might think, 'As long as he does it on a Saturday, why does it matter what happens in training during the week?' That attitude is unfair on those lads applying themselves correctly and running through the proverbial brick wall in a bid to put themselves in contention for the first team. Yes the so-called 'flair player' might produce that little bit of magic to win a game but it's not guaranteed. Every manager I've ever played for has emphasised the need to work hard in training and in every game, because you cannot win a match on skill alone. You could be very talented but having a shocking day, in terms of your technical ability, but if you work your socks off you could still win the game. Your application and commitment might possibly prevent a goal; create a chance or even a lucky goal.

I played with one of the greatest flair players of his generation in David Ginola. He was unplayable most of the time. Ginola wasn't lazy, but the ugly side of the game, tracking and chasing back, wasn't one of his strengths. I'm not saying the France international didn't work hard, he did. He worked his tail off in training as well; a fantastic professional. But he produced on the field. If he wasn't scoring goals he was making them and being a constant threat to the opposition. That was the difference. If they're not producing then they have to make it up with hard work.

Greame Souness had a big problem with Laurent Robert because he felt he wasn't applying himself in training the way he should. Patrick Kluivert was another one Souness had a predicament with I'm led to understand. He was a world class player in his day but by the time he came to Newcastle it seemed as if he'd lost the hunger and wasn't applying himself in training.

There were clubs interested in taking Zigic but he didn't have any interest in playing in the Middle East or Russia, which I understood. His family were settled in Birmingham and he didn't want to leave. The club were desperate to get him off the wage bill so they could get it back on an even keel. We were in the bottom eight, in terms of budget, in the Championship. If we took Zigic out of the equation, probably top four, because that's how big his salary was. I could have brought in seven or eight players had Zigic moved on. Our big striker told me the only place he was interested in going was Spain because he'd played there before. He understood about the club's precarious financial predicament and acknowledged City had to move him on. But he had an affinity for Birmingham and the area he lived in.

My first pre-season at St Andrew's was good. We went to Austria and I didn't want to change too much because, previously, the team had done well. I brought some experienced players into the club: Hayden Mullins, Peter Lovenkrands and Darren Ambrose. Footballers I thought would enhance the squad we already had. We had Marlon King and Adam Rooney up front and I believed Lovenkrands would complement our strikers with his goalscoring record and experience. Unfortunately it didn't work out that well. There was little or no money for transfer fees and we didn't hit the ground running as quickly as I thought. The same could be said about the new signings we brought in.

We didn't get the results I wanted at the start of the season and lost a local derby to Coventry in the second round of the League Cup. City was in a lower league to us and that was a setback. My biggest disappointment was being unable to play Stephen Carr and David Murphy as full backs. They were the best full back pairing outside of the Premier League. Injury ended both of their careers in my first term and it was no coincidence that we got our best results when Murphy played for us.

I had to adapt and change the club's former mentality very quickly. The days of being the highest payers were now gone. The model I used at Huddersfield, of signing young, hungry and ambitious players on loan had been very successful for me at the Galpharm Stadium. I had little choice but to try and introduce the same paradigm at St Andrew's because there was no money available and we now had to cut our cloth accordingly.

The club had taken its parachute payments from the Premier League early just to keep it afloat on a day-to-day basis. Birmingham's loyal supporters were unaware and didn't see a lot of what went on behind the scenes. Understandably, they just want to see results on the pitch. But this is difficult when you don't have the tools to do that.

I felt we did OK in my first season given the circumstances of having a transfer embargo placed on the club. We had a strong finish to the season; losing only four of our last 20, finishing 12th, seven points off the play-offs. The targets or ambition were radically different at St Andrew's to the objectives I had at the Galpharm. At Huddersfield there was money to spend on players and the club was ambitious to gain promotion. At Birmingham the objective was to stabilise the club in the Championship, reduce the wage bill and get on a stable financial footing. But despite that I was confident of turning around the team's performances. Using the loan market, and targeting young and hungry, ambitious players, I felt we could kick on.

I brought in Albert Rusnak and Emyr Huws from Man City, Tom Thorpe, Tyler Blackett, Federico Macheda from Man United and Liverpool's Jordan Ibe. Ravel Morrison came in on loan from West Ham and was an unbelievably talented player. Probably the most naturally gifted player I had. At the time I called him the modern day Paul Gascoigne. Ironically, Morrison didn't know who Gazza was! He came with baggage but deep down there was a good lad in there. He just needed to be guided more than other players. The former Man United youngster needed to be more professional and that is why he was in and out of the team. But I loved him as a footballer.

From the outside people may have questioned why I brought Morrison to Birmingham. It wasn't a case of trying to control him or thinking I'd have more influence than that of Sir Alex Ferguson or Sam Allardyce. I thought if I gave him the opportunity to play more often he might respond to it positively. I saw him play against my Huddersfield Under-18s when he was playing for Man United. He was about 15 or 16-years-old at the time. But he just made some bad decisions. The kid would often come and see me, with head bowed, to apologise for something he'd done. I'd often ask myself whether he ever learned from his mistakes.

Sir Alex has been quoted as saying Morrison was the most talented footballer to come through his academy. That is some statement when you take into account all of the players he's had though his hands as manager at Old Trafford. There were times when he was outstanding for us. I remember we went to Crystal Palace and won 4-0. Shane Ferguson, Redmond, Zigic and Morrison were brilliant on the day

Ferguson did well for me in his first loan spell but didn't make an impact the second time around. I knew him from Newcastle reserves when he was a schoolboy so I knew what I was getting. I also liked him as a boy. He'd just signed a five-year contract at Newcastle and had he lost a bit of hunger? He might have done. Was he experiencing what a lot of young footballers go through when they've made an initial impact? That could have been the case. He moved on to Millwall and he's doing very well for them.

I was excited heading into pre-season in my second year because I'd secured some good players. I managed to sign Paul Robinson. He was, unbelievably, an out of contract player. Robinson turned out to be one of my best signings and I ended up making him captain. He was a great leader and a consistent player.

We had an inconsistent start to my second season before putting a ten match unbeaten run together before New Year's Day. I thought, 'Great, we're turning it around. We've got a good chance to make the play-offs.' But then I get a call from Fulham, who recall Dan Burn, Swansea, who want Kyle Bartley back and Jesse Lingard has to go back to Man United. These were three players who'd played an important part in that run. As a consequence, I had to go back into the loan market. Unfortunately the new loan players didn't have the same impact as the lads they'd replaced.

The second half of the 2013-14 season was tough. I felt as if I'd had my legs chopped off at the knees when the parent clubs called to take their players back. The pressure on me was immense and certainly more so after losing five from seven games immediately after the turn of the year. Me, Terry Mac, Fazackerley and Watto had lots of open debates about football affairs. You name it and we discussed it vociferously and passionately. The morning after we lost to Huddersfield at St Andrew's they decided, after a fiery debate, that our relationship had run its course. Faz and Terry Mac opted to move on.

There were several reasons why the pair left, not one. They had been away from their families for a long time. It was different for me because I had my family in the Midlands. I didn't point the finger of blame at anyone but I asked whether they could have done any better. I asked myself the same question. Don't get me wrong, there were some strong words spoken. It was heated. Did it get out of control? Possibly. Could I have handled the situation better? I probably could. Could they have handled the situation better? I don't know. Only Terry Mac and Faz can answer that. In hindsight I wish I could turn back the clock. I was under pressure because of our poor results and the debate got out of control. Yes, we fell out.

From the outside it was viewed as if the club had made a decision to sack them. It was also suggested Birmingham had sacked Lee Clark's backroom staff to force the manager's hand and get him to resign. Nothing could have been further from the truth. Faz and Terry Mac left on their own conditions and no one else's terms. I didn't tell them to leave. They decided their future lay elsewhere. It was hard for me when they quit. They are two unbelievable guys and strong characters. They weren't yes men and that is why I brought them in to work with me. I have a lot of time and respect for them both. Faz is a fantastic coach and has had a lot of success in his career. Terry Mac has played a huge part in my life. His family and mine are great friends. He was good to me as a player and was there for me from day one when I became a manager. It was incredibly hard to see him go after all we'd been through.

I've since been in touch with Terry Mac and built bridges. The same goes for Faz. We texted each other a few times but it was a good few months before we were sitting around a table having a cup of tea. Our relationship runs deep. Terry's son, Neale, lived with me for a while when I was a player at Fulham. And who is to say that further down the line that, as I rebuild my managerial career, we can't work together again.

There was no time for tears but it was a watershed moment and I had to regroup. Watto came in as my assistant while Richard Beale was promoted to the first team. Beal was the Under-21 manager when I arrived at St Andrews. I liked him, instantly. Good personality, coach and fine understanding of the game. I had no qualms about moving him up when the lads moved on. I think he's got a big future in the game.

We had a few good results after Terry Mac and Faz left but before you know it we've lost five games on the spin and we're sitting in the bottom three on the last day of the season to Bolton. You're thinking how did it come to this? How did we get here? You start to feel a little sorry for yourself because you feel as if you've let everyone down. You continually question yourself. You ask all sorts of questions: is it you or your training methods?

I never once doubted myself although, admittedly, thoughts that I should move on from City did cross my mind. I didn't want Birmingham to get relegated. There were times when I thought maybe someone else should come in for the last few games to try and keep them up. Several high-profile friends and former colleagues said I should walk away. They feared for my health and mental state but I refused. I couldn't walk away. I wanted to be there when things turned around. I was hoping the financial situation would change. If those restraints were lifted I could manage the club properly. At times it was as if I had one arm tied behind my back, a patch over my eye and I was walking in quick sand with a shoe full of concrete.

When we came back for pre-season training the same restraints, in terms of finance, were still in place. The budget was restricted, but I made some good signings; albeit the majority were frees or loans. Clayton Donaldson was one such player who has turned out to be a good acquisition for the club. We lost at Middlesbrough in the season's curtain-raiser before a Wes Thomas goal against Brighton at St Andrew's gave us a first home win in the league in ten months. We went 2-1 up at home to Ipswich in our next fixture only for them to equalise in injury-time. That would have been two wins on the bounce and gone a long way into turning around our luck at home. Our form was inconsistent until a big win at Millwall. We followed that up with a draw at Charlton, before a 1-0 defeat at home to Bolton saw me lose my job.

Our home form cost me my position in the end. The team's record on its own patch was woeful under me, yet it was good away from St Andrews. We had some fantastic results on our travels, but couldn't buy a win in the Midlands. It was horrendous. I got the players in at the stadium for their pre-match meal; let them have it at home and even tried an overnight stay in a hotel before a game to Blackburn. We got pumped 4-2. We tried every conceivable scenario. The players were desperate to turn around our home form and get a win for our fans and me. Not for one minute did I think the players weren't busting a gut for me. That old adage 'he's lost the dressing room' raised its ugly head. If that was the case the players would have played with no fear and freedom at home. They didn't. Instead they were tense, nervous and tentative. It became an albatross around our necks.

I had the players in for training after the Trotters' defeat and before we were due to travel to Blackburn. I even took the usual press conference before the game. To my memory, I don't think I fielded any questions regarding my position. After that I saw my PA and looked into her eyes and knew my time was up. The club secretary, Julia Shelton, and Joanne Alsop, were superb people and close with our families. They called a meeting where I was given a letter drafted up by Panos Pavlakis, who had gone back to Hong Kong, saying, in essence, me and Watto were relieved of our duties. It was quite an emotional meeting. I was leaving a job I loved and wanted to keep.

The majority of the supporters understood the predicament the club and I were in but, ultimately, they want to see their team win. I'm not bitter about the way Pavlakis dismissed me. Some have said it was a cowardly way to conduct business but he obviously had things to do. He had to set up a successor quite quickly, so he clearly couldn't be there.

I've been asked several times whether there was a sense of relief at getting sacked after all I'd been through. But no, that was never the case. I wouldn't have jumped straight back into a job at Blackpool if it was. I was hurt. Being a manager is the next best thing to playing. But when you lose your job it is one of the worst feelings in the world. You actually get sacked in the public domain. It's in the newspapers, television and on social media and everyone's free to comment on it and your ability. This doesn't happen to Tommy the train driver, Sammy the swimming instructor or Bob the builder. You go through a lot of emotional stages. You feel anger, sadness, frustration, embarrassment and suffer a crisis of confidence and self-doubt.

In retrospect, you always feel you could have done things differently. If I had a full deck of cards, undoubtedly, things would've been different. Football is a results driven business and I didn't win enough games for Birmingham at home.

I say our home form cost me my job but there were other mitigating circumstances. Trying to be a football manager is hard enough without having to deal with non-footballing matters. This added to the pressure I was under. I became a spokesman for the football club; something I didn't want. I only wanted to concentrate on footballing matters not the financial situation; money laundering and Hong Kong. I was fielding more questions about politics off the field than on it, while Peter Pannu, the chairman, was working between Birmingham and Hong Kong.

I spoke to the owner on the phone a couple of times during my two-and-a-half year spell in the Midlands. I never met him face-to-face. He never came to a game under my reign because he was under house arrest in Hong Kong. The most frustrating aspect of this was I didn't know the answers to the club's off the pitch troubles. People, fans and the media didn't see it like that and thought I was trying to hide something. The uncertainty of Birmingham's future was a worry to all players, staff and supporters. At the end of one financial year there was a problem with the accounts. They were late or hadn't been submitted. The negativity from that episode spread from the boardroom on to the pitch and terraces. Supporters were concerned whether the club would continue or go into administration and the media were always asking these questions. It was only towards the end of my time in the midlands that Pavlakis came in and that changed. Ultimately he decided my time was up and fired me. But he actually started to make a difference and answer all of those difficult questions about finance and the future of the club. I had a good relationship with Pavlakis as it happens, but he had to do what he thought was in the best interests of the club. He came down to the training ground regularly and it gave the players a bit of reassurance that everything was going to be OK; something they'd never had in my time. I believe Gary Rowett was able to turn around the Blues' fortunes, after I left, because he could concentrate on the football side, while Pavlakis acted as Birmingham's figurehead.

I spoke to Rowett about players over the phone and face-to-face when he was a manager elsewhere. And I'm sure I played against him in my playing career. There is no ill feeling between us. We spoke after I got sacked and he was in the job. I did some punditry for Sky at Birmingham not long ago and Rowett was getting interviewed. There was some implication this would be a problem. I didn't understand why. I lost my job because I didn't get the results they wanted. The club chose a former Blues favourite to turn it around and he did it brilliantly. He's at a fantastic club I have a lot of affinity for. We're not kids in a play ground. He didn't steal my sweets or my girlfriend. I say good luck to him and, to others, grow up. There are some great people at the football club. My whole family loved it. Two of my kids went to school in Birmingham and loved it. They made some good friends.

Ironically, my first win as a Blackpool manager came when my old club visited Bloomfield Road under Rowett. We beat them 1-0. It was a weird feeling because I felt as if City's players were still mine. I didn't enjoy the day at all. I got a mixed reception from the travelling supporters that day. On the whole, City fans gave me great support when I was their manager before and during a game. But they weren't slow to tell me what they thought when a match finished. They showed their frustration and anger. I never had a problem with it. That comes with the territory. You have to win football matches and get results at a big club like Birmingham. I never once felt I was being treated unfairly.

CHAPTER 16
NO, I DON'T LIKE TO BE BESIDE THE SEASIDE

en to 15 minutes into my first game in charge and I heard, "Fuck off Clark, you're worse than Ince!"

The supporter must have run about 50 yards from the back of the terraces to express his disapproval of my managerial skills. It was certainly delivered with some gusto as well: full of venom, vitriol and hate. It wasn't a character assassination, as such, but he let me know in no uncertain terms that I wasn't welcome at Bloomfield Road. I should've realised then how bad things were! Personally, I thought it was a bit harsh because we were playing well. Yes, Ipswich did eventually win the contest 2-0 but it was all level prior to the abuse. Secondly, Paul Ince had the club up to second in the Championship at one stage of his tenure, as Tangerines boss, so he couldn't have been that bad a manager.

It's difficult to articulate or make sense of what happened next because it feels as if it belongs to a *Viz* comic strip story, like Billy the Fish, or a spoof football film such as, *Bostock's Cup* or *Mike Bassett, England Manager* ! You really couldn't make up the hopelessness, incompetence and ineptitude of those running the club. It couldn't have been scripted. In fact, if it was written as a film it would be dismissed as being too unrealistic or a piss-take.

From losing my job at Birmingham to being installed as the new boss of Blackpool, happened in no time at all. I didn't really have any time to feel sorry for myself or lick my wounds. Sacked on the Monday, packed up on the Tuesday and by Wednesday I was at home in Newcastle watching a football match on the TV. A text from an unknown number came through while I was viewing the game, asking, "Is this still your number, Lee?" I thought it was someone from the press, so replied, "Yes," and left it at that. Another text dropped later that night from Karl Oyston saying, "Sorry you've lost your job at Birmingham, thought it was a harsh decision." He then called and, as a result of our conversation, I met up with the Blackpool chairman at his house in the countryside, on the Saturday my old team lost 8-0 to Bournemouth.

Oyston was straight to the point. He asked whether I was up for the challenge and, obviously I was, so he offered me the job. I was well aware the task in hand was going to be difficult but, my ego kicked in and, thought if I save the Tangerines from relegation then it'll do my CV no harm at all. And that was my remit: to keep Blackpool in the Championship. A 3-0 defeat away at Reading had left the Seasiders bottom of the table, prior to my appointment, but that didn't matter to me. I believed I could keep them up. I quickly realised it was an impossible task. I took over from former incumbent, José Riga, a week after my meeting with Oyston and set about assessing what I had to work with at the North West outfit. There was money at the club, despite what people were saying from the outside. Some of the players were on very good Championship salaries. But when the club has a policy of not paying agents, it's difficult to get players over the line.

In the Championship, games came thick and fast and a few days after losing my first fixture to the Tractor Boys, we're in London to play my old club Fulham. This is where the first problem arose. We stayed in a North West London hotel the night before the game. I know driving from one end of London to the other on an evening is a nightmare. Consequently, we got stuck in traffic on the way to the match. Our captain, Tony McMahon, and my assistant, Alan Thompson, jumped off the team coach a couple of miles away from Craven Cottage and ran to the ground to hand in the team sheet. We would have been fined if it was late. This was the start of it all. But in this case, it wasn't Oyston's fault. The club secretary put us in that hotel.

I changed the system to 3-5-2, from the previous game, which we'd practised at Queens Park Rangers' training ground on the morning of the match. Everything was going well. We were 2-0 up against the Cottagers, playing great and had a chance to score a third when McMahon took a swing a Hugo Rodallega and got a straight red card. In the end we drew 2-2 but it was a great point, although it should have been three.

We went to Leeds in my third game. After a horrendous first half, which saw us trailing 3-0 at the break, we turned it around and performed better in the second period. There was a break for a couple of weeks after that and I worked them hard in training. It seemed to bear fruit. And then 1-1 draw at home to Bolton was followed by a repeat result at Rotherham before I recorded my first victory, ironically, at home to my former club, Birmingham. Our mini run continued with a 2-2 draw at Charlton and in the back of my mind, I'm thinking, we could just do it and stay up.

On the pitch it was tough, though, because we didn't have enough players of quality. Yet it was even tougher off it and ultimately, that conspired against my attempts to stave off relegation. It was chaotic behind the scenes and because of that it was just about impossible to find any order or coherence on the main stage. One Monday morning I turned up for training at Bloomfield Road and the big glass windows in the reception had been shattered. Vandals, disgruntled fans or protesting supporters had been firing ball bearings into it with a catapult. I had to sweep away the dangerous shards of glass from the corridors and dressing room before people came in. The club, in its wisdom, only employed cleaners from a Monday to a Friday. Any mess from a Saturday match was just left unattended until the Monday afternoon. You name it: mud from boots, food, drinks, bottles, glasses, crap. It wasn't a good impression at all.

It was hard to create a good positive atmosphere and working environment with the lads. We didn't even have anywhere to change at the training ground. We had to get dressed at Bloomfield Road. On top of that, players had to wash their own boots and playing and training kits. It's easy to see why players became disenchanted There was no fitness coach. It was tough trying to get things done. The chairman was hardly ever there. The people he had running the club when he wasn't there were incompetent. The infrastructure at Blackpool was a mess. I couldn't even get the club to buy some footballs so we could train. I'm thinking, 'Is this for real?' But I'm not joking – there were no footballs. For a football team. A professional one. To train with.

We were getting complaints from other Championship teams about the state of our pitch and, rightly so, and ultimately the FA got involved. It was embarrassing. The club had staged a Rod Stewart concert in the summer and judging by the state of the pitch; it never recovered for the start of the season and got progressively worse. So the pitch was in a shocking state and, on top of that, the training ground was a mess.

I talked regularly with Jimmy Armfield in my office. Armfield was a Seasiders and England playing legend, who also captained his country. Blackpool was his one and only team. He was gutted about the state of his beloved club. Armfield told me the training facilities hadn't changed since his playing days in the 1950s.

Unbelievably, 'progress' is written on the Blackpool crest but that has to be one of the biggest ironies of all time given the current state of the club. There were no home game advantages to the team because fans were turning up to boo and voice their opinion about the owners. There were, "Oyston out!" chants all the way through my first fixture at home to Ipswich. It was bad but it was about to get worse as my time at Blackpool wore on. The atmosphere between the supporters and the chairman was toxic, which I didn't know about at first. But it was becoming more and more poisonous. Obviously when things aren't going well, the manager, chairman or owners are all in the firing line.

I've been asked about unhappy players and unrest at the club. Admittedly, most of the players were unhappy but they never give me any problems. Mr Attitude, Nile Ranger, was probably the only exception. Ranger had been signed by the club on a free transfer. He played in my first game at home to Ipswich and missed a couple of matches until we faced Rotherham where he could have been sent off. He made a couple of challenges I would have been unhappy about had I been on the pitch. United were looking to get him dismissed, so I took him off at half-time.

In training on the following Monday and Tuesday, his attitude towards the staff wasn't acceptable and he wasn't pulling up any trees with his performances. I pulled Ranger into my office for a meeting the following day to discuss it with him and my number two, who had been his coach at Newcastle. I told Ranger he wasn't going to be in the squad for the following game with Birmingham, or any other, until his attitude and performances in training improved. He then informed me of some phantom injury and said he couldn't train on the Thursday, something the physio didn't know about. On the Friday he rang to say he had toothache and couldn't come in. We organised a dental appointment, which he didn't turn up for (it was scheduled for tooth-hurty), and that was the last I saw of him until I left the club.

Ranger was whinging on about his pittance of a contract. But because of his history, no one was going to give him a huge contract. It was a ridiculous low basic wage. If he'd played he would have picked up good appearance money. It was his choice not to turn up, work hard in training and get picked for the team. Had he shown a good attitude and applied himself everything would have taken care of itself. He didn't get fined, like he said, the club just didn't pay him.

I was trying to attract players to the club and it proved difficult. I had to promote some of the academy kids to the first team pool. They were under incredible pressure to perform at a higher level and therefore struggled. In the January transfer window I had players begging to leave the club. These players I inherited were not only sick of the poor training facilities, lack of balls and poor state of the pitch; the club weren't honouring their contracts. Relocation packages, bonuses and other perks promised when they signed failed to materialise. Players were coming to me with these problems. I tried to rectify them but found it impossible.

I tried to bring in a couple of Scottish players. The secretary of the club, Chris Hough, was going to offer them less money than what they were on at Dundee United to come to Blackpool. I wondered what was behind his thinking. They ended up going to Celtic. Later on I found out the guy didn't really have any power. The chairman was the only one who could fix wages. He acted like Johnny big bananas but once we went to meet Oyston to see if he would loosen the purse strings, Hough wouldn't say boo to a goose. He just sat in the corner like a little boy lost.

I didn't feel cheated or let down by Oyston or the club. I could have walked away earlier but I wanted to be loyal to the young players I brought in. I told their parents I would try and get a contract for their kids. Ultimately I couldn't do it because the club had a policy for young players they wouldn't waiver from. Two of these lads: Mark Waddington and Dom Telfer ended up leaving to join Stoke City. They were offered £200 a week by the club and when the lads wouldn't sign they were told to train with the youth team. They were two exciting young talents. Maybe I should have looked after Lee Clark at the time, and walked instead, because I have been tarnished by the whole sorry episode.

I never had regular meetings with the owner but when he was at the ground or in the area I'd go and meet him or he'd come and see me. This will upset a lot of Blackpool supporters, because they hate him, but as a man, having a cup of coffee in my office or a cup of tea in his, not a problem. But when I wanted to talk football or identify players it was another matter. When we knew we were going down I told him we needed to sign players quickly to come straight back up. I identified a couple of Scottish players and a goalkeeper called Richard O'Donnell. We did a deal with his agent and he agreed to sign but Oyston wouldn't pay the agent's fees.

Malcolm Crosby, who was my head of recruitment, had a brief chat with Oyston that went:

Crosby: "The agent's fees aren't that big in the grand scheme of things. They shouldn't be a deal breaker and we should pay it."

Oyston: "Well, you, pay the fucking agent!"

Crosby: "I would but I don't have the money."

This showed the football side of things was wrong because they then struggled as a consequence in League One and are now in League Two after another relegation, while the teams who came down with Blackpool have fared better. Oyston promised things would change in my second season. He said the training ground would be improved but I resigned.

The story about Joe Lewis being dropped, because an appearance payment was about to be triggered, is untrue. It had nothing to do with paying Cardiff a loyalty payment if he played. I didn't feel Lewis was making a sufficient contribution to the team. A lot of players were left out for that reason.

Admittedly, there was a payment due if he had played but I was never told I couldn't pick or play him.

The tale Lewis had to play in a signed shirt, however, was true, and yes it was his signature on the jersey. This manifested itself because our secretary had to double up as the kit man and there wasn't a goalkeeper top for one reason or another. We took one out of the club shop and he wore it against Charlton at home. You can't make this stuff up.

How was I supposed to attract players with all of this turmoil going on? I signed out of contract players, called in a few favours and took a few youngsters on loan, who did improve the team. But ultimately, towards the end, it was just carnage. Most of the Blackpool players didn't have a pre-season so they were unfit. Less than 12 hours before the start of the season they had five contracted players. Agents were having a field day with Blackpool offering out of contract players who couldn't get a club.

I was undecided what to do until our last game of the season got abandoned against Huddersfield. Three minutes into the second half, supporters invaded the pitch, set off flares and began protesting against the owners. Some fans were doing the conga, while one joined in the protest on a mobility scooter. It was surreal. After the game Jimmy Armfield came into my office and I looked into his eyes and saw, sadness. I knew then I didn't get involved in football to go through this. My family couldn't come and enjoy it and games were getting abandoned.

After the match at home to Huddersfield got called off, after 48 minutes, I decided enough was enough. This wasn't an environment where I could work and flourish. Supporters didn't particularly want me there. They thought I was an ally of the owner and his family, which couldn't have been further from the truth. I was employed by them and wanted to do a job to the best of my ability but the atmosphere was so poisonous it was impossible. It wasn't a pleasurable place to work.

The Football League decided the result should stay as a 0-0 draw. It might have been replayed if any of the sides around us could move up, or another team benefitted from another result, but that wasn't the case here. Huddersfield couldn't move up a place and neither could we.

It didn't matter who the manager was, there had to be a big change at the end of the season. No manager was going to keep players who had surrendered so feebly in taking the club down. I stuck to my duties and held one-to-one meetings with the players the day after the Huddersfield match and, basically, culled the squad. I let about 20 players go, including loan signings and those on short-term contracts. It was a tough environment for those lads and there was mutual respect when we sat down to discuss the reasons etc. It was a relief to some of them, especially those banging on my door in January, begging to be let go.

The following day, on Monday, I rang Oyston and left a voicemail message because he didn't pick up. He had an inkling to what it was when he called back. We spoke briefly about the complications, if you like, about the legal side of things and made an announcement I was leaving the week after, despite the fact Thommo and I resigned on the Monday morning.

The owner didn't try to talk me around but said he was disappointed with my decision. Oyston said he thought I'd just stick a tin hat on and get on with it, which is his way. There were no raised voices or emotions running away with themselves. The owner deals with things in a manly businesslike manner. He wasn't petty about things. He understood I'd had a rough ride. He was aware of how I worked. I was very open with him in my time there and he appreciated that.

I didn't tell the staff I'd resigned. In fact, I took them away to Spain for a few days while the announcement was being made. Obviously the staff still wanted to stay there because they needed to work. I also played a part in Neil McDonald getting the Blackpool job and suggested to Oyston to give the position to my former Newcastle United colleague. McDonald wasn't under any illusions about the post and I didn't hide anything from him. I'm guessing he's found it tougher than he thought it would be; but so did I.

Attracting players to Bloomfield Road is one of the biggest problems. With five or six games to go before the end of the season I started planning for life in League One because of our perilous position. I wanted to do what Wigan has ended up doing and jump straight back up. It wasn't possible because of the recruitment process.

I went through a lot of emotions when I finally quit; relief obviously. It felt like a great weight was lifted off my shoulders when I knew I wasn't going back into that environment. There was hurt because the club got relegated while I was manager. The previous boss, Jose Riga, who had won one of his 15 games in charge, said he'd never had relegation on his CV. Looks like he was taking no responsibility for a third of the season under his charge. I accept my part in the club's demotion. I can't ignore it because it is on my CV. Obviously, in hindsight, I should have left the job within the first month.

Several of the players got in touch and said they'd enjoyed playing under me. And if there was an opportunity they would like to work with me again, which was nice to hear. I signed Miles Addison for Blackpool and also brought him to Kilmarnock. He has been impressive since he got to Rugby Park. But the players understood my predicament and the difficulties I was facing. They weren't motivated by the atmosphere. I couldn't have imagined a worst case scenario. The chief scout was washing and ironing the kit. There was many a time when I was sweeping the corridor on a Monday morning. I understood the lower down the league you go you have to cut your cloth accordingly. But this was a former Premier League club in the Championship.

I wish the five or six months of my career spent in Lancashire could be erased from my CV. I'm sure the players from that time are thinking the same. A home match wasn't a home match because it was protests, banners and chants against the owners. The supporters tried to get behind the team but once we went behind they vented their spleens. I can understand their frustrations and anger. We only won three home games all season.

Like all of my former teams, Blackpool is a club rich in culture, success and legends. Arguably the first thing that springs to mind when you mention Blackpool is Stanley Matthews and the 1953 Matthews' final. Stan Mortensen was another great who played there. World Cup winner Alan Ball also turned out for the Seasiders, as did Tony Green. In fact there were four Blackpool players in the England side which lost to Hungary 6-3 in the same year. This was one of the things that attracted me to the club, its heritage. You dream about turning around a famous club down on its luck and reliving the exciting FA Cup runs of the 1950s. I know all about the romance of the 1950s FA Cup because Newcastle famously won it three times, once at the expense of Blackpool. But Blackpool's halcyon days are nothing but memories in the past and will remain there until there is a changing of the guard.

I really fear for the future of Blackpool. There doesn't seem to be any resolution between the supporters and the club's owners. It'll be interesting to see what the attendances will be at Bloomfield Road for the 2016-17 campaign. A lot of fans bought a two-year deal that ended in 2016. Yet the fans are in a

Catch-22 situation. They don't want to boycott the games and see their side go down again, but what can they do? A sensible solution would see fans and the owners getting together to resolve their problems. But I can't ever see that happening. I personally think the relationship is beyond repair. The only resolution for me is if the owners sell up and leave.

CHAPTER 17
CHANGE OF CLIMATE, FOREIGN FOOD AND THE LANGUAGE BARRIER

Kilmarnock won't win the Scottish Premier Football League. I'm not going to patronise or insult our supporters' intelligence to say anything otherwise. The club does not have the financial clout or infrastructure of a Glasgow or Edinburgh club. Some players from those teams have a take home salary of £40,000 each week, while the budget for the whole of my squad is half of that. Mind you, if there's a rich benefactor with Killie sympathies or a rich oil tycoon with a bottomless pit of money wanting a part in a fairy tale, then I'd love to hear from him or her. All joking aside, the SPFL may be out of our reach but there's nothing stopping us from winning a Scottish Cup, a League Cup or qualifying for the Europa League?

Ross County are not a massive club but they have shown you can have success on a limited budget. My big mate at St Johnstone, Tommy Wright, steered his side to fourth in the SPFL last term. That wasn't luck. It was accomplished by hard work. If you have good recruitment and backing from those pulling the strings behind the scenes anything is achievable. My board work tirelessly trying to do as much as they can despite the financial constraints they're under. I'm under no illusion it will be tough, but I'm up for the challenge. I'm excited about my first full season in charge and want our supporters to feel the same way. I'm stimulated by the thought of going to Ibrox and Parkhead to compete with the league's big boys. There shouldn't be any fear factor going into the so-called cauldron of those big arenas. We should embrace it and that's what we intend to do.

I'm targeting a top six finish. It will be a tall order but if we fail and end up in a mid-table position then at least we've had a go. We'll then build on that and go again next season.

I knew a clearout was needed at Rugby Park at the end of the 2015-16 campaign. It's been said in several quarters I've been harsh but Kilmarnock has been slipping down the SPFL by one position, every season in the last seven. I needed to cut loose the dead wood, remove the negativity and freshen up the squad. Seventeen were released and 16 came in. Killie fans have got to trust my judgement. I know most of the new lads will not be known to the supporters, but hopefully by the end of the season they will be fans' favourites. No one knew Anthony Pilkington, Jordan Rhodes, Danny Drinkwater or Benik Afobe when I signed them for Huddersfield. Yet they've all gone on to have success in one way or another.

I'm hoping a few of my new recruits can emulate the achievements of my past signings and, with the help of the more experienced lads like Kris Boyd, I'm sure they will. Kris has been nothing short of magnificent for me since I came to Killie. And against his former club, Rangers, he revealed just what a top class striker he is when netting the opener against the Glasgow outfit.

It's been an emotional period for Kris following the death of his younger brother. I gave him the option to sit out our home fixture with Partick Thistle following the bad news. But he displayed incredible bravery to play in the match and netted a poignant goal in dedication to his brother. Football always takes second place when a tragedy like this happens. It'll get harder for the Boyd family before it gets easier. We just need to make sure we're there for him in any difficult times.

It is fair to say we didn't hit the ground running at the beginning of the new season. It's been a mixed bag so far. We were the favourites to get out of our League Cup group because we were the Premier League team. We're all disappointed we didn't make it into the second stage of the competition. I get the feeling there's been a bit of a witch-hunt up here because the same fuss wasn't made when, the holders, Ross County, went out in the group stage. The same can be said about Dundee, who is classed as a top six side. Kilmarnock appears to have stolen the limelight from those two clubs. Killie is having a torrid time, apparently, when we only lost one game of the four we played in the group stage. That's not to say I was happy with the two victories and draw. The performances weren't good enough. Has it been magnified because I've brought in a lot of English players and they're unfamiliar with the league? It could be. I recently suggested there might be a little bias but I got into trouble with the SPFL. I won't be doing that again. Anyway, being a Geordie I'm closer to being Scottish than most English people. I've always been led to believe the Geordies have a close bond with the Jocks because we're not really English. Geordieland is like a republic, separate from both Scotland and England. Anyway, aren't the Scots just like Geordies but with their brains kicked in? Or is it the other way around?

Seriously, I have noticed a lot of negativity since I've arrived. From my experience this seems to be the way with the Scottish press and media. They all seem to be pushing a pessimistic line. One characteristic that has manifested itself is the obsession to whip up some false rivalry with an opposition manager. One reporter suggested Falkirk manager Peter Houston and I were playing mind games with each other. I responded by saying, "I wasn't very good at school so I don't think my mind operates on that level," or words to that affect. I liked what Houston's team were about and the level he got them to playing at. He was really humble after the play-off game at Rugby Park and complimentary about my team's performance over both legs. I understand what he must have been going through because I've been there myself and it's tough to fall at the final hurdle.

The Lee Clark quitting line was another puzzling one that appeared in the public domain. I wasn't sure where the rumours came from, whether it was from one of the playing staff or a mole within the dressing room. People will think there is no smoke without fire but, regardless, it is still beyond me how whatever was said within the confines of the club has morphed into a story about me intending to quit. It goes without saying we had a mixed start to the season. But that is understandable when you've brought in 17 new players and let more leave. Maybe a player wasn't happy with the way I'd spoken to him and got on to his agent. The agent has then spun a story because he wants an out-of-work manager, on his books, shoehorned into my place. I don't know. Needless to say, I'm going nowhere.

We started the domestic programme with an encouraging performance at Rugby Park against Motherwell. They were a top six side last season and we should have got something from the game. Then we went to Hamilton, one of the teams we're expected to get points from, and won. That was three consecutive triumphs on the road. We got a couple of draws to Glasgow giants Rangers and on the road at Dundee. But the new lads are bedding in. Some of them have found the change of climate a bit difficult, while others have hit the ground running. Most of them haven't experienced Scottish football but they're doing better now the league programme is up and running. There will be a learning process for them and they will get better as the season evolves.

I've been through this myself as a player. The transition when I left Newcastle to go to Sunderland was done with ease. Yet when I swapped Wearside for West London I didn't hit the ground running at all. I was Fulham's record transfer signing yet for the first month I played like a donut. There were mitigating circumstances. I didn't have my family with me at first. It felt as if I was in a foreign place without them and out of my comfort zone. Then after four to six weeks I came into my own and went on to have a successful and happy time at Craven Cottage.

I've brought a lot of young lads to Killie. It will be the first time a lot of them have lived away from their parents. While I know playing in Scotland isn't like swapping one continent for another, there will be a settling in period. I had to make radical changes on the recruitment side of the football club. Kilmarnock has been in the doldrums for years. It wasn't just the performances that needed to change but the characters as well. The whole mentality of the place had to be transformed.

I have the full support of the board and there has been money to bring in players but we have to be realistic. We don't pay transfer fees so we have to employ good housekeeping and husbandry. We were offered a substantial fee for Josh Magennis and had no option but to let him go. I know he was a fans' favourite and they will be disappointed he's gone. But he only had a year left on his contract and could've left from nothing at the end of the season. Allowing him to leave allowed me to be a bit more creative. He was one of the club's highest earners as well. I have to decide whether I use the money the club have received for him on one player, two or three. Magennis was good for Kilmarnock and vice versa. The club allowed him to find his feet and flourish after an early unsettling period of his career at Cardiff, Aberdeen and St Mirren. I had a good relationship with him and wish him well in South London at Charlton Athletic. They're a good club.

One of the biggest challenges I face is reversing the lazy stereotypes of Scottish football. The outside perception of Scottish game is that it is inferior to English football. I've brought several English players to Scotland and, without question, some of them arrived with that mindset. They've listened to pundits, friends and agents saying it's easy up there. Then they've been shocked that the standard is better than what they first expected. A few of them must have believed they could just stroll it, which as you'll know by now, that attitude doesn't was with me. They've been surprised by the tenacity, tempo and never-say-die attitude of the players. A few of them haven't picked up the pace of the game and I need to get them up to speed. They will have to work hard to get there. Some of them won't find their feet and we'll have to move them on. That's just football. Not every player that comes to a club is a sensation. But I'm confident most of the lads I've brought in will eventually find their feet and become a success at Rugby Park.

Admittedly, the SPFL is not at the same standard technically as the English Premier League because the money isn't here. But when you go up against a team like Rangers or Celtic, you soon discover they have very good technical players. I've also seen a shift in attitudes from the English clubs. They've started fishing in the Scottish waters again, after what seems like a long absence, and they're taking players from up here. Magennis has just gone to Charlton, Dundee lost Greg Stewart to Birmingham and Kane Hemmings has gone to Oxford. There is talent up here. It just needs to be discovered, nurtured and developed.

The time between leaving Blackpool and my appointment at Kilmarnock was the longest I'd been out of the game. I didn't think the experience at Bloomfield Road would be damaging. Close friends reassured me future employers would understand. But as time went on I was beginning to think I was soiled goods. I spoke to several clubs such as: Notts County, Doncaster Rovers and York City. Some of them offered me a job while I lost out on a couple. There was an opportunity to go to America and I spoke to a couple of clubs over there but it didn't feel right. There was a chance to go to Newcastle Jets, in Australia, when I was Birmingham manager. The family were interested at the prospect but I was at a great club and didn't want to give that up.

I'm ambitious, hungry for success but also aware a manager's lifespan is short. And the longer you're out of football the more likely it is that people will forget about you.

I took a call from someone I know in the Scottish game saying Gary Locke and Kilmarnock had agreed to go their separate ways, while I was watching a game at my old club, Huddersfield. He asked whether I'd be interested in talking to the board at Rugby Park. I jumped at the opportunity. I met up with the chairman and board of directors, had a look around the stadium and immediately got a good feeling about the place. Everything was positive from the outset. We chatted and I asked the board what they wanted and what targets were realistic. I was happy with the outcome of the meeting and we mutually agreed we would be good for each other. It was a different challenge altogether. For one, I would be working in the top flight of a different country. I knew it would be a tough task to keep Killie in the league when I first arrived. But, while we were fighting to stay up, in the back of my mind I was aware Rangers were coming back into the SPFL. Gers' return meant the Scottish top flight was getting its wow factor back. I was salivating at the prospect of taking my Kilmarnock team to Ibrox to play in front of 52,000. The same can be said about going to Celtic and Parkhead, which holds 60,000. But I had to put that at the back of my mind, for the time being, and keep the club in the division.

The board gave me permission to restructure my backroom staff and I spoke to Alan Thompson. Tommo is a good friend, was an excellent number two to me before and he's first-class at his job. The fact he had experience of Scottish football with Celtic would've been a bonus. But Tommo decided it wouldn't have been the right move for him. I accepted his decision and had to move on. I'm sure we'll work together again sometime in the future.

I needed lads to work with me who knew the team and Scottish football. I'd made several trips up here in the past to scout players so I knew the leagues quite well. But I wanted guys with extensive knowledge of the game up here and that's what I already had in my backroom staff. Lee McCulloch, Peter Leven and my goalkeeping coach Billy Thompson work really well together. They are a good team, enthusiastic and excellent coaches. They are a loyal bunch who work hard so there was no need to change anything.

McCulloch is highly thought of in Scottish football from his time at Rangers and with the national squad. He's popular around the club, with the players and staff. There's no doubt Jig will go on to be a manager in the future. Thompson is another, who played for Gers, and also Dundee. He has an abundance of experience, while Leven is an ex Killie favourite, who spent a lot of his career in the English leagues at MK Dons, Chesterfield and Oxford. They all speak their minds in staff meetings which is crucially important. The only change I made was to bring in Paul Stephenson. He will look after the development side and he's doing a great job.

It goes without saying it was a baptism of fire when I accepted the Kilmarnock position and moved to East Ayrshire. The first five fixtures were against teams in the top six. We were third bottom of the league, cut adrift from Hamilton above us and had only 12 games left to play! Talk about a challenge. I must be a masochist. Most people would have looked at the fixtures and said thanks but no thanks.

I had to sacrifice our last home game of the SPFL season against Dundee after we'd lost to Partick Thistle at Rugby Park. The defeat was a watershed moment. It meant Hamilton had secured their top flight status and we couldn't catch them. I had to prepare the side for the play-offs with Falkirk, despite having a fixture at Dundee and a game playing host to their rivals, United. The game at Rugby Park just got in the way. I left seven regulars out of the starting eleven and then substituted two during the game. In the line-up: I had a right back playing left back, a centre half that hadn't played for a few weeks and a couple of teenagers were making their debuts. It caused a little bit of negativity around the club but I was proved right in the end. We may have lost the first leg 1-0 but we should have won both of the play-off games. There would have been no complaints from Falkirk if we'd taken a lead into the return fixture on our own patch.

I wasn't thinking about my previous failures in play-off games. I was thinking more about the people who would lose their jobs if we dropped down a division. Stopping in the top flight of the SPFL isn't as lucrative as being in the English Premier League but you are better off financially. Fortunately we triumphed 4-0 in the return leg so we avoided the drop. Escaping relegation was a relief. It was stressful. But I've taken Kilmarnock to my heart and I want everyone to buy into the club the way I have. I don't want to see fans suffering or people struggle and have their jobs threatened because we haven't been good enough on the pitch. I can't emphasise enough, that can't be allowed to happen again.

Everyone's picked up on my scarf-waving moment in our play-off victory at home to Falkirk. What's wrong with showing a bit of passion? Football is an emotional game and it was a relief when it sunk in we'd still be playing top flight football. I don't think there was anything wrong with it as long as you show respect to the opposition manager and his staff. I didn't run past the Falkirk technical area; I went the other way. I'm not sure what the police officer thought when I draped the scarf around her neck. I saw one caption on a photo after the game saying, 'Get your scarf love, you've pulled,' which tickled me.

The referee on the day of the home leg was asking me to keep a lid on it. My point of view was, 'Life's too short, man. Everyone just get over it.'

However, it was a bit different in the first game of the new season at home to Motherwell when I got sent to the stands. Apparently, I told the fourth official to... well, to, "Fuck off!" If you look at the footage, there was no aggression and I wasn't even facing him. It is pointless appealing these decisions because the referees' board aren't going to take my word over one of their own, are they? It was only ten minutes into the game. I served a one-match ban in the stands at Hamilton and we won. I like to watch games from the stand, as it happens. You get a better view and perspective up there. I know supporters don't like seeing their manager sitting upstairs. Sometimes it has to be done. But, saying that, when you're struggling you need to be on the touchline to support the team.

Like a lot of the new players I've also had to adapt to my new surroundings, climate, foreign food and language. The square sausage and tattie scone are a little different to what I'm used to eating at home. I haven't been tempted by the deep fried Mars Bar, as yet, although the Killie Pie is something else, delicious. But without question the language barrier has been the biggest obstacle to overcome since my arrival in East Ayrshire. I thought being a Geordie and living close to the borders wouldn't pose too many problems. But I'm still toying with the idea of employing an interpreter. One day a member of staff asked me not to go too hard on a player otherwise he'd start 'greeting.' It went straight over my head. Why would anyone say hello to a bollocking? It didn't make sense. Another member warned me to be careful that a player doesn't go 'chapping on my door.' I'm thinking, 'Why would anyone want to file my door?' My first trip to Aberdeen on the team bus was another occasion where there was a breakdown in communications. The coach driver asked me if I knew Ken. Obviously I didn't know who Ken was. He repeated it again and I still couldn't understand him. Then I thought maybe he'd called me Ken. I said, "No, my name's Lee." It brought a lot of merriment among the staff.

Fortunately, Lorraine, has stepped in to try and resolve the language barrier issue. She's bought me a tea mug with Scottish slang words pasted all over it to help me out. The mug comes complete with Scottish to English translation. Every time I have a doubt about what is being said linguistically I have a quick look at it. Just means I'm forever drinking tea.

All joking aside, as well as building up my Scottish vocabulary, I'm also rebuilding my reputation as a manager. I'm confident I can do well for Killie and the club can do well for me. How long I remain as Kilmarnock boss will be decided on how successful I become. A cup triumph and qualifying for Europe are not beyond the realms of our imagination. Until then we'll keep plugging away until we achieve that goal. And as they say back home, "Haway the Lads! Ken?"

CHAPTER 18
FAMILY, FRIENDS AND STRUCK BY CUPID'S ARROW

Without trying to turn it into a mushy Richard Curtis rom-com, like *Four Weddings and a Funeral*, yes, I was struck by Cupid's Arrow. We all try to pretend we're jack-the-lad and that it'll not happen to us but the so-called angel of love seduce us all. We're all susceptible to her inimitable charms and I was no different.

Me and Andy Cole were doing some promotion work at a shoe shop, Breeze, on Grey Street, which was opposite the Theatre Royal in Newcastle. Lorraine's granddad came into the shop when we were in there and got chatting. He was a big Toon fan. The old fella asked whether we would go and say hello to his granddaughter, who was working in his shop, also on Grey Street, called, Life's Menswear. So I went over and said hello and we had a chat. I'd seen her out and about in town when the lads were socialising so recognised her face. Consequently, every now and then, on the pretence of buying a few outfits, I'd pop in to have a chat. It cost me a fair few bob before I eventually plucked up the courage to ask her out. I wouldn't say I was like one of the shy kids from a 1980s John Hughes film, but I wasn't far off it. This much I can say: it's a lot bloody easier playing in a Tyne and Wear derby!

A month or so later, Lorraine revealed she wasn't the sweet and innocent girl she first made out to be. She exposed a mischievous side when stitching up me, Coley and Steve Watson. Unbeknown to us; she'd sold the three of us the same suit but at different times. The first occasion I put mine on, I'm thinking, 'This is a right bobby dazzler.' And as I set off for the match at St James' Park my thoughts were, 'The lads'll be double jealous when they see me in my new suit.' But when I got there, Coley and Watto were wearing the same one. I couldn't believe it. We all stood looking aghast at each other. The rest of the lads lapped this up, of course, and absolutely battered us, asking whether it was 'a club issue' and when was their 'fitting'. It took a while to live that one down. Every time I bought something new it would start the lads off.

We've got three kids: Jak, Claudia and Bobby. We got married in the autumn of 1998 at Gretna Green. I was a Sunderland player at the time and had a broken leg. We didn't tell anyone other than Watto and his Mrs, who were there with us. But we let all of our close friends and family know we wanted them to come and meet us at Uno's on Newcastle Quayside, because we had something to celebrate. I was best man for Watto in a big church wedding and nervous as anything. I couldn't imagine standing up and delivering some eloquent speech at mine. The thought absolutely terrified me. In fact, it would've ended up on *You've Been Framed* or some other show highlighting the public's gaffes and mistakes, because I would've keeled over, fell in the cake or something daft like that.

Lorraine wasn't too bothered about a church wedding and happy to go with the flow. It was exciting and a bit romantic as well. That's what I keep telling her anyway. Jak and Claudia were both at our wedding, while Bobby wasn't born at the time. It's quite unique for a footballer to get married in October because they generally do it in the summer. I think that was how we managed to throw everyone off the scent.

We both wanted a family and we started quite young. Jak was born just before Euro 96; Claudia came along two years later and Bobby in 2005. I remember watching England against Spain in the Euro 96 quarter-finals at home and jumping up in excitement when David Seaman saved a penalty. I forgot Jak was lying asleep on my chest. To my horror, he flipped off me, one bounce on the bed and before I knew it, he was on the floor, screaming his eyes out. I was beside myself and panicked. I nashed straight to the phone to call Lorraine, worried I'd done some damage. Fortunately, he was fine and it doesn't seem to have affected him in anyway. Hope the social services aren't reading this. I was never destined to be in goal.

My wife and kids are undoubtedly the best thing that has happened in my life. Football is my life but my family is the only thing more important. I get what Bill Shankly meant when he said, "Some people believe football is a matter of life and death... it's much, much more important than that." But I think he meant after family. Jak hasn't followed his old man into football. He trained with a soccer school at Chelsea when he was younger but quickly made up his mind that football wasn't for him and pursued another life. He served his time as a dry liner when he left school and is making a living working in the construction trade. It didn't matter what he did. I would support him in whatever line of work he chose and he seems very happy doing what he does.

Claudia is about to go to university. She is a clever girl academically and I'm not sure what career she wants to carve out for herself at the moment. But as long as she is happy then Lorraine and I will give her our blessing. She was under a bit of stress when revising for her A Levels and we had to walk around on eggshells for a while. But she came through it and we're all extremely proud of her. The world is her oyster at the moment.

My youngest, Bobby, at the time of writing this, is at Newcastle United's academy. Like his brother Jak, before him, he wears football kit as standard issue every day, instead of regular clothes, and kicks a ball about everywhere he goes. Bobby might be at the academy but that doesn't guarantee he will make it. There are a large percentage of people who don't make it. We aren't taking anything for granted. We're not pushing him into football. If it's his dream, so be it. I'll give him advice and tell him it's about dedication and hard work. If he doesn't have those two things, he'll not make it. There are thousands of talented footballers out there who don't make the grade because they don't want to train hard. If he's got the dedication and ability, then he's got a chance; until then we'll wait and see.

My friends are important to me and two of my closest in life and football are Steve Watson and Alan Thompson. I've known them both from the age of six and seven. Tommo's mother, Ann, was my dinner lady and told me off many a time. Mind you, I have been told on more than one occasion that I was a cheeky kid. But I come from Pottery Bank, Walker, in the east end of Newcastle. It's not quite up there with Ronnie and Reggie Kray but it is a tough area. It's survival of the fittest. You have to be able to stand up for yourself. You would get crushed otherwise.

Watto and Tommo are two lads I grew up with, played football with and formed a bond. They are two great guys who have my back. Even when our careers went off in different directions we still kept in touch and our families became close and great friends. We had holidays away and days out with the kids together. I went to see them at Villa when they were there and they came to see me in London when I was at Fulham.

I remember playing at Cambridge United for Newcastle back in the early part of my career. We'd gone to warm up before the match and during this time Keegan had disappeared to the toilet in the Abbey Stadium. Back then they had those big silver urinals. And, when KK came back out, he told us that some regurgitated Black Forest Gateau was lying in it and went ballistic. He wasn't happy at all. After a brief investigation we found out it was Tommo. He missed his pre-match meal for some reason and, because of that, decided to order some Black Forest Gateau an hour before the game. Consequently, he barfed it up.

Watto was the first of us to get a car and used to drive us around. The car would be rocking to Gangsta Rap or Guns and Roses. He wasn't the best of drivers because we had a crash one time on the way to a game, just off Wallsend High Street, but nothing too serious.

You hear people reminiscing and saying, "The best days of your life are your school days." But for me it has to be the times we spent together in the boot room at St James' Park. It was a perpetual wind-up and constant Mickey taking. We'd run wire brushes across each other's hands when we were cleaning the pros' boots; put deep heat in the jockstraps and hide items and belongings. It was daft childish stuff but hilarious at the time. People go on about Man United's class of 92 but our class of 91 were a great bunch of lads to be around.

Me, Robbie Elliott and Watto were all in plaster or injured this day and stuck for transport. We were waiting for Rover to drop off an automatic car at St James' Park because we couldn't go through the gears and press the clutch down. Freddy Shepherd and Douglas Hall bumped into us in reception. Douglas shouts, "What are you three up to? I bet it's no good again." When we relayed this story to Douglas, he threw the keys to his car at us. It was only a Bentley. He said, "My car's an automatic, you can have that." Watto thought he was Ice-T. It was great driving this big black car with NUFC on the number plate. I drove it down a couple of one-way streets by mistake. Watto and Robbie are telling me to drive quickly so the traffic warden doesn't get the plate. I said, "Howay lads, it's the easiest plate in the world to see. How many cars do you know with an NUFC registration?" We drove around all day and had a scream.

Fortunately, we didn't have a scrape or get a ticket but Douglas took it off us the following day.

Sir John Hall, his son, Shepherd and all of the Newcastle directors were great with us. They made us feel at ease and were good people. They let their hair down every now and again but that doesn't make them bad blokes. We all go a bit mental at times. Douglas and Freddy got a lot of unfair criticism. They were both set up in the whole Toongate scandal, and the Fake Sheikh was later investigated for his methods was he not? We all could have fallen foul of that. They both had the best interests of Newcastle United at heart and were two decent men. It would be a shame if they were judged on that regrettable episode because they did a lot of good for the club.

I like to let my hair down like most people and a day at the races on a day off is just the ticket. But when I was at Fulham, Mark Crossley mentioned buying a share in a greyhound. I thought, why not, this could be fun. We had some great nights at Wimbledon dogs and at the horse racing. I was involved in a racing syndicate with interskyracing.com. We had Interskychampagne, which we went to see at Musselburgh, but it lost. The best one we had was Interskyfalcon, which won the Fighting Fifth twice at Newcastle and ran in the Champions Hurdle when it wasn't 100 per cent fit. Then there was Logonintersky. I was involved in this one with Terry Mac and another ten to 15 punters. We went to Tipperary and Jonjo O'Neil was the trainer. Me and Loraine had a trip over after a Fulham game and had a great time watching it win in Ireland. Then there was Logonintersky. I was involved in this one with Terry Mac and ten to 15 others.

The success of Interskyfalcon made us invest in other horses and the prize money we won meant we could have the odd trip away. I went to watch it in the Christmas Hurdles at Kempton, in one of the few times I could celebrate the Festive period because of my bad injury at Fulham. It was never as serious as it was with Michael Owen. I wasn't a big gambler, just enjoyed a day out with friends and family. But when Crossley mentioned investing in a greyhound, I thought, 'Why not? We could have a bit of fun with it.' We paid something like £4,000 each for a leg in Droopy's Okocha with two lads from County Durham who would train it. Incredibly, the dog broke a leg in its first training session, so it never even ran a race! Bloody typical!

The trainers were two good working-class lads who loved to have a pint. One Sunday after a session at his local social club, one of them decided to drive home. He realises, very soon, he can't drive because he is intoxicated beyond comprehension, so pulled off on to the slip road on the motorway to sleep it off. He is woken from his slumber by a bang on the window by a policeman. He winds the window down, and you can imagine what the stench was like. The alcohol fumes would have knocked you out!

The policeman says, "Have you been drinking, sir?"

"Aye, been to the club. Had about eight or nine pints."

The policeman went to his car and returned with a breathalyser and asks, "Will you blow into this please?"

"I've just told you I've had eight or nine fucking pints; why do I need to blow in that? "

Retelling that story tickles me every time I relay it. Needless to say I haven't invested in a greyhound or horse since, but still enjoy a day out at the dogs or races all the same.

CHAPTER 19
THOUGHTS OF CHAIRMAN CLARK

I'm no different to anyone; there would be changes to our beloved football game if I was the head honcho at FIFA. I was saddened by the scandal surrounding the world's governing body. FIFA is supposed to promote the beautiful game of football, yet it has been exposed for rank corruption. It appears figureheads at the top of the corporation have been more interested in lining their own pockets than promoting the good of the game. The whole charade of awarding the World Cup to Russia and Qatar, respectively, raised the eyebrows of everyone, other than the two countries given the right to host the competition. It was obvious it would cause controversy and an investigation. Hopefully some good will come from the exposé and FIFA will be regulated in the future. In its current form, football's ruling body does not send out a good message to the rest of the world.

Sepp Blatter claimed there was a witch hunt by the English press, yet the findings of these investigators into corruption proved to be correct. It is good we can promote football in different countries and continents. And, with it, raise the profile of football, reinvest in those countries and help the economies which are poorer than the rest of the world. This is what was intended when it went to South Africa. But then you read that countries were bribing FIFA and you don't know what to believe. It all leaves a bitter taste in your mouth.

To award the competition to Qatar just doesn't make sense logistically. I've been to the Middle East on holiday and the heat and humidity is extremely uncomfortable just walking around the shops. So what will it be like to play in that heat and in those conditions? Will it be safe for footballers and can FIFA give the same guarantees to supporters as well? My good friend, and former colleague, David Ginola, recently had a cardiac arrest after playing in high temperatures. Admittedly he isn't as fit as he was in his pomp, but he's a former professional athlete. This was just a charity match in the South of France; nowhere near the temperatures of the Middle East. You just fear the World Cup is a tragedy waiting to happen.

I can empathise with all those wanting the World Cup back home in England. It's been frustrating for a nation, who invented the game, that in football history it has hosted only two major tournaments. We sent Prince William, David Beckham and the Prime Minister, David Cameron, to represent us. We didn't even make it to the second round of voting. Why didn't England get to host it? I've got no doubt we didn't get it because of the relationship our FA and English media shares with FIFA. Blatter probably did it out of spite. But hopefully there'll be more transparency now and we can move forward. In the future you hope there'll be a level playing field and everyone will have a better chance of hosting the World Cup or European Championships on merit, rather than who has the biggest suitcase full of money.

On the subject of fairness, a lot has been made about the lack of diversity in football. It has been said several times in the recent past that there aren't enough black managers or coaches in the game. Apparently 25 per cent of footballers across the four English leagues are black or from a different ethnic background. This statistic does not transfer into the coaching or managerial side of the game. It has also been inferred that the game is institutionally racist because of this stat. Now this claim shocked me. I have never witnessed or experienced any of this during my time inside football and hope there aren't any problems with race. I wouldn't allow it if I saw any of it. There's no doubt football was steeped in racism when I was a kid. As a fan I witnessed supporters throwing bananas on to the pitch and heard monkey chants. Many of these people were seen distributing far-right racist literature and peddling propaganda outside of St James' Park when I was younger. These weren't kids by the way, it was grown men and it was sickening.

The Rooney Rule has been introduced in American Football, where at least one black or ethnic minority candidate will be interviewed for a vacant head coach or manager's position. I don't think they need to introduce that in the UK. If they're good enough they will get the job. It's that simple. There are some good black managers out there that have been successful. Chris Hughton, Chris Powell, Keith Alexander, Keith Curle and Paul Ince are just a few off the top of my head, while Les Ferdinand is proving to be a great director of football at QPR. It is a contentious or controversial debate. No one has the god given right to be a top flight, Premier League manager. I'd love to manage a team in the first tier but I've got to prove myself at a lower level before getting that chance. It may never come. That won't be a race issue. You have to be worthy of the right. I haven't earned that right, yet.

I saw Dwight York on television not long ago touting for the Aston Villa job. I know Yorky well. He is a great lad and was a fantastic footballer in his day. What gives him the right to demand or ask for a position at a Premier League club? Aston Villa is one of the biggest clubs in Britain. What qualifications does he have? Is he applying for League One and League Two jobs? Just because he was a great player or played for the club doesn't give him the right to be its manager. He has to earn his stripes.

The same can be said about women in football. I don't think we need women in football jobs for diversity reasons. You shouldn't be trying to shoehorn members of the opposite sex into employment for the sake of diversity. You want the best people for the job. If that's a woman, then so be it. If they have the qualifications and can do it, brilliant. It has nothing to do with sex or race in my opinion. Everybody should have the same attitude.

Admittedly it would be difficult for a woman to get a coach, manager or masseuse's position in men's professional football. But there's no reason why the opposite sex can't be sports scientists, physios, writers and take other important positions within the structure of a football club. You just need to look at what happened to Eva Carneiro at Chelsea to see how difficult the job can be for a woman. Whether that was down to a difference of opinion, a man knowing better than a silly woman, we've all got our own opinions and we know things like that shouldn't go on anywhere, never mind on a football pitch.

I was at Fulham, as a player, when the club had the first professional women's football team in England. The Cottagers were pioneers in that sense. They were well paid and signed some of the best players in the world. The women's football team at Birmingham had strong links to the first team when I was manager. At Kilmarnock, one of our physios is a woman and, when I was a coach, at Norwich a woman was part of the medical team.

Am I surprised there aren't more women officials? No, not really because it is a tough job. Referees and officials get an enormous amount of abuse and scrutiny from, not only the players and supporters but, the press and media. Most men don't want to do it never mind women. Why anyone would put themselves in that position is beyond me. I'd hate to do it. There have been a few peaks and troughs with female officials but overall none have seen it through.

There should be changes to the way we approach kid's football. I would make children's football summer based. We can't coach them in the winter or, rather, we struggle to train them in the colder months. There aren't many football clubs with facilities to train children indoors, apart from a select few Premier League clubs. As a consequence, you have to coach kids on dark nights and when the weather is atrocious. It's impossible to stop and start sessions and go through a routine because they would all freeze to death. And when young lads and lasses are cold, they don't listen. Their minds will be on the weather and when the session is going to end so they can get back inside into the warmth. Admittedly, we don't have great summers in the UK but the climate is warmer. Ideally a children's season should be from March to September or October.

As a manager I take a great deal of interest in the academy system. I think there is room for a bit of the old style apprenticeship in the modern era. At Huddersfield I made sure the academy kids were training with or near to the first team squad so it wasn't a case of us and them. I did the same with the coaching staff. They are important members of staff. I invest heavily in the kids. I've never really had the privilege to buy big name players so I like to develop youngsters. I've given 16 to 17 debuts to academy kids at the four clubs I've managed.

Birmingham City has a fantastic academy. They even have two or three people carriers so they can pick up kids for training. When I was a youngster I had to catch a regular bus at the top of Pottery Bank in Walker, to get into town. Then I had to change and get on another one to take me to Benwell where we trained. In fact, me, Robbie Elliott, Steve Howey, Steve Watson, Alan Neilson and Alan Thompson used to meet up in town for a bit craic before we made our way to Benwell together. And then we'd have a good laugh in the boot room. It was all part of the learning process and we were proud of making sure the pros' kit and boots were immaculate.

Kids today even have sessions with psychologists in place of training. You could say that most players were all amateur psychologists when I played. Is this really beneficial to kids? I believe kids aged ten and under should be allowed to enjoy playing football with freedom, free from any pressures of coaching or systems. The pressure comes very early and they have to learn about it. A lot of these kids are living their fathers' dreams. The dads haven't made it as a professional for one reason or another so these children have that added pressure as well. The rate kids drop out of football or get released is quicker and bigger as well. They also get to feel what it's like being a professional footballer quicker than what we did in our time. And then there's the television coverage. We were lucky if we had one live game a week, whereas now you can get two or three games a night from all over Europe.

I don't agree that young footballers get handed everything on a plate or they don't have to earn it. But I certainly agree a lot of these kids are getting riches and privileges beyond their station. My son's travelled on the first team bus to an away game when there hasn't been a game for the first XI. We were lucky if we got a coach. Most of the time it was a minibus, and if you didn't get there early enough you had to sit on the metal skip in the alley. It would freeze your backside off! And of course after every youth team game we would be back at St James' Park to clean and sweep the dressing room after the pros had finished. There's none of that now. All they have to do is play football.

Another sad aspect missing from the professional game is the abolishment of the reserves. The Under-23s have replaced the second string team, in a format where you can play three over age players. In my day you could play as many first teamers in the reserve team as you wanted. It wasn't always a punishment, although sometimes it was. But most of the time a player needed to get some minutes of game time under his belt.

BLACK OR WHITE, NO GREY AREAS

A winter break for the Premier League and Football League clubs would be a good idea. All footballers would benefit from some mid-season time off. In Scotland the break is from January 1 until January 21. The first week you just down tools and give everyone a week off. Then the lads come back in and do a bit of training in the second week in preparation for week number three. It gives everyone a chance to recharge and get refreshed. It also gives us managers a chance to focus on recruiting in the January transfer window.

The Festive fixtures should be localised like they used to be. I don't know why that has changed but, when I was a kid, Newcastle would be playing against Sunderland, Middlesbrough or Carlisle on a Boxing Day or New Year's Day. Supporters shouldn't have to travel to London or the south coast during the Christmas period and, vice versa, those in the south shouldn't have to make a trek up north. I remember travelling to Southampton when I was the Huddersfield manager. It was horrific for Terriers' fans. For a start it is tough to get transport at this time of the year.

A computer is supposed to randomly compile the fixtures. But surely the powers that be can intervene and rearrange the Festive calendar. Local teams can play each other home and away at this time of year. But if there are no derby games to be played you can play clubs closest to your area. This is just common sense. Secondly, teams are playing on Boxing Day, December 28, 30 and then there's the first round of the FA Cup. Fans aren't getting value for money because the quality on show will be poor. Players aren't workhorses. It is impossible to perform at the top level with high intensity. Even the big clubs in the Premier League with the largest squads struggle to do it. Wouldn't it be a benefit to players, clubs and fans to cut fixture congestion and localise matches?

I often get asked who my toughest opponent was on the pitch. There wasn't just one, there were several. Two of the biggest challenges came when I faced up to Roy Keane and Paul Scholes. Patrick Viera and Emmanuel Petit were another tough pairing to go toe-to-toe with but Keane and Scholes were by far the best. They could do anything: tackle, run, pass and score goals. Midfielders today seem to be labelled attacking or defensive midfielders. I thought they were supposed to do everything. And Scholes and Keane could do it all. They were brilliant.

I remember going to Old Trafford on Boxing Day 1995 with Newcastle and losing 2-0. Andy Cole and Keane scored for Man United. The Irishman was unbelievable that day while Scholes was just phenomenal. And when I met them through Coley, they turned out to be two unbelievably humble fellows.

There were some talented midfielders around in my era. Standing in the tunnel at Highbury, in my day, you'd look across and see Viera and Petit and you think you're in the land of giants. Steven Gerrard and Xabi Alonso at Liverpool were another good pairing and two incredibly humble players. Bryan Robson was one of the best I ever played against. He was coming to the end of his career and I was just starting. He hit me so hard in a game at Old Trafford; I thought I'd been hit by a bus. Can you imagine what it was like facing him in his prime, when he was one of the best players in the world? It doesn't bear thinking about. Robson was the complete player. He could head the ball, tackle, pass it and score goals from deep.

When I think back to my playing days, I have fond memories of standing in the tunnel at St James' Park. This is something else when you hear *Going Home* (*Theme of the Local Hero*). The song seems to whip the crowd up into a frenzy and the hairs, literally stand to attention, on the back of your neck. It is a ridiculous feeling. I always enjoyed playing at Old Trafford and

Anfield. Those two grounds felt a bit special compared to other grounds I've played at. You got a sense of the history of the venues when you ran onto the pitch. It was the same in the tunnel at St James' Park: it was tangible; you could almost touch it. You don't seem to get the same sensation anywhere else. But once the game starts you're never aware of anything on the terraces. So any shouts of abuse are lost on most players because they're focused on the game.

My favourite players when I was growing up were: Kevin Keegan, Peter Beardsley, Bryan Robson and Glenn Hoddle. Hoddle was the England manager who called me up for La Tournoi. He was a nice guy and a progressive, forward-thinking coach. I got on very well with John Gorman, Hoddle's number two. It was all surreal getting to play with, or play for, your heroes. You never think this will happen in a million years.

Gorman tried to sign me for Swindon the year they got promoted to the Premier League. John Deehan wanted to do the same with Norwich. Ironically, Deehan ended up working for me as a scout at Birmingham. He was also our England Under-21s coach when we won the Toulon Tournament in 1993. Led Zeppelin singer Robert Plant was in the same hotel and he celebrated with us. Deehan bought the first couple of rounds for the lads after the tournament. And when he left our company we heard him telling the bar staff his room number so every round after that was put on his bill. The following morning, he battered us and we had to chip in to pay it.

I found Hoddle to be a good coach and tactically astute when I was in the La Tournoi squad. It's a shame he lost his job for religious beliefs. He ensured we qualified for a World Cup and I believe he had stats as an England manager only bettered by Sir Alf Ramsey. Hoddle went for a non-football reason which is unusual in itself. Someone loaded those questions and he answered them honestly. Next thing it's in the House of

Commons and the Prime Minister is involved. It's astounding to be honest and I don't want to talk about it too much because before I know it I'll be dragged into a political minefield. But it was sad all the same.

Being England manager is supposed to be a dream job yet it always seems to end up as a nightmare. The press and media go overboard both ways where the Three Lions are concerned in a major tournament. They say we're favourites, we're going to do this and that and then when their predictions don't come to fruition they go after the manager and decimate him.

Steve McManaman was another terrific player and a great lad. Jamie Redknapp was also in the Toulon squad with me. He was a terrific passer of the ball. That Arsenal team in the late 1990s was excellent: Dennis Bergkamp, Robert Pires, Thierry Henry, Ashley Cole and Ray Parlour, who is a great lad. I would love to have played with those lads week in and week out. Players like them make you look an even better player. The higher standard of player you play with the easier it is. That's why there was no fear factor for me at Newcastle when KK kept bringing in quality players and raising the bar.

Keegan's signings excited us, never mind the supporters. And when we saw them in action it was, *wow*! We'd never seen the likes of Philippe Albert in English football: bigger than a brick shithouse who could do anything with a football. We'd never seen a centre-half like him.

The same can be said about David Ginola. Ginola always wanted the ball in tight areas. Most players flourish with time and space, not the Frenchman. He liked being touch-tightly marked so he could manipulate the defender and beat him. It was easy for me with him on one side and Keith Gillespie on the other flank. Gillespie, on the other hand, loved running on to the ball. He liked to get in a race with a full-back because he had him for pace. Wingers today want the ball to their feet all of the time. You have to use your asset well and Gillespie did that. When he did have the ball at his feet he wanted to get close to the defender and push it past him. He didn't have a trick. He had blistering pace and was an intelligent footballer. We had so much variety in our side.

Today I wonder whether teams and players actually know the strengths and weaknesses of their teammates. I knew how to deliver a ball to my colleagues. I was fortunate my passing ability was one of my strengths and I could pick out a player. It makes the game a lot simpler if you do know what you're good at and it also makes you look like a better player.

There are players out there who like to give it the big one vocally but I was never one of those who got involved with any of that unless they had a pop at me. Robbie Savage was one player who liked to engage in a game of linguistics. He was one of those players you'd like to bump into down a back alley. But that's because he was a horrible so and so on the pitch. Off it he's not a bad lad. There were loads of players like that. He's made a good career out of that now being a pundit.

Savage was part of a barney in the tunnel at St James' Park when Blackburn were the visitors. Graeme Souness was the Magpies boss at the time and tried to calm it down. Savage shouted, "Souness, what have you ever won?" The gaffer's response was, "Just three big ones, son," in reference to the European Cup. There was no comeback from that one. We thought that was hilarious.

If playing at St James' Park, Old Trafford or Anfield were pleasurable experiences then the same can't be said about Southampton. Playing against the Saints, whether it was at the old Dell or St Mary's, has never held many happy memories for me as a player or manager. I suffered two heavy defeats when boss at Huddersfield; one under Nigel Adkins and one under Alan Pardew. We beat them comfortably at home. I scored for

Fulham in a game at the Dell which we lost 3-2. One of my Achilles' injuries happened at St Mary's. When I played for Newcastle, Matt Le Tissier was scoring world class goals from all over the pitch. He'd generally score an even better goal than the one he netted in the match before. Le Tissier was on a different planet when he played us. Then there was the time when Keegan hauled me off; I spat my dummy out and he spanked my arse after kicking a metal bucket.

Southampton is a place I'd put into Room 101 if I got the chance. All joking aside, it is a beautiful part of the country. My brother-in-law, Paul Baker, started his football career down there under Lawrie McMenemy and our family used to go and visit. I can't ever remember winning on the south coast. There was one game when I scored for Newcastle and we were winning 2-0 with five minutes to go. We ended up drawing 2-2. Another time we lost 3-1 when 1-0 up with two minutes to go. It was surreal.

I've never been privy to any premeditated aggression or had any plan to do a player. Although I did once see David Batty lunge in with a two-footed tackle on teammate Brian Pinas. You'll not believe this but Batts was playing in the same team as the Dutchman in training. In fact, he passed Pinas the ball, ran after him and lunged in with both feet. Pinas was a bit of a fanny on the ball, poncing around. I don't think Batts was too enthused with what he brought to the table. We were all in shock at first and then fell about laughing.

Being a professional footballer in the public eye means you're under a lot of scrutiny and criticism all of the time. There was a newspaper article about me with comments made by Sheffield United manager Dave Bassett. In it, Bassett is quoted as saying I hadn't fulfilled my potential. Keegan was furious when it was brought to his attention in a press conference. KK remarked that, "The manager who made that comment would be with his side in the second tier of the football league, while Lee Clark would be plying his trade in the top flight." It didn't bother me to be honest because I saw the way his team was set up and it wasn't football. His midfielders must have had rotating necks because the ball would've just passed them by. If Bassett didn't rate me then it was a compliment in itself. I was in no hurry to play for him or his team.

Apart from the obvious abuse I got from Sunderland fans there wasn't anywhere I got verbally insulted, unless I'd fouled someone. I scored at Millwall once and scaled a fence thinking it was housing Newcastle fans. I nearly shit a brick when I was nose to nose with all those crazy South Londoners. It wasn't the brightest thing I'd ever done. Mick McCarthy was the Lions manager at the time and he called me a, "Fucking idiot," as I ran by. He was probably right. But funny or daft moments like that happen all of the time in football. As I say, everyone just needs to get over things like that and move on. It was obvious by the look on my face that it was a mistake I wouldn't repeat in a hurry.

I remember when we were playing against Liverpool and Milan Baros was coming on as substitute for the Reds. Just as the change was taking place Chris Coleman waved me over. I thought he was going to give me some tactical instruction about Baros.

Coleman says, "Good-looking fucker, isn't he?"

I said, "Who?"

"Baros," he replied.

"Er, aye, not bad," I said.

"OK, get yourself back on the pitch."

I was baffled. Having a strong personality or an idiosyncratic nature seems to be part and parcel of a footballer's life.

Steve Harper had a good one-liner for Lee Bowyer's girlfriend when he was at Newcastle a few years back. Bearing in mind she was an attractive young lady and, it would be fair to say, that Bowyer didn't really possess film star good looks, did he? Harps turned to her and says, "What first attracted you to the multimillionaire Lee Bowyer?" To be fair, that line could have been attributed to several hundred current and former Premier League footballers, me included.

I've been lucky to have played well over 500 matches as a footballer and took part in some cracking contests. One of my most memorable games was, obviously, my debut at Bristol City. Winning the league at Grimsby in 1993 also springs to mind, as well as my last ever Premier League goal against Middlesbrough at St James' Park. Then there was the first time Newcastle went to Old Trafford and got a point in a 1-1 draw. I have fond memories of the Magpies' first season in the top flight after our promotion season. We struggled at first because the standard was higher and we were trying to find our feet. Add that to the fact we lost our most experienced player, Peter Beardsley, to injury in pre-season, didn't help. He would have provided the calming influence on the side. But we quickly learned and finished third in our first season back in the big time. A team doing that, well, it was virtually unheard of, and especially after having only one point from a possible nine. Leicester did something similar in a way but it was their second season in the top flight. They went one step further and won the league.

How did Leicester do it? They did the basics right and have no egos in the team. In the modern game it appears tricks and skills are more important whereas City were more interested in playing to their strengths and getting a result. They have very good players as well, who bring out the best in each other's strengths. Leicester did the nitty-gritty very well and never changed their shape. You're supposed to be a dinosaur if you play 4-4-2 yet they played that way every week. Burnley did the same under Sean Dyche in the 2015-16 season in the Championship. They went 23 games unbeaten. You get people trying to reinvent the wheel but why? The game might have changed in terms of athleticism but the principles are the same.

Playing in Europe for the first time was special. I missed the first game in Antwerp through injury but came on for the second half in the return leg. I also played in both legs to Athletic Bilbao, home and away. And the following season I played against Monaco in the UEFA Cup, where we didn't have a striker and Rob Lee had to play up front as a false number nine.

Playing for Sir Alex Ferguson, Jose Mourinho and Sir Bobby Robson would have been nice. The same could be said about Gordon Strachan. Whenever I've seen or heard Strachan he has come across as unbelievably intelligent, honest and straight as a die. He doesn't bullshit people. There's an unbelievable amount of bullshitters in this game though. The majority of footballers come from ordinary working-class backgrounds and we've had to learn the hard way. We've been brought up to tell the truth and Strachan is a brutally honest guy.

It didn't work out for the former Man United and Leeds midfielder at Middlesbrough but he's still held in high esteem on Teesside because he thanked the chairman for the opportunity to manage the club. He didn't take a penny from them as a pay off, when he could have done. He didn't feel he'd done a good job by his high standards. Yet look at his recruitment work at Southampton and Coventry and he is doing a fantastic job for Scotland with a limited pool of players. I love hearing him talk. He keeps it simple and talks sense. He's commented on how the 2015-16 Leicester side are like the Leeds United team he won the title with in 1992. They had good players in good positions, weren't flash, weren't the best players individually but just got on with the job. Strachan gets criticised for his honesty. Some people said he was being sarcastic or disrespectful. One reporter asked for a quick word. He replied, "Velocity." Hilarious! There aren't enough Gordon Strachan's in the game in my opinion.

CHAPTER 20
I HAVE A DREAM

My old boss and mentor, Kevin Keegan, always believed we should be allowed to follow our dreams or words to that effect. He is right. Why can't we dream? We all should have aspirations, goals and dreams, and I'm no different. Maybe this is a little premature because I still have a lot of unfinished business as a manager. But it goes without saying I want to manage my home-town club before I hang up my boots and sail off into the sunset on an OAP Saga holiday. That's my dream. I have an insatiable appetite for success and this hunger won't be quenched until I succeed. And at the same time I'm aware if I don't become a success I'll never get an opportunity to be in charge at St James' Park. This desire drives me on.

My fledgling career as a number one couldn't have got off to a better start at Huddersfield. I established myself as a young, hungry and up and coming manager. My team played fast-flowing, attractive, attacking football. I felt indestructible. But, before I knew it, I'd gone from being one of the country's most promising, precocious and sort after coaches to one rebuilding his reputation. As I've found out, much to my chagrin, football has a nasty way of kicking you in the teeth when you least expect it. I'm a better manager for the experience at Birmingham and Blackpool but the appointments didn't allow me to flourish. And, maybe, with the benefit of hindsight, I shouldn't have jumped in at the deep end so soon after Huddersfield.

Newcastle was without a manager for much of the 2014-15 season following Alan Pardew's departure for Crystal Palace. The Magpies made the public know they were looking to make a new appointment so I applied for the job, before Steve McClaren got the position. I threw my hat into the ring, simply, because I was an out of work manager. I was contacted by the club and asked whether I'd be interested in becoming a number two to the new boss they had in mind. I'd always seen myself as a number one but, it goes without saying, I'd consider becoming a number two if it was at my home-town club. The proposal was, I'm guessing, put to McClaren and he didn't want to work with me. The former England boss wanted to bring in his own man. That was his prerogative. I accepted that and had to move on.

I know Graham Carr, the Newcastle scout, quite well through Derek Fazackerley. They go back a long way. Carr seemed to have a lot of power at St James' Park in recruiting new players. I'm not too sure many of his players were a success. A lot of those arriving at the club were raw talent that needed to be developed. Arguably, Yohan Cabaye, Demba Ba and Mathieu Debuchy were his only successes. People rant and rave about Moussa Sissoko but where has he been? For me, he goes through the motions and has no fight in him. There's always talk about where he wants to be instead of doing it where he is. He turned up and started playing when a world class coach, Rafa Benitez, arrived at St James' Park. So why didn't he do it for McClaren? And his behaviour during the last transfer deadline window was nothing short of disgraceful. A move was lined up to go to Everton, he agreed, but as soon as Tottenham showed their hand he snubbed the Merseysiders for North London. He didn't even have the good grace to call Toffees' boss Ronald Koeman and tell him. Sissoko wasn't the only one at Newcastle who went through the motions. You can say that about several players in the United squad prior to the Spaniard turning up on Tyneside.

People talk about having pace, power and athleticism in a side. But where was that in the Newcastle team during their relegation season? Furthermore, the squad has not only been short of characters but it's also been unbalanced for years. There were about five or six players at the club who have been bought who fit the number ten or supporting striker tag: De Jong, Cabella, Thauvin, Perez and Mitrovic to name a few. Why do you need several players of the same type in your squad? Not only that but my old team had the same centre half pairing, which took the club down in 2009, playing most of the 2015-16 campaign. It's excruciating that nothing was learned from the last relegation. And it was typical of the team to go to Aston Villa and only come away with a 0-0 draw. You could have scripted it. They had been nothing short of magnificent in the games running up to that. To come back from 2-0 down at Liverpool was brilliant. They would never have come back from that earlier in the season. Yet complacency sets in and the team draw a blank.

I try to get players who are an extension of me. I like them to be honest first and foremost. I have a scouting network that recommends players. I always like to see the player before he comes in. Sometimes that is not possible for one reason or another and in that case, one of my trusted staff will be despatched to run the rule over the player in question and I will back his judgement. You employ a chief scout for a reason and he has to justify his salary. If he doesn't do that he's out of a job. It's quite clear the transfer system Newcastle have had in place didn't work. Mike Ashley used this model for nearly ten years and every season the team has struggled under his tenure, bar one, when they finished fifth. Buying players aged 25 and under so they have a sell on fee is all very well if you want to make a profit. But you'll struggle to stay in the league as a consequence. That has been apparent since United's promotion in 2010. You cannot set out a model like that in stone. You have to be more flexible. For me that has been Newcastle's flaw. They haven't been adaptable. They've been lucky with Cabaye, Debuchy and

Ba. They made money on those and those running the club have thought, we'll keep doing this.

Another thing, you can't keep fishing from the same pond. You have to cast your net out further. If this was a successful way to do business, then why aren't all clubs doing that? They're not, of course. Newcastle and Aston Villa have fished in the French market more than any club and look what has happened to them both, relegation. There are good players in Ligue 1 but there are high-quality players in each league in every country.

What happens if a good 28-year-old becomes available? Ashley said at the end of the 2014-15 season that success is winning a cup or getting into the Champions League. That 28-year-old might be the difference in winning that cup or qualifying for the Champions League. Look at what Jermain Defoe did at Sunderland. The Wearsiders paid around £5m for a 32-year-old striker. The player might not have a sell on but his experience and goals contributed in keeping the team in the top flight. It also ensured Sunderland benefitted from the biggest television money pay out in Premier League history. Now I ask you, which club has employed false economy and which one has applied good husbandry and housekeeping? Newcastle's model has turned out to be nothing but false economy because they were relegated. You need to ask who is accountable. Is it Ashley, Charnley, Graham or is it all three?

Fortunately, Benitez has come to St James' Park. It appears the conditions previous managers were working under no longer apply to him. The Spaniard will be buying and selling his own players, with the help of the staff. Agents will be ringing and, because of that, he'll be having staff meetings to discuss different players. He'll ask who's been flagged up? Who's on our radar? I'm after a number nine, a tall one, or maybe you want a small one. The resources of Premier League clubs are extensive. They can find out whether a player is in your wage bracket, price range or even age group.

I can see why Ashley had that system in place, to be sustainable and sell his product at a profit. The only clubs who are sustainable and successful are the top four clubs who qualify for the Champions League and those who win a cup. They make money from their success and build on it. I don't think Roman Abramovich has even made money from football and yet his team has enjoyed enormous success. I reckon every club has manageable debt and Ashley has to accept that.

Former Newcastle supremo Freddy Shepherd had his critics but he always found resources from somewhere for his managers. They could compete and bring the best players from home and abroad when he was the United chairman. There was a lot of scaremongering he had the club on the verge of bankruptcy but Shepherd was managing all the loans and debt in a structured manner. He was in control. It was only when Ashley took over; the debtors decided they wanted everything paid up. Yet Ashley wanted to do it differently to Shepherd. That was his prerogative. The club still owes money, but only to Ashley.

The whole Tony Jiminez, Jeff Vetere and Denis Wise scenario a few years ago was perplexing. I often wonder what goes on in the minds of owners in this country. They seem to be voyeurs of football clubs in Europe. They want to emulate or copy them. What is wrong with being British? Why do they want to be European? Why don't we do it the old-fashioned British way? If the owner said to the manager, "I want a Head Coach, Director of Football and a Head of Recruitment, but they're your choice, you appoint them," then fair enough. That is the only way it would work. That way the manager won't be undermined because he'll be working with them. He'll bring in people he can trust, can do the job and won't be after his position. We also need to get away from the fact when the team is having a tough time the manager or head coach gets sacked. This way you'll get continuity. There are too many Director's of Football that aren't even in the same book, never mind on the same page as the manager. With this in mind it seems that on the tenth anniversary of his time at the club, Ashley has finally admitted, "Well, this hasn't worked; maybe it's time to give control to my manager."

Steve Morgan, the former Wolves chairman, is a big Liverpool fan. He asked whether I could work in a similar structure. He floated the idea of me being the Wolves coach and manager with Keegan above me recruiting players. I wouldn't have had a problem with that at all. But the manager has to have the final say in what player comes to the club. Keegan didn't have any say in who was coming to Newcastle in his second spell. There was a three-man transfer committee from what I understand of Wise, Jimenez and Vetere.

Keegan was approached and told there was a massive bid in for James Milner in his second spell. KK said he wasn't interested because they didn't have a replacement. The club responded by saying they had Bastian Schweinsteiger lined up. My old boss says if that's the case get Schweinsteiger. Keegan was sceptical of course. Schweinsteiger was at his peak, playing for Bayern Munich in the Champions League. Why would he swap that for a mid-table Premier League team? And because it sounded too good to be true Keegan rang Karl Heinz Rummenigge, an old friend and adversary, from when he played for SV Hamburg in the Bundesliga in the 1970s.

The conversation went something like this:

KK: Hi Karl, it's Kevin Keegan here. I hear my club have put in an offer for Bastian Schweinsteiger?

KHR: Hello Kevin, nice to hear from you. Yes, that's correct. We couldn't stop laughing.

KK: Why's that?

KHR: Well, for one, he's not for sale and two, certainly not for 5m Euros. He's one of the best players in the world. Why would we sell him?

The alarm bells started ringing for Keegan then. He knew the club were bullshitting about Schweinsteiger. It's like bidding £10m for Lionel Messi in his pomp, isn't it? Within a week of this breaking down one of Newcastle's biggest idols had walked away disillusioned after being lied too and undermined.

There was no hint of all the commotion and chaos to come when Ashley bought Newcastle. On the contrary, it seemed like he had good intentions. It was a masterstroke to bring Keegan back to the club. And Chris Mort did a fantastic job initially. He met with supporters, fanzine writers and engaged in open and honest talks about taking the club forward. He arranged a family day for all of the Newcastle staff. My wife, kids and everyone else's families got together at the training ground. There was a fun fair, go carts and other games for the kids.

Mort asked whether I'd be interested in running the academy. He offered me a ridiculous budget to go and get the best kids in the world. While I was flattered and tempted by the offer I saw it as a step back. I've never seen myself working with the kids. I've always seen myself as a number one with the professionals.

It certainly pulled at my heart strings when I was driving to Norwich. I didn't want to leave. But I got offered a chance to become an assistant manager to Glenn Roeder. There was no way I would jump ahead of Nigel Pearson and Steve Round in the pecking order. They were two better and more experienced coaches than me at the time. I was learning from them and Big Sam. But hindsight is a wonderful thing. A few months down the line, Allardyce gets sacked, Keegan comes back and Pearson and Round move on. There was a very good chance KK would have promoted me, given our relationship. I would have loved nothing better than to be part of his coaching staff. Terry Mac, who was closer than anyone to Keegan, let me know I would have been part of his staff. But I wouldn't have liked to see my old boss undermined by Ashley.

It's a hypothetical question and answer but, could I have taken over from Keegan after he left? I don't think I could. I would have been feeling the same as Keegan. My old manager was an inspirational man. He must've been feeling pretty uninspired with all of the restraints put upon him. It would have upset me to see him hurting. I only have fond memories of my career at St James' Park. That probably would have muddied the waters. Fate intervened, fortunately, and I wasn't part of it. I didn't have to make that choice. I read Keegan's quotes and followed the tribunal case for constructive dismissal closely. It seemed he had lost his enthusiasm. That is understandable given the circumstances.

I'm sure Ashley isn't happy that he's approaching a ten-year anniversary in charge of Newcastle and had no real success. He's had two relegations, a perpetual struggle to stay in the Premier League, one season where United qualified for the UEFA Cup and a promotion. You can't really count the promotion as a mark of success because they were first relegated which is a sign of failure.

You can't say he hasn't backed his managers financially, as well, because he has. The owner's biggest mistake, as I've already said, is pigeon-holing himself in a certain transfer market. Ashley has come in and tried to run the club like a business and make it self-sufficient. This is difficult to do with Premier League salaries; transfer fees and the everyday running costs. If you look at Chelsea, Abramovich and the success the West London outfit has enjoyed under his reign. They've won the league, Champions League, FA Cups and League Cups and I bet he's still out of pocket. I don't think he will be making any money from Chelsea and it's hard to see whether the club is paying for itself.

Newcastle's owner has held his hands up and admitted he isn't an expert in running a football club. But he's put faith in other people and you need to ask whether they have delivered. He's been taking advice from people who are supposed to be his friends. We all know the advice should have come from football people. But when you're asking for help from people you are close too, you'd expect them to say, "Mike, I think you should ask football people on how to run a football club."

I was worried about Newcastle's relegation. Until the likes of Matt Ritchie, Mo Diame, Grant Hanley, Daryl Murphy and Dwight Gayle were signed, the team didn't seem to have the same characters to get them back up at first time of asking. But with those signings and Rafa in charge, they do have a chance. He's a world class manager. Apart from a short spell when Keegan came back, this is the first time, in nearly ten years, Ashley has managed to galvanise the club, the city and its supporters.

It's obvious why the supporters don't like him. In Keegan and Alan Shearer, he dismissed two of the biggest icons, heroes and legends, in the club's history. Newcastle United is about its fans. Those supporters have their legends, heroes and icons. You have to respect that. Keegan and Shearer should've been treated with more respect for what they had achieved in their career and at St James' Park. No player or manager is bigger than a football club. But here you have two individuals who come close. They clearly weren't backed by Ashley when they were there as managers. Shearer's Bar is then renamed, Nine, and the ground has a new moniker. You wonder about the politics, who was behind it all and who is advising the owner. It certainly wasn't going to set up a harmonious relationship with the supporters and the club.

Newcastle United lost itself under Ashley's stewardship. The feel-good factor has gone missing. The club should be showing respect to all its former players. They don't want to acknowledge the achievements of the past. I go to other clubs and see ex-players working in the hospitality areas. My wife and I went to see Newcastle play in the Ethihad and were welcomed by players from City's past. They were all smartly dressed in a suit with a club breast badge and tie. You need to keep that connection with the fans of every generation. It was the same at Old Trafford and Anfield. You really get looked after.

A former Newcastle Academy Director, took the photos down of Ossie's class of 91 and the likes of Gazza. The people at the top shouldn't have let that happen. The kids need players to aspire to. You should see how Southampton celebrates their youngsters. And I don't just mean Shearer and the Matt le Tissier's of this world: the players before them like Rod and Danny Wallace. They've unearthed some gems down the years at the south coast club. The Saints are rightly proud of them. I can't get my head around why Money would do it.

Joe Kinnear did a similar thing when taking down photos of Brian Clough at the City Ground when he was manager of Nottingham Forest. It's like committing sporting suicide. He is one of the most iconic men in Forest's history and British football. Cloughy was ahead of the time in terms of being a sports psychologist. He'd take players to the pub before a cup final. Probably wouldn't work today, players would be on to their agents and it would be frowned upon by the media. But all joking aside, he was unique. There is a road stretching between Nottingham and Derby which is named Brian Clough Way. He was loved by both sets of those fans for his achievements. You just don't dismiss a man of that magnitude and you don't write off how a small provincial club won the League and European Cup, twice. You celebrate it. I'm not being disrespectful here,

Forest may never reach those heights ever again but their players could go on to a bigger club and do it. What benefit do you get from doing that? Some people might say you shouldn't live in the past but there is nothing wrong with using it as an inspiration. Things like this need addressing at Newcastle.

I didn't know Kinnear personally but did come across his teams as a player. His team at Wimbledon was quite unique. I was never an admirer of the way they played. In the tunnel at Selhurst Park, Vinnie Jones and John Fashanu would be going ballistic, threatening everyone. If you showed any fear they sensed it. You had to man up and stand up to them. Mind you we never got many good results down there. We had no problem beating them at our place but they were successful at home against a lot of teams.

Sir John Hall had a dream that he would like a team full of Geordies complete with home-town coaching staff. It is a lovely romantic idea but you have to pick the best people and players for the job. You can't just use nepotism and players with links from the past unless they are up to the role. But I think United should have at least one ex-player in the academy coaching set up to help the lads understand what the club is about – its history, culture and what it means to the community, among other things. It's a huge thing to be a part of and you can see that loads of players have just never *got* it. It's the most important part of playing for a club; it's the club's heart and soul.

In persuading Benitez to take a team that has been relegated to the second tier of English football, it looks as if Newcastle now means business. It appears as if they are going to change the structure of how the club is run. In Rafa, Ashley might be able to redeem himself in the eyes of those who felt betrayed or let down. Time will only tell. If he allows the former Real Madrid and Liverpool boss to get on with the football side of the club, without any interference, he might just win over the fans.

Being manager of my home-town club would be a dream job for me and any Geordie. It is one of the most coveted jobs in the world. I don't have a God-given right to manage it because I was part of a successful team under Keegan in the 1990s. On the other hand I am picking up invaluable experience as a manager. I have nearly 500 games under my belt as I write this. I've had highs, lows and craziness. At the moment I reckon people see me as a fire-fighter of a manager because of what I did at Birmingham and Kilmarnock but I've got more than that in my locker.

I created a football team and environment at Huddersfield that hadn't been in place for decades. We brought young players through and sold them to top teams. We developed other players we had on loan from the big boys, several of whom have gone on to win international caps and Premier League titles. So I have other qualities as a manager. One day I'd like to showcase them at St James' Park. For now they're on display at Rugby Park while I turn around Kilmarnock. One day, though, we're all allowed to dream, aren't we?

STATISTICS

PLAYER
Total appearances (inc sub)

	GAMES	GOALS
Newcastle United (1990-97, 2005-06)	240	27
Sunderland (1997-99)	89	16
Fulham (1999-2005)	178	22

MANAGER

Huddersfield (2008-12)	178
Birmingham (2012-14)	116
Blackpool (2014-15)	33
Kilmarnock (2015-present)	30

ACKNOWLEDGMENTS

To every coach, manager and player from St. Anthony's Primary School 1978 to Newcastle United Squad 2006 for helping me LIVE THE DREAM in playing terms. To every player I've coached and managed since – it's been a rollercoaster. I'd also like to thank my publishers Mojo Risin' and Will Scott who helped put my story into words.

Lee Clark

ABOUT THE AUTHOR

Will Scott is also the author of *Pavel is a Geordie* and *Scoop –
The Truth Only Gets in the Way of a Good Story*.

You can follow him on: @willscottwriter

ABOUT THE PUBLISHER

Mojo Risin' is interested in non-fiction titles – mainly football and true crime – anything with an underdog feeling, pop-cultural edginess and the spirit of punk.

You can follow them on: @mojorisinbooks

You can like them on: Mojo Risin' Publishing

And read all about them on: www.mojorisinpublishing.com

MORE FROM MOJO RISIN' PUBLISHNG

THE SAYERS: TRIED AND TESTED AT THE HIGHEST LEVEL

Stephen Sayers, Stuart Wheatman and Steve Wraith
ISBN: 9780993442407
288pp
4pp photographs
£18.99
Published: 31 October 2015
True Crime / Autobiography

Stephen Sayers is one of the most feared men in the country, with a reputation that's preceded him in the dozens of prisons he's served time.

The Sayers family have been known on the streets of Tyneside for decades. No one else comes close to their level and it is widely known that they 'run Newcastle'. Rumoured to be behind countless violent multi-million pound armed robberies, unsolved gangland murders, extortion rackets and organised crime in general, Stephen, his brothers and associates are an unstoppable force.

They've remained tight-lipped about their exploits… until now.

THE MOST TALKED ABOUT CRIME BOOK IN NEWCASTLE

'Stephen Sayers is a man who has earned his reputation the old-fashioned way; on the pavement. His family's reputation is a good one and they are well-respected in London and the rest of the UK. The Sayers are my kind of people.'
Fred Foreman

MORE FROM MOJO RISIN' PUBLISHNG

BY ANY MEANS NECESSARY

Stephen Sayers and David McCaffrey
302pp
£9.99
Published: TBC Winter 2016
Crime Fiction

A promising boxing career in the past.
A horrific crime defining the future.
A desire for revenge that would have consequences.

Tommy Myers had been an up and coming boxer with his future before him. He'll discover that it's impossible to make someone suffer without paying a price.
His sister was the victim of an unspeakable crime that set them both on a path they could have never foreseen.
She'll learn that revenge is an act of passion; vengeance is an act of justice.
Jack Hudson believes sadism and cruelty are the path to true power. He'll be taught that limits are in proportion to your resolve.

From the mind of bestselling author Stephen Sayers comes a new breed of crime thriller.

MORE FROM MOJO RISIN' PUBLISHNG

PAVEL IS A GEORDIE
Pavel Srnicek with Will Scott
ISBN: 9780993442421
320pp
4pp photos
£14.99
Published: 17 December 2015
Autobiography / Football

This isn't a typical footballer's tale of rags to riches; it covers life as a soldier in an Eastern Bloc state under Communist rule where he nearly shot his general and of tales involving the Mafia, guns, drugs and corruption.

Life as a young professional at Newcastle was not without difficulty. Kevin Keegan tried to replace him with several others; never totally convinced by the keeper he inherited from Ossie Ardiles.

His national side fell to a Golden Goal at Euro 96 and he clashed with Dutch superstars Ed-gar Davids and Dennis Bergkamp at Euro 2000. He was also involved in a fierce exchange with Belgium boss Robert Waseige and referee Anders Frisk as the Czech Republic were eliminated from World Cup in controversial circumstances in 2001.

This is a unique and heart-warming account of one of football's good guys: full of comedy, tragedy and heartache that will make the reader laugh and cry in equal measures.

MORE FROM MOJO RISIN' PUBLISHNG

BLOWING MY OWN TRUMPET
Nobby Solano with Will Scott
320pp
4pp photos
£9.99
Published: July 2016
Autobiography / Football

To millions of working-class Peruvians he's the kid who clawed his way out of the Lima slums to become a Premier League superstar, and to Newcastle United fans he's a living legend with a right foot to rival any of the club's fabled wingers.

Nobby Solano had it all… then lost it.
This is the compelling story of a footballer who went from rags to riches and back again; a national icon who saw his wedding beamed out live on state television and his face plastered across giant billboards; the skilful midfielder and accomplished musician who danced to the tune of managerial heavyweights; and a devoted family man who made some bad decisions, took his eye off the ball and was declared bankrupt – despite a decade plying his trade in the richest league in the world.

Nobby's is a remarkable story of an ambitious sportsman who reached for the stars – played alongside many of them – and then suddenly lost his grip. His spectacular descent into debt and despair would have broken most men, but he's never been 'most men'.

MORE FROM MOJO RISIN' PUBLISHNG

NME: FROM THE BENDER SQUAD TO THE GREMLINS; INSIDE NEWCASTLE'S FOOTBALL HOOLIGAN FIRM

Mark Mennim, Stuart Wheatman and Steve Wraith
320pp
£12.99
Published: October 2013
Autobiography / Football / True Crime

The Newcastle Bender Squad, the NME and the Gremlins are three of the most notorious firms in Newcastle United's football hooligan history. They've created match day violence home and away over the last five decades and, in recent years, the Gremlins have become household names in the North East as an infamous gang of thugs with a thirst for fighting, with stories in the press fuelling their fierce reputation.

These firms have been mentioned in many books over the years and now it's time to put the record straight. This is their time to tell their own story…

This book lifts the lid on Newcastle's closely-guarded hooligan firms for the first time. Forget what you've heard on the terraces; forget what you've read in the press and forget what you think you know… this is the real history of violence on and off the terraces in Tyneside. The fashion and haircuts may have changed but the violence stayed the same.